PHOENIX

Phoenix

Policing the Shadows

Jack Holland and Susan Phoenix

CORONET BOOKS
Hodder and Stoughton

First published in Great Britain in 1996
by Hodder & Stoughton
First published in paperback in 1997 by Hodder & Stoughton
A division of Hodder Headline PLC
A Coronet paperback

10 9 8 7 6 5 4 3 2

A CIP catalogue record for this book
is available from the British Library.

ISBN 0 340 66635 8

Typeset by Hewer Text Composition Services, Edinburgh
Printed and bound in Great Britain by
Mackays of Chatham PLC, Chatham, Kent.

Hodder and Stoughton
A division of Hodder Headline PLC
338 Euston Road
London NW1 3BH

Dedicated to the life of
Ian Phoenix
1943–1994

Acknowledgements

The authors would like to thank the following organizations for their help: The Ulster Museum, Belfast; the *Belfast Telegraph*; The Linen Hall Library, Belfast; The *Belfast Newsletter*; and Century Books, Belfast for permission to use the photograph of the Oxford Street Bus Station bombing from *The British Army in Ulster Volume I*, by D. Barzilay (1973).

Contents

List of Illustrations

Ian on duty after the Oxford Road Bus Station explosion in 1972. (*Courtesy of Century Books, Belfast*).

Front page of the *Belfast Newsletter*.

Ian with new sergeant's stripes outside his house in Glengormley.

The young Sgt. Phoenix having a tea break in the Belfast sunshine.

The *Belfast Telegraph*, 18 December 1973.

Ian with his children returning from a fishing trip in their old ferry boat.

With his toddler daughter on the beach on the Isle of Man, 1972.

Ian and a beekeeping friend during his 'beekeeping phase'.

Section Two

Ian at a parachute display he organised for a charity garden party.

At peace in the wilds with gun and dogs.

The wine labels on the crate of personally labelled wine presented to him by his friends in the SAS.

The devastated Loughgall police barracks after the IRA bomb had been detonated.

Dead terrorists after Loughgall.

The Cap'n with his colleague Bob Foster.

The last photograph taken of Ian by Susan.

The final picture of Ian and Susan with her parents.

Foreword

by Susan Phoenix

When I married Ian Phoenix he was a fiery young paratrooper. Twenty-six years later he had matured into a mellow, loyal and wise friend for many people. To me he was still full of fire and enthusiasm when the occasion called for it, but this was tempered with a lot of hard-won worldly knowledge which, his colleagues tell me, made him an excellent strategist in the war against terrorism.

After he was taken so tragically from me I knew that he would have expected me to complete the things which he would have considered unfinished. Always conscious of his early military training, he liked ends tied up and often left me the day's 'force orders' as he left for the office. For this reason I started to look at his notes and personal diaries which had become increasingly detailed in the five years or so before he died. I knew that he planned to write a book when he retired. We had often discussed this, and the children and I teased him during his regular rewrites of the same first pages on each of our summer holidays. He felt strongly about many things in his career, and indeed about worldwide anti-terrorist tactics. Never a man to mince his words, there were things which he wanted to say at a high level because he sincerely believed that the average politician did not adequately understand the psychology of the terrorist.

I was still uncertain as to whether I could embark upon his final task for him until I realised that other people were including him in their books and that I would rather make sure that his story came from me. Recalling our conversations about Jack Holland and his wife, it seemed somehow right that I should ask Jack to help in this task. Ian had recognised a couple whom he felt to be honest and objective. Jack's coming from different religious and cultural traditions made him a balanced and appropriate choice for me, and I have continued to find this to be very much the case as he and I have marvelled together at Ian's notes in a combined admiration for the work of the RUC and the special forces.

Ian was not an ambitious man in the normal career terms, but as he grew older and his frustrations developed at what he perceived to be inappropriate policy from 'above' he really wanted to be in a position to influence, or at least be heard, where he felt that he had a contribution to make. In the simplest terms – 'He cared' – when he made a decision it was because he believed it was for the good of the whole community of Northern Ireland. He did not care from which section of the community a person came; he believed in the individual's right to live a full life without intimidation or fear.

He also (as this book illustrates) respected the men and women who worked with him. I often took great pride in helping him to draft proposals for medals and honours to be bestowed upon his colleagues, all of whom he assumed were his friends. He would have been so proud to know that his final team were awarded commendations after he died. He would *not* have been surprised that the final medal eluded him.

I am grateful to have been allowed to love and keep Ian for twenty-eight years of my life. He has left me a legacy of two wonderful children, lots of good friends, and memories which will sustain us all in the years ahead as we all move forward as he would have wished. This is my medal to him.

Introduction

by Jack Holland

At eight o'clock one June morning in 1994 my wife, Mary Hudson, was in the kitchen sleepily making breakfast when she heard on the Northern Ireland news the words 'the funeral will take place today out of his home of Detective Superintendent Ian Phoenix . . .' A photograph of him flashed on the television screen. She was stunned, not knowing whether she was more shocked that he had died or that he had been a policeman. When she came up to my study she was pale and shaken. 'Ian's dead,' she said. 'He was killed in that helicopter accident.' I looked at her surprised and perplexed. 'Our Ian Phoenix? That couldn't be. They were Special Branch and intelligence officers on that flight,' I replied. 'It was definitely Ian,' she insisted. 'It was his name and his picture on the morning news.'

The Ian Phoenix we knew was a hearing-aid sales-man – or something of that nature. But when we thought about it we realised that his job description had always been kept rather vague. We knew only his wife, Susan, was a psychologist and they had owned a shop which sold hearing-aid equipment for the deaf.

Mary immediately telephoned Susan. 'Susan, is it true?' she asked. I could see by her face that it was. It was Ian's picture she had seen on the screen among the list of the dead from the Chinook crash a few days earlier. With her customary generosity and grace Susan replied, 'Your call has made my day. I didn't know how to tell you about Ian. I didn't want you to think that we had wanted to deceive you.'

We had met the Phoenixes in 1992. They had responded to an advertisement we had placed in the *Belfast Telegraph* when we were trying to rent our house in Italy for part of the summer. They had taken the house – in Trevignano Romano, a pretty lakeside village just outside Rome – for September. When they returned to Ireland later that month, having left the place in better shape than they'd found it, we were very impressed with them. We became fast friends when they invited us out to their home, a converted farmhouse on the Antrim coast, overlooking the channel between Scotland and Ireland. Ian was sitting in the main room by the blazing fire when we came in. Within seconds I had a glass of good wine in my hand and we were chatting about Italy, wine, their trip to Trevignano and the drawbacks of living in Northern Ireland – we had returned there

the year before after spending five years in Italy.
Before that we had spent nine years in New York,
my wife's home town. We were not finding the move
to Belfast an easy transition. The grey, rainy weather,
the low skies, and the long winter nights seemed all
too accurately to mirror the sullen, suspicious aspect
of the place. Mary in particular was suffering from a
feeling of isolation. She found in Susan a kindred spirit
– one who, as an Englishwoman, had also endured the
experience of being an outsider in the small, narrow
world that was Northern Ireland.

By that stage Ian Phoenix knew a lot more about me
than I did about him. He knew that I was a journalist
and novelist. Susan recalls that one day during their
trip to Italy in 1992 she was cooking in the kitchen
of our house, wafting the garlic-filled aromas into the
street in the hope that the locals would be impressed.
Ian was perusing the library in the main room when he
exclaimed, 'Fuck me! Come and have a look at this!
Bloody hell! I don't believe it!' He had plucked from
my shelves the autobiography of a former chief of staff
of the Provisional IRA. It was an autographed copy. He
had noticed the stack of books on the Northern Ireland
problem, most written from a decidedly nationalist
viewpoint. Included among them were a few I had
written myself. 'It's a pity I can't tell Jack what I do,'
he lamented at one point to his wife. 'We could have
some really interesting political discussions!'

We never did have those discussions. Ian Phoenix

could never reveal to me his role as a detective superintendent of the RUC Special Branch, in charge of a top-secret surveillance unit dedicated to putting behind bars some of the people that I, as a journalist and writer, met with regularly. Although he was decidedly diffident in political conversations, it did strike us that the little he said showed he had a keen awareness of the 'situation' – something most middle-class people in Northern Ireland lack. Unbeknown to us, Susan and he often lamented the fact that, because of the dangerous world they lived in, he could not openly and honestly associate with many people to whom they felt drawn.

We saw each other on a few occasions after that first meeting. I recall saying to Mary, 'It's funny we don't hear from the Phoenixes more often, because we seem to get on so well together.' She and Susan corresponded, exchanging observations about the difficulties they had faced adapting to life in Northern Ireland. Ian had been urging Susan to meet with Mary more often, because he felt it was too dangerous for him to form a friendship with me. But Susan had said she could not build a relationship upon a lie, even if it was one that was necessary to keep everyone safe. Mary and I did not realise it at the time, but our friendship with the Phoenixes was another victim of the Northern Ireland 'troubles'.

The last evening I spent with Ian was on 4 February 1994. He and Susan came to dinner with another friend, who is a prominent Northern Ireland journalist, and his wife. I was preoccupied with a book I was writing – a history of the Irish National Liberation Army, a dangerous republican splinter group. I think we talked about it all evening. Ian said little, mostly just listened. Later, as he drove home, he confessed to Susan that the evening had been difficult for him – that he had felt at times he should tell me the truth. But he was concerned with the consequences. If the people I was meeting knew of my connection to him, it would put us both in danger.

For some reason or other, that night I picked up my camera and, as the Phoenixes were leaving, insisted on photographing them. Ian at first refused, but then relented. I caught him as he was leaving through the front door. He would never return. Four months later he was dead.

Only through his death have I got to know Ian Phoenix better. That is one of the sad ironies of our friendship. I realised as I learned more about him that we were rather similar, in spite of coming from different 'traditions'. We both came from poor, working-class backgrounds – mine was Catholic, his Protestant. We both left home early, seeking broader horizons – he joined the army; I took the academic route and went to university. We were both to a certain extent outsiders in our own land, marrying foreigners. By coincidence, we even had children born to us within a day of each other in the same hospital.

Our paths had crossed then, and they would cross again as he pursued the same paramilitaries whom I would chase as I attempted to document the story of the Troubles.

On his trip to Trevignano Romano, as he and Susan perused my library, she picked up one of my novels (just recently published) and said, 'Our landlord writes books.' 'Maybe he'll write mine,' Ian had replied with a smile. It was a wish he repeated to Susan shortly before he died.

The following pages are the result of my efforts to fulfil that wish.

Prologue

The Killer Fog: 2 June 1994

The folly had gone through several transformations, but now Detective Superintendent Ian Phoenix had finally settled on what it was – a sun lounge for the dogs.

He had returned home early on Thursday 2 June 1994 to prepare for the top-secret security conference he was to attend that weekend in Scotland. He was scheduled to leave for the conference that afternoon. After lunch he worked on cutting old glass he had just acquired to modify for the folly he was building in the garden of his home, nestled in the countryside high above the Antrim coast, overlooking the Irish Sea. His English wife, Susan, meanwhile busied herself organising the holiday they were to take when he returned. Every so often she would check the time and go out to the garden to remind her husband that he needed to get ready to leave. 'For God's sake, Ian, you've been building that damn thing for months,' she said at one point. 'You can finish it after our holidays.' 'But I've got this nice new glass-cutter,' he kept replying, going back to work. 'Just give me another few minutes.'

Ian Phoenix was not much looking forward to the conference. He was happier cutting glass for his folly. In fact he had talked to Susan about not attending at all.

The conference was a yearly event that brought together military, police and MI5 intelligence officers prized for their experience and expertise in the war against terrorism in Northern Ireland. For over a decade Phoenix had been a key figure in under-cover operations directed mainly at the Provisional IRA. Since 1992 he had been head of a recently developed Royal Ulster Constabulary specialist sur-veillance unit.

Ian had enjoyed the previous year's helicopter trip and the opportunity to walk the heather-clad Mull with his colleagues. He had, however, felt the emerging tensions between the different security agencies involved in Northern Ireland. When another police officer who was not originally scheduled to go in 1994 had insisted on being included – it was something of a prestige event in the intelligence world – the detective superintendent thought he had found the excuse he needed to back out. Phoenix had offered to let him take his place. But in the end his senior officers had pressed him to attend.

After lingering over his work in the garden as long as he could, he appeared at the door of the little office Susan had in the front of the converted farmhouse, saying he was already late. 'Why didn't you tell me what time it was?' he asked with mock innocence, which was belied by the mischievous glint in his eye. The flight was at five-thirty, and it was already after four.

He packed a suit-carrier which a few months earlier he had bought for his son's twenty-first birthday ('Nice present, dad,' his son had smiled, 'I knew you always wanted one') and the leather satchel that he took with him wherever he went, whether on mountain walks or to top-secret security conferences.

Susan had offered to drive him to the RAF base at Aldergrove Airport, just a few miles north of Belfast, where a Chinook helicopter was waiting to transport him and the twenty-four other participants in the conference to their destination – Fort George, near Inverness.

They drove west over low hills and through green pasture-lands towards the airport. It was a grey, sunless afternoon. He spent most of the trip talking about the problems his wife was experiencing in raising funds for a project that was dear to her heart. She was a developmental psychologist, specialising in programmes for

3

the deaf. She was trying to develop a video unit for the deaf, but she was short of funds. Though it was a potential all-Ireland project, involving both Catholics and Protestants, and offered the possibility of creating jobs, so far she had managed to interest neither the Irish nor the British government.

As they were waved through the first set of security gates into the RAF base, Ian had a brainwave. 'Why don't you write to Richard Branson? He's a man of vision,' he said. He insisted she send a letter off as soon as possible. Susan did not argue. Ian was an expert at delegating tasks, and did so with the quiet authority of a man for whom it was second nature. She smiled and promised him she would 'follow orders'.

As they went through the second security gate, Susan noticed someone looking a little lost. She pointed him out. 'Maybe he's off to the same place as you,' she suggested. Her husband recognised him as one of the intelligence officers attending the conference. 'So he is. He's a typical Brit – lost as usual,' he said, reminding Susan in his usual bantering manner that she was a Brit too. 'He'll get there eventually.' Then he softened. 'Listen, if he's still wandering around when you go back, Susan, you'd better tell him the way.'

They drove past several Wessex helicopters parked on the runway. Susan pointed these out – 'Look, they're all ready for you!'

'No, not those wee baby ones,' Ian replied. 'We're

going in a Chinook. You know – the jungle stuff!' He had always loved the exciting sound of helicopters in jungle warfare, and he spoke of the Chinook with affection.

They pulled up at the hangar. He kissed her, then climbed out, the suit-carrier slung over one shoulder, the leather satchel in the other hand. She sat in the car for a moment, watching him. They had been married twenty-six years. She had met him in 1966, when she was a Queen Alexandra's nurse working in a military hospital in Aldershot. In those days he was a young, dashing Irish paratrooper, well tanned by the desert sun, and she was a rather shy English girl, fulfilling a lifetime's ambition to nurse and 'see the world'. (The nursing 'world' had so far been limited to Aldershot and Germany until she had been swept off her feet by her Irish beau.) He had brought her back to his homeland, and, despite all its murderous problems, with which he dealt almost every day of his life, through him she had grown to love the place.

He was still a handsome man at fifty-one, she thought as she watched him walk towards the small reception hut where the other men were gathered, putting on their orange survival suits and waiting for the bus that would take them to the helicopter. He was of trim build but broad-shouldered, with silvery grey hair, a ready, generous smile and a straight gaze. As usual, she wished he wasn't leaving her, even if it was only for a couple of days. And, as usual, he did not look back as he disappeared into the hangar.

She swung her car round and drove back towards the gates. She did not see any sign of the lost Englishman they'd passed a few moments earlier. The military guards recognised her and waved her on. Then, as she drove through the second gate, she did see two young men who were obviously lost. They were standing around, waiting for directions to the hangar. She pulled up alongside them and rolled the window down. 'Are you travelling to Inverness?' she asked. They nodded yes. 'I'm Ian Phoenix's wife. Hop in and I'll give you a lift to the hangar.' They gratefully accepted her offer.

She drove back to the hangar with her fresh set of passengers. They thanked her profusely for that little act of hospitality. 'I wished them a pleasant weekend,' she recalls. 'I can still see their smiling faces as they leaned down to say thank you.' She looked past them into the depths of the hangar, hoping to catch a glimpse of Ian. The bus had arrived that was to ferry them to the Chinook helicopter waiting on the runway. Her husband was somewhere in the crowd that was already boarding the bus, but she could not see him. Once more she started her car, and drove out of the security area. She was going to Belfast to keep a dinner appointment with their daughter.

Just before 5.20 p.m the bus rumbled out of the hangar to the helicopter. At 5.20 p.m. the passengers boarded the helicopter. Their baggage was placed along the centre of the aircraft's cabin without being put through the security X-ray.

Altogether there were twenty-nine people on board, including the pilots and two loadies.

The struggle in Northern Ireland was just about to enter its twenty-fifth year. Since August 1969 the situation had gone through several drastic transformations. The chief topic on the agenda of the 1994 conference reflected one of them. The intelligence chiefs were meeting to discuss the growing power of the Protestant/loyalist paramilitary groups. In the previous two years the two main loyalist terrorist groups, the Ulster Defence Association (UDA) and the Ulster Volunteer Force (UVF), had been killing more people than the Provisionals. In November 1993 the British police had intercepted a massive arms shipment in Teesport that was destined for the UVF. It was known that the latter had acquired explosives. The potential for a further escalation of violence was there, and the security services had to decide what were the best tactics to deal with such a possibility.

This problem could become especially acute in the light of another momentous change that was on the horizon. None knew this better than Ian Phoenix. Since he had been in charge of the unit, for the past eighteen months, he had been aware of contacts between leading members of the Social Democratic and Labour Party (SDLP), Northern Ireland's main nationalist party, and Sinn Fein, the political wing of the Provisional IRA. Members of both had been engaged in secret talks. The police knew that the British government had been in contact with the Provisional IRA. Indeed, one of the MI5 agents at the NIO who was on the flight, seated not far from Detective Superintendent Phoenix, had been involved in behind-the-scenes talks with the Provisionals within the past year. The Provisionals were talking about calling a cessation of their campaign of terror. The two sides had been exploring various possibilities. What concerned the RUC was the possible reaction of the North's loyalist paramilitaries if they thought a deal was being done between the British government and the IRA. All hell could break loose.

This was a cause of unease among the RUC Special Branch. The unease had been deepened by a further development. For the past year the intelligence services had been shaken by a dispute over the role that MI5 was to play in the war against Northern Ireland's paramilitaries. In May 1992 the agency had taken over the running of counter-terrorism operations in Britain. Since 1993 it had been attempting to bypass the RUC and centralise control of certain Northern Ireland surveillance operations by running them from MI5 headquarters in London. Detective Superintendent Phoenix was among those who were resisting this move most strongly. He did not trust

MI5, which he thought was operating according to its own agenda. He believed he had the support of the head of the RUC Special Branch, Assistant Chief Constable Brian Fitzsimons, who was with him on the flight. But Fitzsimons was due to retire soon, and Ian had expressed concern that some senior officers were beginning to waver under sustained pressure from MI5. As a result of these machinations, there was an air of uncertainty within the ranks of the Special Branch, many of whose officers were suspicious of the British government's long-term intentions in Northern Ireland.

At 5.42 p.m. the Chinook climbed into the sky, its huge twin rotors battering the air and raising a minor dust storm around it, its passengers seated in two rows facing each other along the side of the craft. The meteorological information showed that the weather would be adequate for flying by Visual Flight Rules for most of the trip, but that as the helicopter passed near Machrihanish airfield near the Mull of Kintyre – at the southern tip of the long peninsula on the west of Scotland – there was haze and a possibility of fog which could reduce visibility to 500 metres.

As the enormous helicopter carried its precious cargo eastwards, Susan drove down towards the city of Belfast, which was, as ever, under a grey canopy of cloud. She was mulling over in her mind the letter she would write to Richard Branson as she headed towards her dinner date with her daughter.

Flying at a low level, the Chinook began its sea crossing near Carnlough, a pretty coastal village with a distinctive white stone harbour, not far from where Ian and Susan Phoenix lived. The bottom of their garden overlooks a cliff-lined coast beneath which stretches a lonely, rocky strand. From the strand, on a clear day, the Mull of Kintyre is easily visible, rising up on the horizon. The detective superintendent's favourite way of unwinding was to stroll hand in hand with Susan, their dogs running beside them, along the strand and the cliff paths, looking over the cold choppy waters of the channel between Ireland and Scotland. Often they would watch the sudden fogs that could so quickly envelop the huge round head of the promontory towards which the Chinook was now flying at over 100 miles per hour.

As the helicopter neared the Mull the weather conditions deteriorated rapidly. A thick grey fog snaked around the headland, enveloping everything. At around 6 p.m., the helicopter entered the fog bank at a speculated 140 knots per hour, creating a mystery which has yet to be satisfactorily resolved. It flew past the Mull lighthouse, with its landing-pad to the north. Behind the lighthouse rise the first low, gradual slopes of Beinn na Lice. The name means Hill of Stone, and the mountain rises to a height of 1,400 feet, the highest point on the Mull's southern tip.

The evidence suggests that the helicopter was travelling in a cruise climb – a gradual ascent –

when the pilots seemed to have realised for one split second that something was disastrously wrong. The nose of the Chinook was raised up just before it slammed tail first into a rocky outcrop at an elevation of 800 feet on the Hill of Stone. The Chinook then split in two main sections. The greater part of the aircraft came to rest on a ridge 700 metres further up the hill and the remainder slid back down the heather-clad slopes, thirty-five metres away from the main section. As the Chinook was torn asunder, its aviation fuel ignited, creating a huge fireball, engulfing everything in its path and starting a fierce blaze which was still burning when the first stunned witnesses arrived at the scene of the devastation at about 6.04 p.m.

Susan Phoenix had finished dinner with her daughter and, having declined an invitation to go to the cinema with her and her boyfriend, was driving north towards home. As usual, she was listening to BBC Radio Ulster. As she went through the northern suburb of Greenisland the news flash came. 'A military Chinook helicopter has crashed on the Mull of Kintyre while carrying security-forces personnel to a conference in Inverness,' said the newscaster. 'First reports suggest there are no survivors.'

'No, no, no,' Susan screamed, clinging to the wheel of the car.

The rest of that evening was a blur. But one thing was clear. For the last quarter of a century her life had been entwined with that of Ian and through him with the brutal war of ambush, assassination and terror that was known euphemistically as the 'Troubles'. Now her life had been changed for ever. She clung to the wheel of the car, frantic to find out what had happened, seeking new bearings.

She knew this: that the bearings for the future lay in the past. And, naturally, it was to her past that she turned, and would turn again, to seek Ian's strength, comfort and understanding.

Chapter 1

Thank God
for Rosemary Dwyer

When Susan Phoenix first met Lance-Corporal Ian Phoenix of the 3rd Parachute Regiment he spun her a line about his childhood, painting a beguiling picture of a boyhood spent riding horses barefoot along the beach. In fact the lance-corporal was romancing somewhat. He was born in 1943 in Granville, an obscure village in Co. Tyrone, Northern Ireland, not far from the border with the Republic of Ireland but at least forty miles from the nearest beach. Bare feet certainly did figure in his childhood – he often walked on them to school. He came from a family of eight brothers and sisters. His mother, Maggie, was the caretaker of the local school and cleaned house for the vicar in nearby Castlecaulfield. His father, Willie, worked as a lorry driver for a linen mill. Ian was raised in a small slate-roofed cottage with no running water. Water had to be carried from the tap behind the schoolhouse and stored in enamel buckets in the scullery beside the old jaw-box sink. Along with his brothers and sisters, he helped to tend the Tilley lamps and keep their wicks clean. The nearest town of any size was Dungannon, where he went to secondary school.

Ian Phoenix's relationship with his parents was typical of that found within rural, Irish families, where the father often remains distant, emotionally uninvolved with his children. One of the few memories Ian had of his father was of going with him to the pub. At Willie Phoenix's urging he would have to stand on the bar and sing. The boy would always give the patrons a grand bow in response to their applause. He squirmed with embarrassment when relating this tale in later life. However, Mr Phoenix related to his son in other, more important, ways. He introduced Ian to his lifelong hobby of game shooting. They would roam the hills around Granville hunting rabbits and pheasants for the pot.

If Ian did not speak much about his father, about his mother it was a different story. His home, though modest, was always filled with the sound of her singing and the smells of the apple pies and soda and potato bread she baked on an old black coal-fired range. When she was away visiting friends in England, she always put Ian in charge of the goats, which he also had to milk. Mrs Phoenix was highly thought of in the village, and had a gentle, self-deprecating sense of humour that her son would inherit. He would also inherit her tradition of raising goats – years later he would try raising them in the farmhouse which he and Susan converted into their home.

Still, even without riding barefoot on the beach, his upbringing was colourful enough. Growing up in the 1940s in rural Ireland, he caught flickering glimpses of a world that was passing. It was a world where people still gathered at night in each other's houses for impromptu sessions of dancing, singing and story-telling. It was a world without electricity where ghost stories and tales of the 'Other World' of the fairies still enthralled the young.

There were times when that Other World did not seem so unreal at all. Ian and his chums spent much of their free time playing on the shores of Eskragh Lough and the bog around it, discovering dark pools and secret paths that led to mysterious little islands. Though not far from his home, it was a desolate area. During a game of hide-and-seek, he once lost his companions and went searching for them along a bog road. Dusk was falling. Suddenly a small man in a tweed jacket and plus-fours and a country hat appeared walking along the road and passed the young boy. When Ian turned to ask him if he had seen his friends, the little man had vanished. Years on he often recounted the tale, which helped reinforce a superstitious streak in him.*

It was near Eskragh Lough that Ian began his career as a detective, in a manner of speaking. During the summer of 1953 the level of the lough dropped due to water being drawn off for use by the Moygashel Textile Mills in nearby Dungannon. Ian and his friends noticed something buried in the peat. As they scraped away the crumbling soil, they exposed the length of two dug-out canoes. Each was slightly over twenty-four feet long. At the same site a series of wooden piles was found, as well as several stone querns for grinding corn. These were the remains of an ancient Irish stilt village which once stood in the lake. The Ulster Museum acquired the canoes, and in 1961 an analysis of them appeared in the *Ulster Journal of Archaeology* which dated them to the Late Bronze Age. For his pains, Ian was given sixpence by the museum. (Unfortunately, attempts to preserve the canoes failed, and by the late 1960s the museum had disposed of all but the stern-board of one of them.)

Ian's curiosity was also taking him in other directions. He began experimenting with making wine. His first effort was a concoction made from blackberries.

---

* The author had a similar experience on a bog road in Co. Roscommon in 1965. On that occasion the diminutive stranger was also seen by the author's hiking companion in an encounter which took place in the early hours of the morning on a very bleak stretch of road, far from any human habitation.

He bottled and buried it. Later he dug it up, opened it, and passed it round a group of his schoolfriends, who proceeded to get rotten drunk and then violently sick. Unfortunately this incident seems not to have discouraged him. Throughout his life he would continue experimenting, making wine from elderberries, and champagne from gooseberries. Most infamous of all was his pea-pod wine, which one friend who was exposed to it described as having a bouquet of sweaty socks. Many years later, when he was a police sergeant, he received a Christmas card from his colleagues in the station where he was based which summed up their reaction to his attempts to rival the Rothschilds. It read, 'Dear Sgt Phoenix, we LOVE you but we HATE your wine.'

During his childhood, one of Ian's most influential relationships was that with his grandfather, John Turbitt, from whom he would derive his love of soldiering. Turbitt had been a soldier in the Boer War, during which he had been wounded in the leg by a spear. Later, he joined the Irish Fusileers. At the outbreak of the First World War it was drafted *en masse* into the British army with the Ulster Volunteer Force, a Protestant militia which had been formed to oppose Home Rule for Ireland. They were sent to the front, where their men distinguished themselves by their bravery. Granda Turbitt was again wounded in battle. However, he remained undeterred. When the Second World War began he again joined up –

this time as a cook. He survived both wars, to reach ninety-nine years of age.

Unfortunately the old man's war wounds caught up with him, and after several bouts of gangrene he had to have both legs amputated. It became Ian's task to push Granda Turbitt in his wheelchair to the pub every Thursday night. There the old soldier would get so drunk on dark rum that he would slide on to the floor, and Ian would have to haul him back into wheelchair. 'Now I'm really legless,' his grandfather would mutter, with his rather grim Ulster sense of humour.

Ireland's own troubled past soon brought itself to the attention of the young boy. He discovered a Martini Henry rifle hidden in the rafters of his house. It dated back to the early days of the UVF. He liked to march around the fields with it on his shoulder, and to set up ambushes in the laneways. But he was not the only one who liked to play at soldiering in the area around Granville. Ian and his friends discovered a group of would-be IRA men drilling in an old roofless shed in a remote field. Ian's gang, which included Catholics and Protestants, gathered behind some nearby bushes. When the drilling began, they hurled clods of earth into the shed. As the irate IRA trainees came racing out to see who was attacking them, the boys vanished into the trees.

One of the Catholics who had been part of Ian's gang later joined the Provisional IRA. In the early

1970s he blew himself to bits when the bomb that he was planting exploded prematurely. Ian Phoenix would spend the best part of his life disrupting IRA activities of a rather more serious kind than went on in that old shed.

In his middle teens Ian must have become aware of what he referred to often as his 'puny body'. He found an old Charles Atlas book and proceeded to 'work out' with the help of an abandoned cart axle which he found in a deserted farm shed. This was another pastime which he was to continue throughout his adult life, with an increasingly sophisticated array of equipment.

A bright and adventurous boy, Ian Phoenix was not encouraged towards a studious life. He loved to read adventure stories from his collection of second-hand books under the flickering lamplight in his bedroom. In 1959, aged sixteen, he left secondary school and spent a year studying at the Dungannon Technical College. After that, he took on a series of jobs, which succeeded only in boring him. For a short time he worked as a coffin-maker, then in a dye works. But he wanted action. He applied to join the Royal Ulster Constabulary – the Northern Ireland police force – but was rejected because of his age.

There were few options open to him in Northern Ireland in the late 1950s. For an imaginative and ambitious youth growing up at that time the place seemed moribund – socially as well as economically, and even more so in the remote rural areas than in Belfast and Derry, the main cities. For both the Protestant and the Catholic working classes there were three basic routes to a better life. University was one. Because Catholics were traditionally discriminated against in the major industries, they tended more so than Protestants to take advantage of the provisions of the postwar Education Act, which gave the poor access to higher education. Then there was the emigration route. Thousands headed for the ferries that carried them to England, and many thousands more ventured further afield – to the United States and Australia. Finally there were the armed services. These had a strong appeal to both Catholic and Protestant teenagers who were keen to escape the smothering confines of their own very conservative society, see the world, and perhaps learn a trade at the same time.

In January 1961 Ian read an advertisement in Northern Ireland's main evening newspaper, the *Belfast Telegraph*. It read, 'PARATROOPERS WANTED. Minimum service, six or nine years.' He applied immediately. Much to his amazement, a few weeks later what he described as a 'Rolls-Royce of an army jeep' arrived at his door with 'a large, hard-bitten paratroop sergeant-major at the wheel'. According to Ian Phoenix's own account of the event:

> He immediately launched into his well-rehearsed sales drive, and after an hour of hard talking I was convinced

that this was the life for me (all nine years!). A bottle of whiskey was produced, and he and my father then settled down to the more serious side of life, drinking, hunting and shooting. Not only did he get me but also a black Labrador pup worth thirty pounds.

Over the next few weeks there were further visits, mostly for tots of whiskey from my father. Eventually I was given a ride in the jeep to Lisnelly army barracks in Omagh, where I underwent the basic army medical test and was berated by the local recruiting officer to join the Irish Guards instead of the Parachute Regiment. When that failed, he stood back, had another look at me, and cajoled me to put down the Irish Guards as my second choice, anticipating I would fail the para training. In hindsight, the army must have been desperate for recruits when two recruiting officers were vying for my skinny body to swell their regiments' ranks. In fact they must have been desperate or getting a fat commission for every new sucker enticed into the service.

A few months later, the recruiting officer, Sergeant-Major Ray Hallus, came back one more time to the Phoenix home. He brought with him a one-way ticket from Dungannon to Aldershot, the headquarters of the Parachute Regiment.

Ian Phoenix set off to begin a new life 'lugging my tatty brown suitcase with four changes of clothes and wearing the standard Irishman's blue suit'. Following in the footsteps of countless thousands of young Irishmen before and since, he caught the night ferry from Belfast to Heysham.

'Eventually I arrived in Aldershot after having said about 2,000 times, "Excuse me, but can you direct me to . . .,"' he recalled years later. First impressions were not good. 'It was a dirty, grubby place,' he said of Aldershot station, 'with as much character as a wart-hog's watering-hole. At least you could get a drink at the latter.' However, there he found a sympathetic para who bought him a coffee at an espresso bar and then directed him on 'the final stage of my quest to the land of the Red Beret'.

So it was that on 26 April 1961, on his eighteenth birthday, Ian Phoenix found himself sitting in the back of a Beverley transport aircraft several hundred feet above the ground. He was petrified. The parachute dispatcher did not help. He was a burly soldier from the South of Ireland, with a thick brogue. He knew the trainee para was an Ulster Protestant. When it was Phoenix's turn to take the plunge, he grabbed him by the scruff of the neck and shouted, 'Get out to fuck you dirty wee Orange bastard', before hurling the young lad into the icy slipstream flowing under the plane.

Student nurse Susan Cheshire was sitting in the NAAFI in Aldershot one day in the autumn of 1966 mulling over the disappointment she had recently suffered. A planned holiday in Ireland with an Irish nurse, Rosemary Dwyer, with whom she worked, had fallen through. Susan had been looking forward to it

– she had never been to Ireland. Indeed, at eighteen, her holidays had been limited to those planned by her railwayman father. As a railman's 'dependant' she had been able to travel to several European countries, usually wearing the home-made dresses provided by her mother's skilled dressmaking. Otherwise, at that point in her life the most exciting thing that had happened to her was drinking two Babychams in a row. She had passed her 'O' levels and was a 'smart' girl who had been involved in the Duke of Edinburgh's Award scheme for something more unusual to do, so her father's ambition for her was that she should follow in her big sister's footsteps and get a secretarial job in a railway office. In fact she had shown an aptitude for the sciences, and her headmistress had suggested to her father that she should study to be a medical doctor. But Mr Cheshire had intimated his concern that this would mean many more years of expensive study, during which family finances would be stretched. Susan knew, however, that her kind-hearted parents would have supported her ambition had she insisted.

Susan eventually went her own way. She put on a Queen Alexandra's Royal Army Nursing Corps uniform and became a nurse, leaving behind a warm and loving family in Peterborough who were to support her, from a distance, in her many new lives in the years to come.

As she sat in the NAAFI – known as The Round-about Club – she was disturbed by a commotion. She was not surprised. Earlier, word had rippled through the young nurses stationed at the Cambridge Military Hospital that the 3rd Battalion of the Parachute Regiment (3 Para) was back in town. It brought with it a reputation of the sort that had accompanied the Vikings in their visits a few centuries before. Senior staff advised staying away from the paras. 'They are the loving and leaving kind,' the young nurses were solemnly warned. A more experienced colleague described to Susan how after taking just one drink from a paratrooper she was surprised to find herself unconscious, under the table. 'They slip you Mickey Finns,' she said, shaking her head.

A young paratrooper came racing into the NAAFI club, dashing between the tables. Much to her surprise, he sat down next to Susan. 'What shall we talk about?' he asked without introducing himself, as if they were old friends. He glanced around nervously. Lance-Corporal Ian Phoenix was a little breathless, having just escaped from the custody of the military police while on his way to jail for some minor misdemeanour or other. He had jumped out of the back of their Land Rover and run for his life. 'How's about biology?' he went on, before Susan could respond.

That was the wrong opener to a girl who had not long ago passed her 'O' level in the subject. 'Fine,' she answered, and proceeded to give him a lecture on the life of the cabbage white butterfly.

Nurse Cheshire's confidence on the subject of the cabbage white butterfly could not completely hide the fact that she was a bit in awe of the handsome young man with his dark tan and rather cocky manner, wearing a flashy gold Rolex watch on his wrist. The fugitive paratrooper soon had her spellbound with tales of the Borneo jungle and the Radfan Desert. He told her about jungle campaigns against terrorists in Malaysia, of how he had broken his back in a parachute jump, and threw in a few stories of the fleshpots of Singapore for good measure. There was even a tale attached to his Rolex watch, of which he was extremely proud. He had come by it through rather unconventional methods. On his first overseas posting, in Bahrain, a fellow paratrooper called Arthur had decided after a few drinks that he'd like to raid the NAAFI shop at the RAF base in nearby Mahararragh. He climbed on to the shop's roof, dug a hole through its asbestos ceiling, and dropped in. He filled a big towel with all the watches, Schaeffer and Parker pens that he could carry. He displayed his loot for sale, back at the para's base at Hammallah. From the horde Ian Phoenix picked out the gold Rolex watch and parted with twenty pounds.

Among the loot was a pile of handkerchiefs. 'Well, what's with the hankies, Arthur?' the thief was asked. 'Oh, I really don't know. I just used them to wipe my fingerprints off the place, and then I thought that maybe they would get my prints off the hankies so I brought them too,' he replied.

Ian was the most worldly, experienced man Susan had ever met. But what interested and delighted her most was that he was interested in talking to her. To her, he seemed so exotic and confident. She was whisked off her feet by an Irish paratrooper who appeared to think he was the bee's knees.

'His line of patter was so outrageous that it took me a couple of years before I could really tell if he was spinning me a line or just practising his blarney,' she says. Among the tales he told her were those about his childhood in Ireland – riding barefoot on the beaches of Granville, Co. Tyrone. She did not know that it was a small village a few miles from the Irish border and many miles from the sea. ('The back end of nowhere' as Ian later admitted).

When Susan happened to mention the fact that her planned holiday in Ireland had fallen through, Lance-Corporal Phoenix invited her over for a few weeks to meet the folks. She accepted.

The trip was one of the happiest in her life. They passed the first part of it with Ian's sister and brother-in-law in Kelly's Caravan Park in Portrush, a seaside town on the windswept north Antrim coast. In the evenings, they adjourned to a pub which had a barn at the back, where a singsong took place on bales of hay. 'I thought I would burst with happiness at being in such a different environment with people who – unlike myself – all seemed to be able to sing,' Susan recalled.

They went grouse-hunting in Donnemanagh. Though she couldn't sing, she could shoot – and had a marksman's certificate from the Duke of Edinburgh Award scheme to prove it – so she thought she would be able to cope with this. Then Ian handed her a five-shot Browning automatic rifle. As the grouse flew up from around her feet she fired once. 'For God's sake, keep shooting,' he screamed as the birds flew away unharmed. She hadn't realised she had four more rounds in the clip. It became a family joke, to be related several times in the years to come.

As evening approached, they found themselves alone, walking over undulating peat fields. They stopped to rest by a bank of peat stacked up to dry. There they made love for the first time. 'He was fierce and gentle at the same time,' she recalled. 'That holiday cemented our love and almost complete dependence on each other for our happiness for the next twenty-eight years. I can still feel the love and happiness that started then. Thank God for Rosemary Dwyer!'

From that moment on they set about organising their joint ambitions to make a shared life together. Their plan was simple. She would finish her SRN training, and he would complete his nine-year tour of duty. Then they would return to Ireland together and make a new life for themselves.

Shortly after their meeting in Aldershot, Lance-Corporal Phoenix was sent off to the mountains of Kenya on a map-reading exercise. He began writing to her almost at once.

He already seemed rather weary of certain aspects of army life, as some of his letters show. From Kenya he wrote (turning to Morse code when necessary):

> Sorry Susan, but I've picked the wrong day for writing as I am sick as a sea-going parrot about this stupid army and all the cross-eyed --... .--...--.--.--. .... that run it. Since coming out here all I've done is scream up and down the slopes of Mt Kenya like a demented being with a compass and a map. Right now I'm about 1,000 ft up with a trainee signaller and have lost interest in every damn thing except you. We are supposed to move from RV [rendezvous point] to RV but I've said to hell with it. This is as far as I go for another four days.

In fact Lance-Corporal Phoenix's group was the only one to locate its target during the course of the exercise, having picked up a few tracking tips from the local people. A Kenyan army officer came up to him afterwards and said, 'A fucking excellent job, Phoenix.' Thirty years later, he still looked like a proud young soldier when he related the tale to his son.

Phoenix's love of wildlife and exotic countryside was evident in other letters which Susan received at that time. He told her that she would love the place, because he was aware of her love of art and painting:

> At night the sky is full of stars so low one feels like plucking them out of it ... every night the usual crew and myself lie out on the grass discussing every subject we can think of, I can assure you that's a hell of a lot. (That's enough of that, Phoenix!) You know the day your first letter arrived, when it was handed to me I was nervous as hell before opening it. I'm not quite sure why or maybe I do but I'll not admit it (coward!) ... Just getting used to the climate as the air is somewhat thin at this height (gasp!) ... I took a patrol out yesterday for a little walkabout, the Major told me to keep them on the tracks as rhino and buffalo roam this area. He should have had more sense, the fool, as Phoenix took them hunting. You see we carry live rounds for protection against the animals like these. Now I have my doubts as to who needs the protection, the animals or us! ... keep writing, Susan, I don't mind if it is gibberish – I like reading it. You're the most lovable headcase I've ever known. So I'll finish now and lie on the slopes as mournful as a sick parrot along with the others and have five minutes' silence for our absence from the 'shot [Aldershot].
> Love Ian

He also promised to take her to Kenya in the future, when they could be like the tourists he had seen watching the feeding lions in the game-park lodge. Seemingly during a R & R (rest and recuperation) period the rangers tried to wake the sleeping paratroopers at dawn (along with the paying tourists) to see the animals come down to the waterhole. He commented 'It would have taken more than Billy Smart's circus to wake us after that exercise!'

If training exercises in Kenya left Ian somewhat frustrated – possibly because he couldn't shoot *all* of the game – his memories of the Borneo jungle were much more satisfactory. And it was as a young paratrooper preparing for jungle warfare in the 1966 Borneo campaign, that he first came into contact with the SAS, at its jungle school at Tootong in Brunei. Here Ian developed sufficient knowledge of medical skills for him and his pals to be able to pose as medical students to impress the local girls on leave in Northern Ireland. His tracking ability, later to be developed in Kenya, was initiated in this training-ground. Several of his colleagues from that time went on to join 22 SAS in Hereford. He did not because he refused to sign on to extend his contract from nine to thirteen years. Later he would spend some of the most challenging years of his career in the RUC coordinating SAS operations.

Lance-Corporal Phoenix loved to regale Susan and later his young family with tales of his jungle experiences. He always said that the jungle was a strange and extremely difficult operating environment, in which some soldiers could not function at all. He knew a soldier who had won a George Cross for rescuing two Gurkhas from a minefield which he had crossed to save them, but in the jungle the same man went to pieces. When Phoenix was leader of a four-man reconnaissance patrol operating deep in the Indonesia/Borneo border area one of his men used to wake screaming during the night with the overwhelming feeling that the jungle was closing in upon him. Ian later told his son that while operating in the jungle over long periods he felt that man regained something of his animal ancestry – a kind of sixth sense. He recalled one occasion when he was bending by a jungle stream to wash a mess tin and suddenly felt someone watching him from within the surrounding jungle. The alarm bells were ringing in his head as the hairs began to prickle on the back of his neck. He slowly finished washing the kit, packed his rucksack and rejoined his mates, all of whom were already standing with taut faces ready to go, having sensed the same thing, though no one had said a word.

The now almost extinct tribe of Poonans, a gentle and charming people, were another source of information and interest for the D Company patrol groups. Even in the 1960s the Poonans were already showing signs of dying out as a result of interbreeding. Their babies rarely survived after the age of five. The chief used to offer inducements to the paratroops if they would sleep with his daughters, to try to improve the 'stock'. It is unclear whether anyone took up the offer, but what is certain is that the army's medical training was very useful to the Poonans, who received antibiotic injections and had teeth extractions for the first time.

Ian's own children were later given tuition in how to brush insects off the body in the jungle to avoid being stung or bitten. He also taught them to recognise a variety of animal tracks in mud paths, and passed on the lesson that shaving in the jungle was not a good idea as cuts could become infected (and perfumed shaving-soap could be detected by the sensitive noses of the enemy).

In Bahrain Ian served under men with whom he would later meet up in Northern Ireland. One of them was Colonel Farrar Hockley. On one occasion Phoenix and his squad had been ordered to build a camp, to keep them occupied. After three days of being navvies in tropical temperatures they were so fed up that they mutinied and downed tools. They sent a delegation to Farrar Hockley, who was their commander, protesting at the 'slave labour'. He was not only sympathetic to their plight but also arranged a week's rest for everyone.*

Another figure with whom Ian became acquainted

---

* As major-general, Farrar Hockley later became commander of ground forces in Northern Ireland during the period which saw the birth of the Provisional IRA. He was to make a famous announcement in January 1971 in which he named five men as leading members of the Provisionals, accusing them of orchestrating street riots and inciting violence. This is believed to have provoked a showdown with the new group which was preparing to launch an all-out campaign against policemen and soldiers.

was Major Peter Chiswell, the company commander for the Borneo campaign, who became Commander, Land Forces, Northern Ireland in 1982. Members of D Company link his name to that of Charlie Moon, their tame monkey. The little monkey often disgraced himself after being regularly fed on medical-kit dexedrine and stale beer. One such occasion happened to coincide with a visit by Peter Chiswell to their jungle billet. As the well-liked and respected officer began to address the men, the little monkey, who was nursing a hangover in the rafters, disgraced himself by releasing a stream of monkey pee on to the officer's head.

International relations were first noted by the young Ian Phoenix as he met American Vietnam veterans in Borneo and Singapore. He recalled the absolute incredulity expressed by one such soldier that the British patrols were operating for many weeks without air support deep in alien jungle territory. The patrol groups would see a helicopter only when they were dropped into the jungle and when they were airlifted out many weeks later. This was very different to the heavy air support which the Americans had provided for similar patrols in the Vietnam War. During 'friendly fights' in the NCOs' club in Singapore (very close to the famous Raffles Hotel), Ian was quite aghast to learn that the Vietnam 'vets' reported having raided their own medical packs in order to get 'high' during their jungle-warfare stints. Feeding drugs to a little monkey was one thing, but abusing one's own body and brain in the field was anathema to a professional soldier. Ian reported spending his twenty-first birthday in the same Singapore club fighting with yet more 'vets' who insisted on annoying him with stories of their junkie habits in the field. He later regretted wasting so much valuable time in the Far East in such escapades when he could have been exploring more of the Eastern culture. As a middle-aged man he became very interested in collecting oriental teas and taking his family to visit the places that he felt he had missed during those ingenuous early years. Ian and Susan were to celebrate their daughter's twenty-first birthday by visiting Singapore and Malaysia with their children in a slightly more sedate style.

Ian's later love of France may have begun during some joint exercises with the French paratroopers in the 1960s – although one doubts that there was much of an *entente cordiale* when during one such exercise Ian's pals decided to liven up some mock grenade attacks by wrapping plastic explosive around the thunder-flashes. The resulting 'mini-bombs' succeeded in blowing the French paras completely off their feet, not to mention what it did to their eardrums. He maintained that this was where he first heard the expression '*c'est la guerre*', while all concerned chortled with delight at the shocked expressions on the young French faces.

On another Anglo-French exercise Phoenix witnessed some particularly poor decision-making by senior officers. A joint parachute drop was to take place over some part of rural France, but the weather proved to be highly unsuitable. Apparently problems arose when neither the French nor the British officers in charge were prepared to give orders to cancel the drop, for fear of ridicule by the other. The young paratroopers were rightly terrified and disgusted but obeyed orders as they were trained to do. Although Phoenix landed badly he walked away unharmed in comparison to his peers, many of whom could be seen lying around the drop zone with broken bones sticking out from their shattered limbs. He saw one of his friends with both shin-bones broken and protruding from his flesh. When asked if there was anything Ian could do for him, the man just shook his head and continued looking morosely at his destroyed legs. Ian believed that for commanders to risk the lives of so many men for personal pride, ego and vanity was deplorable. It was a lesson for his own later decision-making in the police.

When the young paratroopers returned from their worldwide tours and military exercises they often found themselves not only bored but with pockets emptied by their foreign pleasures. Back in Aldershot their resourcefulness came into play to increase funds and add some spice to life. Ian enjoyed labouring jobs on building sites, which both helped his level of fitness and prepared him for one of his later hobbies of folly-building. One bunch of para pals at this time secured the job of demolishing an old cinema. They built up small teams of workers, some knocking down walls or cleaning bricks, and others clearing and selling the timber. One enterprising team of two mates discovered an old safe in the former manager's office. Their excitement was great, because they had been in the D Company explosives group and knew *exactly* how to blow it open – or so they thought. They applied the explosive and hid behind a desk as they fired the detonator. When they extricated themselves from the remains of the shattered desk they were quite surprised that their miscalculations had blown the whole thing through the wall and out into the middle of the car park. It was unfortunate for them that it was just opposite the police station – *more* promising para careers were blighted.

The legacy of stories from those early days would be with the Phoenix family for many years to come. Ian often referred to himself as 'Phoenix' as the letters and personal diaries testify, often poking fun at himself and life's strange turns.

A turn of fate changed the long-term plans of Susan and Ian around the Christmas of 1967. Susan had invited Ian to spend Christmas with her family in Peterborough, where he planned to ask formally for her hand in marriage. They knew that she was to be posted to the British Military Hospital in Munster (BAOR) in January, and they wanted to be officially engaged before she left. Her family were quite shocked that the dedicated career-girl seemed to be willing to give everything up for this young Irishman, but as usual, they supported the decision in a somewhat bemused way. She recalls having cried all the way to the airport when she left Ian for Germany, because he had got up at the crack of dawn to kiss her goodbye yet again. However her parents became even more bemused and shocked when, after three months in Germany, Susan returned to plan a wedding. 'As a result of too many *earth-moving* goodbye scenes' before she left for Germany, she discovered a baby daughter on the way, possibly because, as she told her parents, 'nice' girls didn't use contraception in those days (despite the sister tutor's advice to 'never trust a paratrooper').

Susan's return to England from Germany was a wonderful reunion, in spite of the efforts of officialdom. She arrived alone at Heathrow Airport, clutching her army discharge papers and with a single foreign purchase – a wedding dress made of German lace. The customs officer charged her import tax on the dress, leaving her with just enough money in her purse for the train fare to Aldershot.

She went to the Johnsons – people she hardly knew – who kindly offered her a bed until Ian was due to return from an exercise, later that night. The look on his face as he came through the door just after midnight, scooping her into his arms, symbolised the rest of their lives together really. The overpowering love that they were to feel for each other for twenty-seven years made them almost oblivious to others at that time. And in times of crisis for the rest of their lives together the intensity of the emotion that they felt for each other seemed to step in and cushion them from too much hurt. Lying in each others arms, they would say, 'This is all that matters, isn't it?'

On 2 March 1968 they were married in St Paul's parish church in Peterborough. The wedding went off uneventfully, despite her parents' tiny terrace house being crammed to the rafters with relatives from Ireland, Susan's family, and as many of Ian's para friends as could squeeze themselves in. The local pub, frequented by railwaymen, had never witnessed such a stag-night, as paratroopers entertained the locals along with Susan's mesmerised relatives.

The reception was held in the family home because Mr Cheshire was paying for a honeymoon in Devon rather than a posh hotel reception. The newly married couple spent several happy days wandering the blustery sea fronts of Teignmouth. When their money ran out they moved to a cheaper boarding-house to enjoy a few more days of quiet togetherness. Then, the honeymoon having been extended as long as their meagre budget allowed, they returned to Aldershot in a borrowed car packed with their wedding presents. Once established in their married quarters in Somerset Square they set out to have their first lunch in town. Unfortunately funds were again low and they pawned

Susan's nurse's fob watch to raise the two shillings and sixpence needed to buy two mixed grills in the local café.

They spent happy months in the house in Somerset Square, where the quarters were built around parade-grounds like barrack squares. Their 'house' was the top two floors of a three-storey building. The baby's pram had to be bumped up two flights of stairs to the living-room. The open fire always crackled a welcome, and the well-polished brown lino was scrubbed with pride. There was an old gas copper (water boiler) in the kitchen which had a vicious kickback when being lit with a match. The Phoenixes had many a sooty face while running backwards from this flame-belching monster. They felt they had reached the height of luxury when they were able to afford a tiny Baby Belling electric boiler. Washing was carried down the two flights of stairs, in an old army-issue wicker basket, to be dried on the communal clothes-lines in the centre of the square.

Mrs Phoenix senior – ever concerned about her son's welfare in the wilds of England – would arrive from Ireland for a visit complete with parcels of Irish butter and dead chickens already rotting from the long journey. There was an old pine kitchen table which she loved to scrub until it was pure white – 'to get rid of the old English grime'. She taught Susan to make Irish soda bread and tattie (potato) bread, so that she could get a 'daicent cup of tea' with hot buttered farls and not 'an old cup in your hand like the English give you', according to Maggie Phoenix.

Like many mothers-in-law, Susan's, although very helpful, was not always welcome – especially when she insisted on staying up to greet her son on his return from long-distance exercises. Susan always liked to meet Ian alone for each of their much coveted 'reunions'. There was one occasion, however, when Susan was glad to have his mother there on such an occasion. They were both waiting for Ian's return from an exercise in Libya when they heard that a planeload of paratroopers had been killed in a crash at the Libyan airfield. The pilot had been doing a low-flying goodbye 'buzz' of the airfield as he took off. Several tense hours passed before the women heard that the dead paratroopers were in fact from the Royal Horse Artillery – it was not Ian's turn. When a dusty, black-tanned Ian eventually returned with half of the Libyan Desert in his kit the whole family thanked God many times over for their luck. Ian, like most men who risk their lives on a regular basis, always felt a tremendous sense of humility when fortune smiled on him – as it did on this occasion, and would do many more times in the coming years.

In September 1968 a baby daughter was born after Susan had gone through a difficult and prolonged labour. The baby almost entered the world as a passenger in an army Land Rover. The usually cool Ian had been unable to find an ambulance to get his wife to hospital, and in his panic he commandeered the army vehicle, complete with driver, for the journey. The mother-to-be was kneeling in pain on the front seat as the very worried Ian leaned over from the back reassurring her that it was probably 'all in her head'. This was his favourite way of dealing with pain – always assume that it is psychosomatic, unless proved otherwise. To a woman about to give birth, it seemed a trifle unsympathetic, to say the least.

Being a father proved congenial to Ian Phoenix. He was quite besotted with his daughter. On a Sunday morning he would put her in her pram and join the large number of other paras pushing prams on their way to the local pub for a pre-lunchtime drink. No one seemed to mind being seen in this 1960s 'new man' role – perhaps because there was a relaxing drink at the end of it.

During his time in Aldershot Ian returned to his favourite Malaysia and the Middle East for several exercises. Then shortly after their first child was born, Ian and Susan heard that there was to be an 'accompanied posting' to Malta for two years. They were delighted. The idea of teaching their baby daughter to walk and talk on a sun-kissed island, rather than in the grey garrison town of Aldershot, seemed idyllic. The MFO (Military Freight Overseas) boxes were packed with their few household possessions and sent to RAF Hendon. Their two-month-old baby was packed into her quilted sleeping-bag (made by granny

41

from material bought in Peterborough market) and then tucked carefully into the baby carrier. The families and men (in full uniform) travelled together for such overseas postings. There was excitement and a buzz of chatter as the snow-capped Alps were seen from the air for the first time. As the propeller-driven Britannia aircraft made a rather bumpy landing at RAF Luqa, a large metal sheet forming part of the overhead luggage carriers fell into the aisle, missing baby Phoenix by inches. But shock and panic turned to relief as the baby continued to smile and coo her way on to the island where she was to learn not only to walk and talk but also to eat a mean curry.

Malta taught the Phoenix family quite a bit about Mediterranean life. Their married quarters were in Guardamangia, a few miles from the capital, Valetta. The local hospital was at the end of the street, and they would watch the splendid horse-drawn hearses with their plumes and velvet drapes make regular sorties. In fact in 1969 the Maltese hospital seemed to have hearses permanently parked outside. This perhaps was not surprising in the light of what happened to a neighbour. He was a young soldier and slashed his wrists in an attempted suicide. His attempt almost succeeded, thanks to a young Maltese nurse in the hospital who devoted her attentions to cleaning his blood from the floor rather than to tending the wound. Susan's recently abandoned nursing training came in handy for this young man.

The local baker used the ancient brick ovens in the thick wall of his house to produce the massive mishapen loaves of delicious rough country bread. The shape never mattered to baby Phoenix, who before they reached home had usually eaten most of the bread by sneaking handfuls of the hot dough from her pram basket and into her mouth.

Ian himself would catch the local bus into camp at around 6 a.m., returning for lunchtime and a 'siesta' before completing the day's work at around 6 p.m.

It was in Malta that the Phoenix family started to appreciate good food and wine for the first time. They made friends with a couple who shared their knowledge of the catering and hotel industry with them. Christel was German and Alfons was Irish, and they had two young daughters. They were a generous couple with a wide knowledge of food – Alfons, who was a skilled chef at an exclusive hotel on the tiny island of Comino, produced the most mouth-watering rabbit stew with an aromatic sauce of garlic, local wine and fresh herbs. When eating out, the young Phoenix couple were fascinated to see the response when Alfons would send a 'complimentary' glass of wine to the chef in appreciation of the meal. It was to be a tradition that Ian continued in later years when dining all over the world with his growing family. He was always delighted when the complimented chefs reciprocated with interesting new delicacies to be tasted.

The Phoenix home began to be considered as

a home from home for the single soldiers in the battalion. There were always a meal, unlimited drinks and a listening ear for young men who appreciated good fellowship. Their baby girl learned to walk on the beaches of Malta being dangled from the arms of a variety of macho men who liked to play 'uncle' when no one was looking.

The young soldiers found the cheap beer and spirits available in the island's duty-free NAAFIs too hard to resist. This led inevitably to wild drinking bouts, which proved the only source of argument ever to rear its head in the Phoenixes' marriage. Susan quickly learned how to sober up drunken paratroopers. She felt it her duty to deliver timely lectures on the error of overindulgence – though she never had any illusions that her remonstrations were taken seriously. However, even in the midst of drunken abandon her husband's pals always treated her with the utmost respect. Her concern for Ian was not that he drank alcohol but that it made him very ill the following day. (He was to discover in later life that he suffered from a genetic syndrome which may have contributed to his post-alcohol sickness.) Susan was not the kind of woman to keep such concerns to herself, but nor was Phoenix the kind of man to let the boozy camaraderie of army life interfere with the relationship that mattered most to him and gave him the emotional haven he needed – one that in years to come would help keep him sane. In any case, in later years as his taste buds became more discerning and his common sense developed he discovered the pleasure of good wine and a clearer day-after head.

While Phoenix was sent off on military exercises all over the Mediterranean and Middle East, Susan developed a close friendship with Christine Coghill, a young woman from Edinburgh, whose husband, Jimmy, was in the same unit. The two friends used their husbands' absence to explore the island, enjoying the delights of Phoenician architecture, the wild figs plucked from roadside trees and the cappuccino in the Valetta town square, while pushing baby Phoenix in her well-worn blue pram on and off the local buses. The young wives would nudge each other nervously as they saw the Maltese travellers crossing themselves before the bus left each dilapidated stop. Christine moved into the Phoenix house in Guardamangia during their husbands' overseas tours of duty. It helped ease their loneliness, and doing the chores together also enabled them to take off on their island explorations more quickly. The division of labour worked well: Susan cooked and Christine excelled at housework.

Phoenix quickly made the local butcher an ally, thanks to the weekly bottle of whisky (cost ten shillings) which he brought him from the camp NAAFI. Susan traded it for a pound's worth of meat – enough to last a week. The pigs in Malta were fed on pigswill containing an aromatic amount of garlic, leading to garlic-flavoured pork chops. The whole family, including the baby, developed a predilection for garlic which was to stay with them all of their lives. The garlic and herbs first tasted on Malta would one day be grown in Ian's greenhouse in the far different world of Co. Antrim, Northern Ireland.

By the autumn of 1969 the Phoenix family were preparing to leave the Mediterranean sunshine for the green fields of Ireland. Ian was to be demobbed at the end of his nine years in the Paratroop Regiment and fulfil his boyhood ambition to become an RUC officer.

Susan and Ian had discussed several other options before he took the final decision to leave. Many of his old colleagues were joining the SAS. However he was adamant that he would not extend his army contract for another four years, and this was a prerequisite for the SAS at that time. The couple had already agreed that they would not like to bring up their family in an army environment, with all of the separations and uncertainty that this would inevitably bring. They explored the possibility of Ian joining foreign police forces, which would enable them to continue to travel as a family, but applications to Rhodesia and Hong Kong were turned down because he was too old. They even considered becoming Kenyan wildlife officers. But realism for once was in concert with boyhood ambition, and Ian decided that the Royal Ulster Constabulary was his best option.

Susan and their toddler returned before the winter set into Britain, to avoid a shock in temperature change for the child. It was, however, shock enough for her to be dressed in proper clothes for the first time after her previously sunkissed life. Susan had borrowed her friend Christel's sewing-machine and had carefully sewn a little red leather coat with matching hat for her daughter to wear on her return to Britain. It took Susan some time to realise that the child's screams on the flight from RAF Luqa to RAF Brize Norton were the result of the unfamiliar heavy clothes. Once the clothes were removed, peace reigned on the aircraft.

Susan was sad as she watched Ian's back disappearing into the RAF hangar after helping her and their child on to the plane. She wanted him to turn and wave, but as always his motto was 'Never look back.'

She arrived at her parents' home in Peterborough on 7 October and settled down to await the arrival of Ian for Christmas. There was no time to dwell on the past, only to look forward to their new future. Susan and her daughter missed Ian painfully, and both cried secretly in their shared bed at night. In the daytime she arranged for Ian's application forms for the RUC to be completed and booked his interview, which would take place in the local police station in Peterborough. Life was busy if somewhat cramped in the tiny terrace house. New winter clothes were being sewn and knitted by the ever-industrious granny.

Arrangements for the move to Northern Ireland were discussed at length. Everyone was overjoyed when Ian returned in December with the last of their luggage, though there was a question in his heart, wondering whether they had made the right decision. The transition into civilian life was a big one for them all.

The winter weeks proved long for the Phoenixes as they craved some privacy and a home of their own. They kept themselves busy by decorating the house for Susan's parents and borrowing her father's car to visit her sister in Leicester. A flu epidemic hit the local hospital, and Susan volunteered her nursing skills along with many other retired and former nurses.

While they had been in Malta Ian and Susan had not been able to save much. As Ian waited for his joining date for the RUC he was forced to 'sign on' for the first time in his life. But financial assistance was only obtained with difficulty. It seemed that the Social Security staff found it hard to comprehend that an ex-serviceman needed money. Fortunately, Susan's parents were generous. Phoenix dreaded the weekly visit to the local dole office and the indignity of standing in line as he waited to sign his name. He often passed the time in the queue by helping newly arrived Pakistanis who were confused by the forms and asked for his assistance.

It was to be the first and last family Christmas shared by both the Cheshire and the Phoenix families. Susan's mother was thrilled to have all of her grandchildren and both daughters with their husbands together at such a festive time. Susan's sister, Pauline, and her two daughters added to the fun and giggles as the three little girls opened their presents on Christmas Day. Everyone stood outside on New Year's Eve to hear the railway engines, just across the road from the terrace of houses, sound their whistles to mark the arrival of 1970.

Across the Irish Sea forces were in motion that they knew little or nothing about. But they would change the Phoenixes' lives, and those of thousands of others, for ever.

Chapter 2

On the Beat in the Black North

(1970–78)

On Saturday 2 May 1970, Phoenix, his wife and their daughter boarded the 6.18 p.m. train from Peterborough to Heysham, from where they crossed the Irish Sea. He was to report to the RUC training depot in Enniskillen. They were sailing into the worst crisis in modern Irish history.

In 1970 the situation in Northern Ireland was deteriorating almost on a daily basis. Two years earlier a civil-rights campaign demanding an end to discrimination against the province's Catholic minority had been met with counter-demonstrations from Protestant extremists inspired by the Revd Ian Paisley. Riots and deaths followed, with the RUC losing control of the situation, forcing the intervention of the British Army in August 1969.

After a government inquiry, the RUC, traditionally dominated by Protestants, had been disarmed, and its militia, the B-Specials – perceived as a sectarian force and feared by Catholics – had been abolished.

The force that Ian was joining had never been an ordinary police force. It had been born out of the Irish conflict in 1921: after the partition of the island, it had been specially set up to defend Northern Ireland against IRA attacks. This meant that it was as much a paramilitary force, armed and equipped like an army, as a police force. The 1969 reforms were an attempt to make it more appealing to Catholics and as such loyalists had viciously opposed them; ironically, the first RUC man to die violently in the 'Troubles', Constable Victor Arbuckle, was shot by a Protestant gunman as he tried to prevent a Protestant mob from attacking Catholics at the foot of the loyalist Shankill Road area of Belfast in October that year. But the reforms had come too late. The social turbulence had stirred up deadly forces that had lain dormant for years and that would soon emerge again, bloody and violent.

However, such concerns were far from their minds as the young family tried to adjust to their new environment. Politics did not impinge upon them, nor did they influence Ian Phoenix's desire to be a policeman. Other things struck them as more important at the time. When they had left England the sun was shining and summer was on the way.

Susan and her daughter were wearing lightweight cotton clothes as they warmly kissed and hugged the Cheshire family goodbye. When they met the Granville household the weather was cold and grey, and the hugs were not so forthcoming.

For Susan, who remembered only the previous Irish welcome in the holiday atmosphere of her pre-marriage days, the experience was traumatic. Her first letter to her mother, two days after arriving in Granville, near Dungannon, stated that she now felt like an alien in a household that was very different from that of her own family in England. People did not openly hug or express affection towards each other. They initially considered her somewhat eccentric when she put her arm around Mrs Phoenix's shoulder for a quick cuddle as she would her own mother. It was also an upheaval for Maggie Phoenix to have a new daughter-in-law from England and small grandchild suddenly dropped into her well-ordered routine. She had to come to terms with what may have appeared as a rather bossy young English woman who did not seem to know her place. Over the years, the friendship between the two women was to develop into mutual love and respect, but in those early weeks inevitably there were difficulties: cultural differences often brought clashes in the kitchen.

Susan soon discovered that Ulster was something of a patriarchy, where women were expected to be submissive in their interactions with men and the world in general. She was used to open and frank discussion with her friends, treating men and women as equals. The Dungannon of 1970 was definitely a man's world. The men of the family were always given precedence at the table and expected to have the last word. Maggie Phoenix would eat soda bread to allow the menfolk more meat.

But it was not planned that Susan and her daughter would stay in Granville for long. The training sergeant at the RUC depot had found the young family a flat which was near to the depot and would, in theory at least, keep them close together as Ian underwent his basic training, and when they eventually arrived in the ancient town of Enniskillen on the banks of Lough Erne in Co. Fermanagh the couple were looking forward to having privacy for the first time since leaving Malta. The little room at the top of a dark and creepy house on the edge of the main road was not, however, what they had envisaged. The landlady, a local corsetier, was pleasant enough but did not seem to realise the needs of a young family with an active toddler to look after. There were no domestic facilities in the bedsit, no running water or refrigerator, and the only daylight filtered through tiny sash windows on to drab furniture which consisted of a huge high bed and wardrobe. There were a tiny two-ring cooker and kettle, with a plastic basin to transport all water and slops down two flights of stairs to the bathroom sink for disposal. The couple comforted each other by lying with their daughter all cuddled together in the giant bed. Unfortunately, once Phoenix had settled his family into this gloomy room he had to report to the depot to begin his intensive three months of training. He could expect to spend only the weekends with them. After a long kiss at the top of the murky staircase he walked away with a lump in his throat, knowing that the week would feel like an eternity before they were all reunited.

After the hanging around in Peterborough for months, Phoenix was glad to throw himself into the training, and eager to meet his new colleagues, most of whom were young men just out of school or college. The commandant was Superintendent R. T. Killen, and the training officer was Chief Superintendent John Hermon, later to be chief constable of the RUC. Though it was not easy for the ex-para to go back into the classroom after nine years of active service, he was keen to do what had to be done to fulfil his long-postponed ambition to become a policeman. He became so thin and wiry during the intensive training that he earned the nick name of 'cap and boots' – it being reckoned that there was very little in between them.

Not all the demands of training were to his liking, of course. His least favourite was the police driver's course. He turned to his wife for help with his driving practice in his father's car. As they careered around the narrow country roads, they narrowly avoided veering into ditches as he changed gear by focusing on the gear stick rather than the road ahead. He failed the initial police driver's assessment. Susan was not surprised. But he persevered and eventually passed his civilian driver's test in Dungannon – where, luckily for Phoenix, in those days there were no traffic lights and very little traffic.

Right from the beginning of his police career Phoenix demonstrated certain attitudes which stemmed from his military training. One was a belief in the need for solidarity among the men of the unit. During training, one officer, Ronnie Flanagan, from Phoenix's squad lost a close relative. As a result, he monopolised the depot payphone talking with his grieving family. This irritated another recruit who hassled him while he was on the phone. The harassment continued the next day as Ronnie and Phoenix were marching out of the depot gates in squad formation. Tempers were frayed, and soon fists flew. Ronnie promptly decked the other recruit. He was called in front of the commandant and was told he was to be dismissed from the force. Luckily for him, Phoenix had organised a group of fellow recruits to send the other recruit to Coventry – refusing to talk to him, treating him like a leper. 'Right, you bastard,' the former para told him, pulling him aside. 'Go to the commandant and explain what happened or else it'll be like this for another month.' He did. Ronnie's RUC career was saved. He later rose to the rank of chief constable and would recount this story, with affection, to Susan following Ian's death.

From their room at the top of the bleak house Susan and her baby daughter could see the trainee constables taking their daily run along the loughshore. She strained to pick out her husband, in his regulation white T-shirt and black cotton shorts, longing for the weekends when he would return with a batch of stories about the depot. While waiting, she passed each day walking around the old streets near the town's historic centre, pushing the little blue pram which had seemed less tatty in the Maltese sunshine. Their twenty-month-old daughter was missing her daddy and seemed to cry more than before. After always having been surrounded by lots of love and happy company, it was clearly upsetting for the child to be alone with her mother in such a grey environment so soon after enjoying the Mediterranean sun. Mother and daughter were desperate for some genial company, and their lonely hearts ached for Phoenix and his good-humoured presence.

Susan became deeply depressed during her lonely days wandering in this unfriendly environment. Food and milk quickly turned rancid in the stuffy little room without a refrigerator. She attempted to stay outdoors as much as possible. She tried to strike up conversations with other young mums in the local park, but they did not reciprocate – either because they were suspicious of her English accent or because they were not interested in potential new acquaintances: she could not judge. After her previously active and fulfilling life, she felt rejected and unhappy for the first time. She knew that if she did not find a useful lifestyle she would begin to resent Phoenix 'having all the fun' in his new career. She tried joining the local library and losing herself in her favourite pastime, but it proved impossible to read away her unhappiness. She tried to hide it so that at least they could share some pleasant weekends together.

However, Ian sensed immediately that his wife was not happy. He knew Enniskillen was a bleak place to live and asked her if she wanted to go back to stay with her mother while he was in the depot. If she left she would not see her husband for three months, because they could not afford to travel back and forth for short visits. They were both miserable when they were parted for long periods. A compromise was reached when Ian's next weekend came up. They agreed that wife and child should return to stay with the Phoenix family in Granville, where Ian could make weekend visits more easily, and Phoenix's brother was sent to transport them from the dreary Enniskillen house. But Susan left with a feeling of guilt that she had failed as a wife because she could not stay near her man.

As on all of the other occasions when things did not go according to plan, she looked for the positive aspects. She devoted herself to her daughter. She made flash cards (although she did not know then that they were called that by the educationalists) and drew the accompanying pictures to teach the little girl her first written words. She wrote articles for the English newspapers and magazines, and also wrote letters to the local papers. This unwittingly upset some of Ian's family, though what she wrote was usually no more than a description of some difference between English and Irish cultures which had fascinated her. She borrowed her father-in-law's car (much to his disgust) and took Maggie to the seaside in Warrenpoint or to market in Portadown.

She also devoted herself to getting to know her mother-in-law and her unmarried sister-in-law, both of whom became real friends. Maggie Phoenix taught her to make home-made jam from the juicy black-berries which were piled into her red plastic rain hat as she pushed the faithful old pram around the lanes of Co. Tyrone. It fascinated her that her mother-in-law still did her weekly baking session in the old black range of the tiny family home – soon to be demolished. Granville had been redeveloped, with a smart new public housing estate springing up, and Maggie and Willie were allocated a semi-detached house with large gardens at an end of the row nearest to the new village school, where Maggie continued to 'caretake'. But she did not consider the new-fangled gas cooker suitable for baking her popular apple cakes and griddle-baked soda bread. Instead she lugged all of her baking ingredients – the soda flour, buttermilk and fresh eggs – to the disused house at the top of the village and relit the fire in the old range to produce her mouth-watering week's supply. She was a woman who did not welcome modern conveniences. Her Sunday lunches were always a dish of thick home-made broth followed by a huge roast of beef accompanied by copious amounts of potatoes – boiled in their skins and peeled at the table – with cabbage, which, after being boiled to a pulp, was often fried. Tinned fruit, home-made jelly and vast amounts of creamy yellow custard rounded off the meal.

It was not long before rural life came to an end for Susan and her daughter. Phoenix graduated from the RUC training depot in July 1970 and became Constable 10042 – a number he would keep for the rest of his life. He was told that his first posting as a probationer constable was to be with B Division, based at the Springfield Road RUC barracks in West Belfast. The Phoenixes were in for yet another big change.

The Springfield Road RUC barracks sits smack in the middle of the IRA stronghold around the Falls Road, but B Division also takes in large working-class Protestant estates to the north. It was then a district of mostly poor families living in Victorian housing, where the majority of people used to earn their wage in nearby linen mills. But by the late 1960s and early 1970s these were closing down. The new estates, such as the loyalist Highfield estate at the

top of the Springfield Road and the nearby nationalist New Barnsley estate, were desolate, windswept
developments with few amenities, where anger and
frustration had ample opportunity to fester. Today
the peace line – a large corrugated-steel wall – runs
down one side of the Springfield Road, separating
the two communities. But in 1970 the area was still
mixed, with daily confrontations and riots between
Catholics and Protestants, as well as mob attacks
using petrol bombs and bricks on police and army
patrols. In 1971 it was to become the scene of far
worse violence, which would make it one of the most
dangerous postings in Northern Ireland.

As Constable Phoenix settled into his new routine,
his wife and little daughter would go around the
streets of Belfast, visiting estate agents and dreaming
of the first home they were to have to themselves
since Malta. Exactly twelve months after leaving the
island they found a house in the wind-blown heights
of Glengormley on the outskirts of North Belfast.

The city of Belfast sits in a basin on the banks of
the River Lagan, at the head of Belfast Lough, a cold
and choppy inlet of the Irish Sea, bounded to the
west and north by basalt hills. The Cave Hill, with its
sheer cliff of grey basalt known locally as Napoleon's
Nose, dominates the northern fringe of this low range.
Glengormley lies in a little valley between the back of
the Cave Hill and Carnmoney Hill, overlooking the
waters of Belfast Lough. Originally a village, after

the war Glengormley had expanded with an estate of semi-detached red-brick houses, and it was in one of these, with a tiny garden front and rear and a wasteground beyond it, that the Phoenixes made their first home.

Glengormley was a mixed community of Protestant and Catholic families. The 'village' was the centre, with a collection of small shops, a post office and chemist's. There was one doctor's surgery, which was later to develop into a modern health centre as the population expanded. Catholic and Protestant schools and churches nestled comfortably together, and the local children played amicably in the quiet culs-de-sac as they arrived home from their respective schools.

It was a question of starting from scratch. Having lived an army life for so long, the family had little in the way of household goods. They bought one bed for their daughter and a sofa. They could not afford a second bed at the time, so for the first six months in their new home they bunked down on the floor, sleeping on cushions and pillows.

The Phoenixes had much to occupy them in those early months, gathering furniture, making friends, and working out how Ian would make the journey to his job in the Springfield Road on a daily basis. At first they were very casual about their new situation and personal security did not bother them, so Constable Phoenix would cycle to work.

As the Provisional IRA stepped up its campaign of violence in the first few months of 1971, tension between the working-class Catholics and Protestants increased. On 13 May rival crowds gathered near the top of the Springfield Road. Phoenix was dispatched with Sergeant Bell and Inspector Nurse from the station. He found a situation which in many ways was a microcosm of the whole Northern Ireland crisis. According to Constable Phoenix:

I got out of the car and approached the Protestant crowd of about 50 to 60 men and youths from the Springmartin and Highfield estates. They were in a field and on the Ballygomartin Road and were throwing stones and waving a Union Jack at a similar sized crowd of Catholics from the Ballymurphy and New Barnsley estates. This crowd were further into the field. I told the Prod. crowd to move off and was told by one of them that I should move the other crowd along as there was a shotgun in the crowd. I again told the Prod. crowd to move along and then I went over to the Catholic crowd who were about 50 or 60 in size. This crowd were also throwing stones and waving a Tricolour. As I approached this crowd two adults met me and said that the other crowd had started it and that one of them had a revolver. I told the crowd to get out of the field and to remove the Tricolour. With the help of two adults we started to move the crowd back. As we were beginning to move one of the adults said, 'Look out!'

I turned round and was struck on the right temple by a large stone thrown by a youth from

the Protestant crowd. I remained with the Catholic
crowd to see if they were going to keep moving
which they appeared to be doing. I then went back
and chased the remainder of the Prod. crowd. The
army then arrived and we cleared both crowds out
of the area.

Phoenix was sent off to hospital with a severe bruise
and a large swelling on his temple. For several days
he had headaches. It used to amuse him afterwards
that his first injury on duty was at the hands of
so-called loyalists. From local Catholics he had so far
received only abuse – some of it even complimentary.
Once during a search of a house, when Phoenix was
accompanying the soldiers, the woman whose things
were being turned upside down began to shout and
hurl insults at them. The young constable tried to calm
her down. 'As for you,' she screamed, turning towards
him, 'you can fuck off as well, you handsome black
bastard!' The RUC were used to angry civilians calling
them 'black bastards' because of the uniform they wore
then, but rarely were they called 'handsome'. It was a
back-handed compliment that in the years to come
Phoenix liked to repeat.

Because of his experience in the Parachute Regiment, Ian was given the task of liaising between the
police and the army. When a new regiment arrived in
B Division he went out on patrol with them, helping
them to familiarise themselves with the district and its
main 'players' – those whom the police had identified

as dangerous and who had to be watched. A batch of photographs – many taken surreptitiously – of those under suspicion was kept in the station. They included photographs of some men who were later to become prominent in the Provisional IRA, such as Gerry Adams, Joe Cahill and Jimmy Drumm.

In 1971, 3 Para, Phoenix's old unit, was stationed in Springfield Road police station. It was under the command of Lieutenant Colonel Peter Chiswell, with whom Phoenix had served in Borneo. The two had a reunion which, much to Phoenix's horror, was reported in a local paper, with photographs. Chiswell was quoted as saying, 'It is certainly an amazing coincidence. I never expected our paths to cross under such circumstances.' The last time Phoenix had seen Chiswell, the latter was being pissed on by a monkey in the jungle. This little anecdote was kept out of the papers.

In spite of the gathering chaos, the police tried to maintain as much of an air of normality as possible. Towards the end of May the police and army held a supper and social night in the Springfield Road barracks. It was the sort of social evening that Ian and Susan both enjoyed, where a black military humour pervaded the jokes and conversation. As they were leaving the station at the evening's end, para sergeant Mick Willets was at the station sergeant's desk. He leaned over to wish them goodnight. His battalion was due to leave the province the next week. Mick had served with Ian in Borneo, Bahrain and Malta. At twenty-seven, he was the father of two children and was looking forward to getting home to see them. 'Bye, Mick. Enjoy your home leave – *if* you all survive,' Susan said, continuing the dark humour of the evening.

A few days later, on 25 May, Constable Phoenix was chatting with Sergeant Willets at the rear of the enquiry office near the station entrance. They were getting ready to go out on patrol. A group of civilians, including four women and three children, were nearby. Inspector Ted Nurse was chatting with them. A car pulled up suddenly at the entrance. A dark-haired young man, said to be in his mid-twenties, got out carrying a suitcase and walked quickly to the station. He must have seen the women and children standing in the reception area as he dropped his lethal load of gelignite weighing between twenty and thirty pounds in the hallway.

Phoenix heard a thump coming from the main entrance hall. 'Get out of the way. There's a bomb!' a policeman shouted. He had spotted the fast-burning fuse. Guided by the police, people began to run towards a corridor to the side of the sergeant's desk.

'Come on. Down here,' Phoenix shouted across to Mick. But the sergeant hesitated, glancing at the bomb. He came out from behind the desk, placing himself between the bomb and the others. Phoenix was dropping down on the corridor floor, his hands behind his head, following safety procedures, when there was a terrific bang and a cloud of dust enveloped everything. He was flung forward along the corridor. Seconds later he staggered to his feet. The back of his head was bleeding, his right leg was badly bruised, and his hands were cut. An eerie silence had descended on the scene. The women and children, huddled in the corridor, were dazed and silent. Bodies lay in the debris. Phoenix drew his gun and staggered past a smashed outer office. Through it he saw an elderly lady standing in a side-street staring at the bombed station. Then a young man suddenly stepped quickly across the main road. The constable aimed his weapon. Was it the bomber? He hesitated. No, he decided, as the civilian turned down a street.

Phoenix made his way to the entrance area, where he saw Sergeant Willets lying with the back of his head gaping open. A metal chunk from a locker hurled across the room by the force of the explosion had struck him. Covered in dust, the constable clambered over the rubble-strewn entrance and stumbled into the street, looking desperately for the bombers. But they had disappeared. Instead he found a scene of devastation. The front wall of the building had collapsed. Cars had been flung across the road. A woman lay covered in broken glass in the smashed window of a grocery shop. Her baby's pram was up-ended, its wheels spinning. It was empty. The two-year-old boy who had been sitting in it seconds before was lying in the rubble, his skull fractured.

Local people had gathered outside and began to help clear the debris, offering what assistance they could. Ambulances began ferrying the injured to the nearby Royal Victoria Hospital. Lieutenant Colonel Chiswell was with Sergeant Willets, who was taken out on a door to the ambulance. A crowd of youths were waiting to greet them. They started to jeer and scream obscenities at the badly wounded soldier. Said Chiswell, 'My reaction was one of total disbelief that anyone could be so inhumane.'

Bleeding badly, Sergeant Willets was rushed to the emergency operating-room. Twenty-seven others were treated for injuries. Apart from the para sergeant, the two-year-old local boy had suffered the most serious wounds.

Susan's neighbour, Jackie, came to her with the news that Springfield Road police station had been hit by a bomb. Since the family did not have a telephone, Susan unthinkingly pushed her friend to one side as she raced to Jackie's house to call the hospital. But it had no news of her husband. She returned home and waited nervously, tuning into every news broadcast. Then a police Land Rover pulled up at her house. She rushed out. 'Constable Phoenix asked us to tell you that he is all right,' said a policeman who had been sent from the local station. She flung her arms around him and kissed him.

Later that evening Susan heard a car stop outside her door. Opening it, she found her husband standing on the doorstep, still enveloped in chalky dust from the explosion. His face was covered with grime, his eyelashes caked. She was overjoyed to see him alive and not badly injured. When she went to hug him, he looked at her angrily. 'Why are you looking so happy? Willets is dead,' he growled, coming into the house.

Sergeant Willets had died after two hours on the operating-table. He was the eighth soldier to die in Northern Ireland, and the first member of the Parachute Regiment.

Lieutenant Colonel Chiswell was determined that Willets's death would not go unmarked. He organised the first – and last – military funeral for a British soldier that Northern Ireland was ever to see. On 28 May a procession of ten military vehicles followed behind a gun-carriage on which rested Willets's coffin, draped in a Union Jack, with his red beret and his gloves sitting on top. Chiswell had had the gun-carriage brought in especially from Aldershot. The cortège wound its way with dignified defiance through the republican strongholds of West Belfast, pausing for two minutes outside the now-boarded-up police station where the Sergeant had been fatally injured. Ranks of RUC men were drawn up along the Springfield Road to give the soldier his last salute. Among them was his old army friend, Constable Phoenix.

The bombing of Springfield Road shocked Northern Ireland. The attack had been carried out with no thought for the ordinary people, most of them Catholics, who had been waiting in the reception room. Their lives were callously put at risk by the Provisional IRA, which liked to pose as their defenders. Unfortunately, the Springfield Road bombing would soon be forgotten as the violence deteriorated into even more brutal and bloody acts.

Sergeant Willets was posthumously awarded the George Medal for his actions. Several police officers were also given medals. Phoenix quietly refused his. Accepting it meant going on television, being interviewed by the media, getting his picture in the paper. Looking at the growing crisis all around him, he knew that this was not a good idea. Already, his security and that of his young family had been compromised. *Republican News*, a Provisional republican news-sheet, had published a story which drew attention to the RUC man seen riding in the observer's seat of an army Land Over. He decided to apply for permission to carry his regulation firearm home when in plain clothes. 'I am on liaison duty with the army,' he wrote in his request, filed on 12 June 1971, 'and come constantly into contact with the more subversive elements of the community. I am constantly in areas of trouble and have been threatened on a number of occasions . . . In case someone is foolish enough to back up their threats, I would like to be prepared on

an equal basis if firearms or similar are to be used.'
He also mentioned the *Republican News* story.

The chief constable agreed to his request, and Ian
Phoenix became possibly the first police constable in
Northern Ireland to be granted permission to arm
himself when off duty. Meanwhile, when Susan's
father heard that Ian was using a pedal bicycle to
make the journey to work each day he provided a
little moped for him.

The situation continued to worsen throughout the
summer of 1971, and policemen, both on and off
duty, increasingly became the target of destructive
forces in both communities. One night, after finishing
a late-duty shift, Constable 10042 was put-putting his
way on his moped along the Ballysillan Road which
runs through a loyalist area in North Belfast when
he found himself surrounded by a hostile crowd of
youths. Though he was armed, he did not want to
have to use his weapon and tried instead to reason
his way through. But the mob was out of control and
attempted to drag him off. He drew his Ruger pistol
and cocked it, forcing them to back away. On arriving
home, Phoenix expressed disgust with himself because
he had had to resort to drawing his revolver to get out of
the situation. Susan was just pleased to see him back
in one piece.

A few months later, on 11 November, his gun
could actually have cost him his life. He was on
his way down the Springfield to report for duty. He

was out of uniform. As he approached the station, an army vehicle pulled out. Two Provisional IRA gunmen stepped on to the road as he was passing and opened fire on the vehicle with rifles. The gunmen were within a few feet of him. As they disappeared down a side-street, Phoenix was about to pull out his gun and open up on them when he noticed Scottish troops racing out of the base. It took him a split second to realise that if the troops saw him, an armed man in civilian clothes, they would not hesitate to shoot him. So he took a deep breath, kept his weapon in his pocket, and lived to report what he had seen.

The young couple were almost relieved when the moped was stolen by the local paperboy. They replaced it with their first car, a beaten-up turquoise Mini bought for thirty pounds (slightly more than their monthly rent), which was again replaced by Mr Cheshire when he first saw the sorry picture that it presented. 'You can't drive that bundle of rust – it's not safe!' he exclaimed. He gave them a deposit for a shiny new Mini Clubman which gave the family more freedom and Phoenix some degree of protection as he drove to work each day.

The crisis hit Northern Ireland with full force on 9 August 1971, when internment without trial was introduced against suspected IRA activists. Over 300 were arrested. But the operation was based on poor intelligence, and provoked the wrath of the nationalist population, leading to inter-communal rioting and gun battles. Springfield Road came under sustained attack, and gun battles raged throughout the city. Barricades were thrown up in the Catholic areas. Susan would listen to the police channels on her transistor radio as she waited for Ian to return from long hours of duty. She was amazed at the cool voices as they reported violent acts against their lives. A superintendent could be heard saying, 'Yes, that's two wheels we have on fire now, boys – keep up the good work. Gunfire reported, heads down!' as his Land Rover careered down the Falls Road to one of the many incidents. Fires burned out of control, casting a lurid light over the otherwise darkened streets.

Catholic families still living in Protestant areas were driven from their homes. Early on the morning of 10 August, Phoenix was on mobile patrol with 2 Para in the working-class Protestant housing estate of Highfield, at the top of the Springfield Road. It was a particularly poor estate, which had seen sectarian incidents even in the 1950s. A crowd of about forty thugs attacked two Catholic families, the McK's and McC's, who still lived there and told them that they had to leave their homes by midnight or be burned out. Phoenix's patrol arrived and gave them protection from the mob as they removed their furniture and belongings. The families told him that they had been offered temporary accommodation in Clonard Monastery, about two miles away.

The para commander said he could not escort

them, as he had to continue on his patrol, but the families followed behind the Land Rover as it wound its way through the estate. When they reached the Springfield Road junction, gunmen opened fire from several different points. Phoenix's vehicle pulled to a halt. He jumped out and ran towards the two families, some of whom were crouched behind their car. A woman and her young daughter were still in the car, and as they were getting out another burst of fire erupted and the constable pushed the child to the floor and covered her until it stopped. Then he escorted the families straight to the police station, where he made tea for them. They were sheltered in a nearby church hall for the night.

Later that night he was called to an army post a mile or so up the road from the station. Nearby he found the body of a fifty-year-old woman lying in the road. Her face had been shot off by a stray army bullet. She had been caught in the crossfire during a shoot-out between soldiers and the IRA. He took the body to the hospital morgue. That night he came home smelling of formalin. It was to be a familiar aroma on his uniform whenever he attended autopsies where a police presence was requested. He shared his disgust with Susan that the so-called 'defenders' of the Catholic population callously disregarded the lives of the local people. He was always angry when he saw lives wasted in this way. Even at that early stage in his career he voiced his frustration that the government did not use appropriate propaganda to illustrate such double standards of the IRA.

Over the next week Phoenix was caught in gun battles on a daily basis as he moved through the darkened streets of the district, clearing barricades with the army. On one occasion the station came under such sustained fire that he could not get out of it when his duty ended and had to spend the night there. Some indication of the temper of those times can be gleaned from Constable 10042's notebooks:

8.8.71 On duty at 8.30 p.m. Could not get into station as it was being attacked. Brought in by Con. D. Confined to station until 12.30 a.m . . .

10.8.71. Heavy shooting, Beechmount area, Falls Rd area . . .

11.8.71. 1 Para attacked barricades at 3 a.m. In S/Field Ave. Firing from further down street. Woman injured at 8 Earlscourt St, barricades pushed aside on street and side-streets . . .

14.8.71. Reported explosion T[aggert] M[emorial army base] . . . reported second explosion from area upper S/Field . . .

17.8.71. Expl. at about 11.05 p.m. Later found to be at McCausland's car hire . . .

12.9.71 Large crowds at Falls/Whiterock . . . also crowd of 1,000 with stones approaching towards A[ndersons]town . . . rival kids stoning at bottom of M1 . . .

13.9.71. Toured the area, all quiet except for odd stone-throwing incidents and reported shots . . .

16.9.71. Went to Whitehorse Inn ref. bomb scare.
Found to be hoax . . .
17.9.71. About 7 or 8 shots fired at station by light
semi-automatic weapon. Report of woman injured
across road from station. Went across with Woman
Const. N. Woman called Mary (?) badly shocked. Some
of the crowd became abusive to myself and N. Left
them and went back to the station . . .
28.9.71. Standby in station. Shooting at 9 p.m. at
station. Fire returned, two known persons hit. Off
duty 11 p.m . . .
2.10.71. Appears two bombs thrown from a lorry at
sentry post and a burst of fire directed at sentry. No
injuries, Out at 10 p.m. Toured general area. All quiet.
In at 12.15 a.m. Off duty at 12.30 a.m.

Susan decided the family needed a break. It had
been a hard and gruelling year. On 26 August,
Constable 10042 filled in his annual leave sheet.
They hired a car and set off for the South, which
Ian had never explored before, eager to get away from
the troubles. They took a tent with them, camping
in the lush countryside of Co. Wicklow and then
heading west to the bleak boglands of Connemara.
Unfortunately their tent had to be packed sodden into
the car as it rained every day. Their young daughter
seemed very relieved to get back to her own warm
bed at the end of their vacation.

They arrived back to find that the husband of
a Catholic family living in the same street as the
Phoenixes had been interned. Susan vowed that she

would help the woman, if necessary, as she had been left with her children and no support. Local Protestants warned Susan not to help 'Fenians', but she continued to befriend Catholic and Protestant alike. Her neighbours were of all religions and, apart from the known republican family, everyone continued their street coffee-parties and combined bonfire nights for Halloween.

The growing sectarianism seen in Belfast helped inspire her to go to the local youth club and see if there was anything, however small, she could contribute to help the city as it seemed to be tearing itself apart.

She became a youth leader at the Carnmoney Parish Youth Club, which in those days was frequented by both Catholic and Protestant teenagers. There was rarely trouble unless outside gangs came from the town to try to break up the mixed community. She took the teenagers on decorating projects in deprived areas all over Belfast, and persuaded Ian to go along to the youth club's camping weekends to empty the latrines and help with assault courses.

She became friendly with Elizabeth Jones, the wife of the local Church of Ireland vicar. Elizabeth was an unusual woman who could speak Irish and who got Susan involved in prison visiting, which in turn led to ferrying the wives of prisoners to Crumlin Road Prison in Belfast. This meant that, while Phoenix was battling the IRA in West Belfast, Susan may have been busing the families of suspected IRA and

UVF men out to visit their husbands. She drove into some of the toughest republican areas in the city at a time when the Provisional IRA could seal them off almost at will. She always got on well with the women and children, and enjoyed their animated chat as many expressed relief at how much further their housekeeping money stretched when 'the men are away'. She provided transport for the families to take their toddlers to the NSPCC playgroup in University Street. Her own young daughter shared her morning toast with the children of IRA, UDA and ordinary criminal prisoners. Susan was appalled at the poverty she saw around her, and even more at the irresponsibility of some of the parents, who would park prams outside local pubs and leave their babies in them while they were inside drinking. Ian also commented on this as he did the rounds of the streets, and he often told his wife that he felt tempted to take the children home with him.

Unfortunately, Susan was forced to bring her service to an end when a group of Provisionals approached her one day in the Lower Ormeau area of the city and warned her not to come back. Their reason was not because her husband was a policeman (which they did not know) but because she drove a minibus with Carnmoney Parish printed on it – an area of the city they assumed was Protestant and therefore suspicious.

The rest of 1971 became a blur of riots, shootings

and bombings, which Phoenix noted in the matter-of-fact language of police statements. But the job did have its less serious moments. On the night of 31 October he was on duty at the Royal Victoria Hospital's casualty ward, awaiting the custody of two men who had been slightly wounded after failing to stop at an army checkpoint. One of the two, a Mr McC, whom Phoenix described in his statement as a 'foul-mouthed, nasty, aggressive lout', was sitting up on a stretcher in the corridor shouting obscenities at the soldiers and police.

'You British bastards, you murdering fuckers,' he cried to all around – conveniently forgetting that the policemen and nurses around him were in fact as Irish as himself. He paid no heed to the nurses who tried to get him to keep quiet, and his ranting and raving was beginning to upset a young woman waiting in a nearby cubicle for treatment. Phoenix approached him and asked him 'to keep quiet'. 'You're another British bastard,' he cried as he grabbed the constable by the tie and tried to head-butt him. 'To protect myself,' reported the policeman:

I hit him on the chin and pushed his head down on the stretcher. Some soldiers then restrained McC. He then threatened me that he would get me later. I cautioned him and told him I was charging him with assault. To which he replied, 'I'll fight you and you can caution me in court.' He again said 'the most I'll get is a couple of months and then I'll get you.' 2 a.m. caution administered.

A few months later Phoenix was embroiled in a dispute between neighbours in the Beechmount area, which lies just off the Falls Road. A Mrs Mc., described as a housewife, claimed that her neighbour, a man called Gorm, began to throw stones at her. Soon he was joined by his son, who also began to hurl stones at her, according to her statement, which continued:

> The caretaker of St Rose's [Secondary School] tried to stop them and had no success. I said, 'You have picked on the wrong one now and I will see you go the whole road, policewise.' Then Gorm's son said, 'You fix us and I will fix these next door. He then lifted a big piece of rusted material and threw it through Granddad K's window. I was throwing stones at the Gorms by this time. Some of the kids went and told my husband and he then came down. Gorm's son tried to kick my husband and then ran. The father jumped on my husband's back and I trailed him off. My husband then ran after the Gorm's son. I had the old man on the ground restraining him from hitting me. The army came on the scene.

Phoenix learned that the Gorms believed that their neighbours had it in for them, and that the older Gorm was given to fits of depression and heavy drinking. Both wanted to leave the district but couldn't. After the father and son had returned from being charged with assault at the police station they found all the windows of their house smashed. On 23 March the elder Mr Gorm was fined five pounds at Belfast magistrate's court for assault. A charge of disorderly behaviour was adjourned for twelve months.

While Constable 10042 was in court grappling with the Gorm situation, Northern Ireland's fifty-year parliament at Stormont was in its death throes. On 30 March 1972, the day after Mr Gorm was sentenced, it was formerly suspended by Westminster and direct rule was imposed. It was a decision which in the long run would have tremendous implications for Northern Ireland and for security policy there – implications that would have a profound effect on Constable Phoenix's life as a policeman.

Security policy was at the heart of the dispute between Unionists and their British overseers, and would remain there. The British government had ended the life of the Unionist regime when Brian Faulkner, the Northern Ireland Prime Minister, had refused to agree that the control of the security forces should be in the hands of London. The RUC was supposedly discredited in the eyes of the Catholic population. The Unionists had used the British army as a blunt instrument to try to restore law and order in the Catholic areas, but this had further alienated the Catholic community, allowing the Provisional IRA and to a lesser extent the left-wing Official republican movement to flourish as never before. Britain could no longer trust Unionist stewardship of the army and police. Nor could it any longer accept the monolithic political structures which had kept the Ulster Unionist Party in power for fifty years. With the suspension of Stormont began the slow, painful dismantling of Unionist hegemony in Northern Ireland.

The immediate reaction of the Provisionals was to maintain their campaign of violence. But now that the Unionist government was out of the way the British decided that it could deal directly with the Provisional leadership. In early July a group of Provisional leaders – among them two young IRA bosses from Belfast and Derry, Gerry Adams and Martin McGuinness – were flown secretly to London to meet with the man who had been appointed Northern Ireland Secretary of State, William Whitelaw. A temporary halt was called in the Provisionals' campaign. But the talks were brief and unproductive. The truce broke down, and within two weeks the Provisionals had launched their bloodiest offensive yet.

On Friday 21 July 1972, at 2.20 p.m., the first bomb went off in Belfast. From then until 3.37 p.m. there were a further twenty-one explosions, using a total of 2,000 lb of explosives. They killed eleven people and wounded a further 130. The worst bombing occurred in a bus station near the city centre, where seven people died, including two soldiers, two youths who worked as parcel boys, an old lady, a young girl and a bus driver. It took a while to establish the identity of the dead, they were so badly mutilated. The day became known as Bloody Friday.

Phoenix was among the policemen sent to help clean up the carnage. In the bus station, pools of blood dripped into the drains; a dark pall of smoke hung over the ruins; the stench of scorched flesh filled the air. The police and ambulance men picked up bits of bodies from the wreckage, including a mutilated head. One report described vividly how a fireman was forced to shovel up a 'lacerated and sodden lump of lifeless humanity' to be placed in a plastic bag.

A shocked ambulanceman commented, 'I've seen most of them, but this is the worst.'

Phoenix's overwhelming reaction was a deep feeling of sadness. After Bloody Friday, he came home and said in a calm voice, 'I've spent the day putting bits of people into plastic bags. There must be something better than this for our country.' His military training had come into play and he had tried to help the younger policemen who were traumatised by what they had seen. His reaction was one of overwhelming sadness that his fellow Irishmen could do such things to other human beings.

One of Ian's old friends from 3 Para, a Scottish Catholic, was unable to cope with the stress of duty in Belfast. The constant rioting, coupled with the bombings and shootings, had left him on the verge of a breakdown, and he began to question his role there. Ian brought him home to try to keep him calm, and Susan offered a family environment and a bit of practical counselling. In order to counteract the horror of daily life, efforts were made to bring people together. Susan's youth club organised a friendly football match between members of 3 Para and local teenagers, both Catholic and Protestant. It worked so well that the paras' commanding officer, Lieutenant Colonel Chiswell, sent flowers to her as thanks for helping his men get to know the ordinary people of the city in a relaxed and informal way. It must have looked odd in the quiet Glengormley Avenue as two burly paratroopers jumped from their Land Rover carrying a dainty bouquet to the delighted Susan.

Phoenix remained in Springfield Road until 1973. He survived another two potentially deadly attacks.

In late 1972 the Provisional IRA acquired a supply of RPG-7 hand-held rockets. Theoretically, this gave them the power to destroy an armoured car or severely damage a base. On 28 November a rocket hit an RUC station in Belleek, Co. Fermanagh. It went through the steel shutters and killed Constable Robert Keys.

On 1 January 1973 Phoenix was station duty officer. In nearby Colligan Street, which is directly opposite the barracks, a unit of Provisionals got out of a car and fired an RPG-7 across the Springfield Road. It slammed into the sergeant's office. Phoenix was hurled off his feet by the explosion. He was lucky to be alive – the office near which he was working was extensively damaged, and several people were badly injured.

Thirty days later, along with Constable D, Phoenix was leaving the side entrance of the station, which exits on to Violet Street. As D stepped out, a Provisional gunman with an Armalite rifle opened fire, hitting him in the arm and leg. Phoenix dragged him in. Later, four Armalite rounds were found in 11 Violet Street, a vacant house that had been taken over by the sniper.

One of the last tasks Phoenix undertook in Springfield Road was of a somewhat less serious nature. On 26 March 1973, accompanied by a unit of the Coldstream Guards, he searched premises on Wilton Street, in the loyalist Shankill area, where it was suspected an illegal sheeben, or drinking den, was in operation. The premises were used by the Wilton Street Ladies Social Club, but, according to Phoenix's report, they 'had all the appearances of a drinking club. There were tables and chairs in both the downstairs and upstairs parts of the premises. There was also a kitchen and a bar, full and empty cases of beer and spirits, a small till and glasses and all the other items that go to making a drinking club.' The most impressive evidence of all that the Wilton Street Ladies Social Club was more than its title suggested was the amount of drink found on the premises. Phoenix listed what was carted away to the police station: '9¾ dozen bottles of Black Label, 7 dozen and 11 bottles of Harp, 2 dozen bottles of Tuborg Ordinary, 3 unopened bottles of Bacardi, 2 unopened bottles of vodka, plus 1 bottle ¼ full, 4 unopened bottles of whiskey plus 1 bottle ¼ full, ⅓ of a bottle of Black Rum, 4 unopened bottles of Nobility Cream Sherry plus 1 bottle ⅓ full . . .'

A Mrs McC of the Top House pub on the Shankill Road told Phoenix that she had sold the drink to the Wilton Street Ladies Social Club so that they could have a 'jolly night'. Elizabeth G, a twenty-five-year-old housewife who was the secretary of the club, told him 'every Saturday night we have a ladies meeting in which husbands are allowed'. Whether this was an attempt to shift the blame for having so much drink on to the ladies' menfolk, Phoenix did not say. But he concluded in his usual laconic manner: 'As for the amount of drink ordered and the remainder that was seized, either it is a very big club or the ladies are exceptionally heavy drinkers, and at the rate they consume vast amounts of drink it *must* be a danger to their health.'

A few weeks before this there had occurred another more momentous event in Phoenix's life. In February 1973 he had become the father of a baby boy. This time, there had been no army Land Rover to take them to the maternity hospital: Susan was driven there by a very nervous husband. At first they went to Carrickfergus Hospital, but their son was proving to be an awkward little customer, trying to see where he was going rather than cooperating and entering the world in the conventional manner. As a result,

Susan was rushed to the larger maternity unit at Larne District Hospital for an emergency Caesarean delivery. Jackie once more proved a good neighbour and babysat their daughter until Ian's mum could get down from Granville.

Shortly after this Constable Phoenix reached a different milestone in his life and was promoted to sergeant. He had spent just three years as a constable – less than half the usual time before promotion can be expected. He was transferred to York Road RUC station in North Belfast.

North Belfast was one of the most dangerous areas in Northern Ireland. Approximately one-fifth of all the murders that have occurred since 1969 have taken place within this cluster of Catholic and Protestant districts. Unlike the west of the city, the boundaries between the two communities were not clearly marked in the north. Tough republican strongholds such as the New Lodge Road rubbed shoulders with hard-line loyalist areas like Tiger's Bay. Roads and streets wound through Catholic and Protestant zones. Some, like the Crumlin Road, became notorious as the haunt of assassination squads prowling for victims.

Phoenix's duty was much the same as it had been in Springfield Road – beat patrol, liaising with the army, dealing with all manner of situations from confronting drunken youths to dodging snipers' bullets. But as sergeant he was frequently put in command of small patrols and was expected to take charge of certain situations. This he did with alacrity. Within a few weeks of arriving in his new posting he was involved in a battle with a mob of about twenty drunken Protestants who had been beating up a young man outside a café. During this scuffle, a reserve constable was thrown through a plate-glass window, and Phoenix himself was knocked to the ground and kicked by a gang screaming 'black bastards' whom he then 'dispersed' with his baton. The animosity directed at the police by working-class Protestants was if anything worse than that which they were subjected to from Catholic crowds. Throughout the 1970s poor Protestants were increasingly resentful that what they had regarded as 'their' police force was prepared to act against them when necessary. They were also aware of a growing economic difference between policemen, with steady jobs and a stable income, and themselves. Policemen and their families gradually began moving out of the more traditional working-class Protestant areas and into the suburbs. As a result, the gap between working-class Protestants and the RUC steadily increased. The ill-feeling which this helped to create would remain a regular factor in Phoenix's life as a policeman on the beat. To this day it is a somewhat paradoxical feature of policing in Northern Ireland that many working-class Protestants – who once identified with the RUC so strongly – are now to a large extent alienated from the force.

The dangers of North Belfast were brought home

to Phoenix on the night of 16 October. He was the supervising sergeant at York Road. There was an unusually heavy turn-out for duty that night, with sixteen constables and reserve constables reporting in. Unfortunately, there were only twelve flak jackets available. Sergeant Phoenix donated his own to a constable who had to patrol the dangerous Duncairn Gardens area. At 7 p.m. that evening he detailed Reserve Constable William Campbell and Reserve Constable McK for duty in the area of Queen Victoria Flats and St Aloysious School, near the Antrim Road. Both men volunteered to go out without flak jackets.

Reserve Constable Campbell was twenty-six. He worked in a chemical factory and was the father of two baby boys, one of whom was then just six months old. Around 9 p.m. the policemen heard gunfire near the Capitol Cinema on the Antrim Road and went to investigate. They were in the forecourt of the cinema and just turning into a side-street when gunmen opened fire on them from a car, spraying the pavement with a sub-machine-gun. Reserve Constable Campbell was hit in the back and stomach, and a twelve-year-old schoolgirl, Rita Montgomery, was shot in the leg. When Phoenix arrived on the scene, Campbell was being given first aid. Shortly afterwards an ambulance arrived. Campbell asked the sergeant if he would take him home to his wife, as he felt sure he was dying. However, a doctor told Phoenix that the wounded man would be all right. He was then rushed to the nearby Mater Hospital.

After taking witnesses statement and handing them over to detectives, the sergeant went to the hospital to check on the wounded man's condition. Phoenix was shocked to discover that it had deteriorated rapidly. He wrote in his statement, 'I immediately went to North Queen Street [station] to contact a police woman intending to fetch his wife. At this time I was informed that R/Const. W. Campbell had died. Accompanied by Woman Sergeant S I went to his home and informed his wife and relatives.'

Phoenix's statement betrays no emotion, but he was badly shaken by the incident – particularly when he went to the dead man's home and found his newborn son lying on the sofa. He thought of his own young son, then just eight months old. Although realistically it would have been too late, he blamed himself for denying the dying man the opportunity of spending his last few moments with his wife.

A few days later Sergeant Phoenix wrote a report on the lack of adequate equipment – a situation that had contributed to the loss of a policeman's life. He noted that because of the shortage of flak jackets at York Road station many policemen customarily locked theirs away after duty so that 'by reserving their own personal jacket they are assuring some measure of safely and hygiene for themselves'. Phoenix's career would be a long-running battle with senior officers over lack of preparation and failure to provide the necessary equipment to ensure that jobs get done properly, with minimum risk.

Almost exactly two months after the murder of Reserve Constable Campbell, Sergeant Phoenix was on mobile patrol near Duncairn Gardens when a sniper opened up on his car. 'Fuck me, that was meant for us,' he yelled, as a high-velocity bullet tore up the road in front of them. The driver braked and Phoenix ordered the three other men on his patrol to fan out. He drew his pistol and ran across Hillman Street towards a derelict house from where he thought the shot had come. Constable F radioed for army assistance. Meanwhile, Constable K and a military policeman, Sergeant G, who was an observer with the patrol, provided cover as Phoenix searched the entry at the back of the street. The three then searched the vacant house and found nothing. As they were moving into the next street a small boy approached Sergeant G and told him that he had seen two men with a gun run into a house in nearby Spamount Street. Phoenix asked him if he could show them the house. He did. The police burst in on 239 Spamount Street to find two youths and a woman in the living-room. The woman said, 'I don't know these two. They just came in.' Sergeant G escorted twenty-one-year-old Francis Goodall outside, while Phoenix questioned Michael Reeves, aged seventeen. Convinced they had the right men, he asked Reeves where the gun was hidden. He took Phoenix into the parlour and pointed to the sofa. Under it was hidden a dark-painted .303 rifle – the sniper's favourite weapon. When Phoenix escorted Reeves outside he discovered that his patrol had already left the area and he was immediately surrounded by a hostile crowd. The old military training came to the fore once again as he holstered his revolver and cocked the .303 to the young prisoner's head. 'Come any nearer and I blow him to hell!' was the sentence that ensured their safe passage to the Limestone Road, where he hitched a lift with a passing army Land Rover.

Goodall and Reeves were eventually brought to York Road station for further questioning, and according to Phoenix 'valuable information was gained from both of them'. This led to the arrest of Francis Collins, another Provisional IRA gunman, later that evening. Collins had been implicated by his colleagues and was charged with supplying the weapon for the attempted murder. He was held for four months but was released on 15 February when charges were withdrawn. He was interned as he left the court room. Police suspected that he was the quartermaster of the Provisional IRA's third Belfast battalion, which covered the north of the city.*

* Collins continued his paramilitary career after being freed from internment. Throughout the 1970s he was involved in numerous bombings and shootings. On 9 May 1976 he was arrested with another well-known North Belfast Provisional, Laurence Marley, but

Ian almost immediately wrote commendatory reports praising the reactions of his patrol on that night. It was to be a feature of his leadership that he always ensured that good work was rewarded by commendations or medals wherever possible. Sadly his own senior officers rarely reciprocated with similar commendations for Phoenix's work. But in 1974 his supervising inspector wrote a very heartening report on his progress. It noted:

> Sergeant Phoenix has continued to prove his worth as a young NCO at this station. He has five men on his duty division, all with less than two years' experience, but it is largely due to Sgt Phoenix that this is the most active and successful division here. The recent incident at Hillman Street when his division was fired upon by two gunmen whom they later arrested is but one instance of good enthusiastic police work of which Sgt Phoenix was the mainspring ... Sgt Phoenix is not afraid to take on cases of his own and by his example encourages the men under him to do likewise.

This report was duly endorsed by the chief inspector. He wrote of Officer 10042 that:

was released after questioning. In the late 1980s he turned to ordinary crime. In 1989 he was charged and convicted of armed robbery. Sentenced to seven years, he was released in 1994. On February 1995 he was arrested in connection with the £37,000 robbery of a Securicor van. Again he was released. His luck ran out, however, on 18 December 1995, when Provisional IRA gunmen shot him dead, accusing him of being a drug dealer.

he is not afraid to take command on the ground and to make a decision, which was very evident on 17 December 1973 when his patrol was ambushed ... This led to the capture of a terrorist and I may add that I am also very delighted in his manner of interviewing suspects. I have no doubt if he continues as at present, he will be a credit to the police.

Chief Inspector, York Road

It was these reports which helped his supervisors to recommend that his rank as sergeant be confirmed after his twelve-month probationary period. This was in spite of the acknowledgements that his written reports needed to 'continue to improve'. This was to be a trend in his future police work: Ian was always an excellent operational officer, but senior ranks would occasionally express concern that his sardonic humour was often applied to his written analysis of situations.

A year after the Phoenixes moved into their Glengormley home the owner offered it to them for £690. At the time, they were paying twenty pounds a month rent. They decided to buy, and borrowed the deposit money from Susan's parents – much against her husband's instincts, for he hated being in debt. He had been reared in the old-fashioned working-class morality which was ruled by the simple maxim that if you can't afford something you don't buy it.

In spite of the Troubles, for the first few years the Phoenixes had managed to shut out from their life together the violence that swirled around them. According to Susan, when Phoenix came home he 'shared the funny things with me, and the sad things. He never talked about the dangers.' She did not know that he had been shot at by a sniper until she read about the incident in the newspaper. But she could not but be aware of the threats he faced on a daily basis. He never went to work without kissing her goodbye. 'That was my safety precaution,' she says.

However, the dangers did not end for the RUC man when he reached home. The Provisional IRA grew steadily more ruthless in its targeting. At first the Provisionals, following their claims to be an 'army', attacked only on-duty members of the security forces. There was initially some resistance to the proposal that off-duty policemen and soldiers should also be targeted. This resistance was partly for propaganda reasons. When the Provisionals murdered three off-duty Scottish soldiers in March 1971, after spending the night drinking with them, there was fierce condemnation from within the Catholic community, as well as from the usual quarters. But by early 1972 the brutalising effects of the violence combined with the opportunistic nature of the Provisionals' tactics to widen the concept of a 'legitimate target' to include defenceless men at work and their families at home.

In January 1972 an off-duty reserve constable, Raymond Denham, was shot dead at the factory where he worked in Waterford Street, a few blocks from Springfield Road police station. Just over two weeks later, on 28 January, an off-duty constable was shot dead as he worked on his car in a garage on the Oldpark Road in North Belfast. The Provisionals also began booby-trapping policemen's cars. A few miles from Glengormley in the suburb of Greenisland a police sergeant, Frederick Robinson, was killed when a bomb exploded under his car on 19 March 1974. The Provisionals were also operating in and around Glengormley. On 26 January 1974 snipers shot dead Reserve Constable John Rodgers at the junction of the Carnmoney and Antrim Roads, not far from the Phoenixes' home. Eight months later Inspector William Elliott was shot dead by loyalist gunmen in the Protestant working-class housing estate of Rathcoole, which borders on Glengormley.

The policemen who lived in the Glengormley area at that time organised a local vigilante rota between themselves. This entailed the off-duty men doing plain-clothes foot patrols to protect the homes of their colleagues who were at work. Susan recalls that it also entailed making an awful lot of hot whiskey toddies for the 'vigilantes' as they returned from plodding through the snowy winter streets.

At this time, Susan said, they felt that the violence was closing in on them. Ian had spent several of his night shifts guarding a wounded colleague who was unconscious in the Royal Victoria Hospital after being shot at his own bedroom window. His wife sang haunting Irish folk songs to him in her native Gaelic language. (One wonders if the population realised at that time that there were indeed Catholic policemen suffering at the hands of their co-religionists in the IRA.) Early one morning the Phoenixes were roused from their sleep by a banging on the front door. It was about 2 a.m. Phoenix did not look out the window – he remembered his hospitalised colleague and the favourite tactic of the Provisionals of shooting people as they peered out. He told Susan to get his shotgun, while he armed himself with his pistol. He told her to cover him while he went downstairs to the door. She was in her nightie, lying at the top of the stairs in the marksman's prone position, the shotgun aimed at the door. Her husband stood behind the door and, gun in hand, gently opened it a crack. A gloved hand came in and dropped Phoenix's pay cheque on the floor. It was a fellow police officer who had been on the late shift and, in those days before direct banking, thought he would do Phoenix a favour by delivering his pay cheque on his way home. Susan remembers thinking how ludicrous this was as they all collapsed in laughter. What a way to live! The people in England would not understand how they lived, she thought, 'But we just accepted it.'

On another occasion, near Christmas, they were watching television when there was a loud bang from the back of the house. Phoenix grabbed his gun and, in a defensive position, went round the back while

Susan commando-crawled along the floor towards the staircase and their precious little daughter. Phoenix came back. There was nothing. Then they both rolled on the floor in hysterical laughter as they saw the remains of a large balloon that had burst near the Christmas tree. It was a further indication of the kind of tension under which they were forced to live. Susan began thinking of moving out of the city altogether.

They spent their spare time driving around the countryside. It was on one of these excursions that they found themselves on a quiet part of the Antrim coast, with a rocky, lonely shore and a view of Scotland in the distance. They liked the area and began to explore it. By chance, while driving up a laneway they came across an old, deserted farmhouse that was for sale. It sat on a hill, with primrose-covered fields around it that sloped down to the sea. It was a windy spot, but the Phoenixes fell for it at first sight.

The last owners had been an old sea captain and his wife. He had kept cows in a byre at the back of the house. He was known as a local character and named the cows after local women. When the Phoenixes moved in they found the names 'Kathleen' and 'Ella' written over the byre where he used to milk them. It was reported that he never bothered to chase his chickens for the pot: he just used his shotgun from the kitchen door. The house was about a hundred years old and had been built by a man who had once owned a ship's chandlers in Belfast. It was now in need of renovation, but it looked like an exciting new 'project' to the energetic young couple.

The family moved into a borrowed caravan in the garden of their new home during the summer of 1975. The move came at the same time as Phoenix was made the divisional training instructor for R and P Divisions. He was stationed in the town of Carrickfergus, with its magnificent Norman castle overlooking Belfast Lough. It was a quiet posting, and Phoenix saw little action. He was also made responsible for reserve-constable training and development.

Phoenix's training methods were often unconventional, and certainly never dull. He liked to organise realistic 'stop and search' exercises for the young probationers and reserves. He managed to persuade Susan and an experienced reserve policeman (their friend, Ned) to use a builder's van stuffed with illegal ammunition and mock sticks of dynamite for one such evening exercise. Susan and Ned pretended to be ordinary motorists who were stopped by the trainees at a vehicle checkpoint in Carrickfergus. Unfortunately the young policemen failed to find any of the illegal bounty under the care of the suspicious-looking couple. Phoenix's later dressing-down for such sloppy police work was not recorded. His drill sessions were already feared by the local lady reserves, who had not yet learned that his bark was worse than his bite. One woman recalled how they would stand on parade while Sergeant Phoenix would walk along the ranks to inspect their uniforms. She remembers one of his favourite questions while he flicked hairs from shoulders: 'Slept with the dog last night, did we?'

The local reserves were recruited from all sections of the community – farmers, teachers, builders and unskilled workers. They were valued by Phoenix not only for their service to the community through the police but also for their friendship, and for the skills they could bring to his often inept DIY attempts. Many family jokes emanated from his attempts to 'do it himself'. He loved labouring, and the couple spent many happy hours stripping plaster and ceilings as they made their plans for the future. Refixing things was a different matter. As Susan and he struggled to renovate their old 'house with potential' it became more of a moneybox into which all of their funds disappeared. They were very grateful for any of their new friends' help with the never-ending tasks, but they often wondered if it would have been cheaper to have paid professionals to do the work rather than continually rewarding their helpers with thankyou parties – although the parties were more fun, and many of the friends made in those years were to stay with the Phoenix family for a lifetime.

They lived in the caravan in the garden for the first six months, while the heavy work was carried out. Helpful neighbours supplied locally caught lobsters, which were boiled up in the old tin bath over the open fire in the garden. (All hot water came from this source while they lived in the caravan.) They went fishing with their new friends, and learned the satisfaction of dropping a trace of fishing-line with several hooks attached over the side of a little boat when the mackerel and herring were about. The line would be reeled back into the boat pulsating with fish that were dropped into the hull for the pan that night. The local fishing-boats were always ready when the cry went out 'the herring are up.' The Phoenixes could stand in their garden and count the boats as they bobbed about below them. On still nights they could hear the fishermen chatting to each other across the still and misty waters of the Irish Sea. Had it not been for Ian's chosen career and the everyday dangers he encountered it could almost have been described as an idyllic lifestyle, with their own crops in the large garden, goats to milk, and chickens, geese and ducks to rear for their eggs.

It was at this time too that Susan got the surprise of her life when on her seventh wedding anniversary Phoenix came home and told her that she would always remember this night. 'Why?' she asked, excited because this was a rare occasion indeed, since her husband rarely made a fuss about such events. 'Because I need you to exercise your artistic talents and draw a sub-machine-gun on here,' he said, producing a blackboard. 'It's for tomorrow's weapon-training class.' She should have known.

All was far from pastoral bliss, however, and Phoenix did see action, even in Carrickfergus. He became involved in a riot on 11 July, during the Orangemen's biggest marching time. A gang of fifty or more youths had been stoning the Catholic church, and Phoenix confronted them with the help of only a young constable (coincidentally another ex-paratrooper) and a reserve policewoman. The young Constable had just been clobbered with Union Jack flag pole, opening a wound on his head which required fourteen stitches. Phoenix turned to Constable C, saying, 'Have you got your baton with you?' 'Yes, Sergeant.' 'OK. Well let's get this lot dispersed then!' As usual, the Phoenix method of dispersal was direct and determined, and around fourteen rioters were hospitalised – one for every stitch in the young constable C's head. The two-man baton charge was considered a huge success, although local loyalist leaders were never too sure whether Phoenix was not really a 'Fenian in disguise'. After arresting the ring-leaders, some of whom turned out to be local councillors, Phoenix was amused by their outlandish claims that they were just 'investigating reports that policemen had been throwing milk bottles at innocent Protestants'.

Phoenix would remain in Carrickfergus for three years, before being promoted to inspector and transferred back to Belfast – at the insistence, it would seem, of a senior officer who thought that his potential was being wasted in the training branch. Ian held this officer in high esteem for ever after. He was to spend just one year more on the beat, in Tennent Street police station in the fiercely loyalist Shankill Road area. He arrived there with a reputation as an 'ex-para fitness fanatic', as one of his colleagues who would later serve as his detective sergeant discovered. Phoenix had previously been nicknamed the 'roadrunner' in York Street, because of the speed at which he did his foot patrols.

The new colleague recalls arriving at the station one evening for duty, having had one pint of lager. 'Ian came into the enquiry office,' he remembered. 'He asked me if I had been drinking. I replied that I had one before starting duty. He then went to his office, returning with his flak jacket on, and told me to put on my overcoat and flak jacket and come with him. This done, he then led me on a beat patrol through the night around the boundary of the whole of the Tennent Street subdivision – down Tennent Street, up the Crumlin Road, through the back alleyways of the Ardoyne [a dangerous Provisional IRA area], across into Forthriver, and back down the Shankill Road and into the station. He still looked cool and refreshed, while there wasn't a spot on my body that didn't drip with sweat. He just looked at me and said, "Let that be a lesson to you. Don't drink before you come on duty again." It was

Ian Phoenix discipline – as a lesson learned rather than through the discipline procedures in the force's manual.'

On the morning of 3 February 1978 Phoenix was caught in an IRA ambush. The Provisionals attacked and shot two military policemen outside the Crumlin Road jail. Phoenix arrived with another policeman fifteen minutes later, and was searching the area for the gunmen when a bomb went off in a vacant house as he passed it. He was just twenty-five yards from the blast and was blown off his feet. He suffered from shock and a ringing (tinnitus) in his ears which rendered him partially deaf for the rest of his life. Phoenix reckoned he had experienced some 300 attacks in his eight-year career as a policeman on the beat in the black North. The bombing of 3 February was to be the last. For the rest of his career he would be undercover in the Special Branch (SB).

In the years immediately after they bought the farmhouse, the Phoenixes devoted most of their spare time, energy and money to fixing up their new home. One day, as they rummaged through the old attic, they discovered a poem that had been written about Robert Kane, the original builder of the house. It was written after he had drowned in an accident on Dufferin Dock in Belfast on 4 December 1897, and describes his house and the countryside around it:

And there the white rocks do shine
  Washed by the rolling sea
And the bean blossom's scent so sweet
  Floats on the gentle breeze . . .

And at its base where rabbits graze
  O'er many a hollow and few may know
That since the days of Adam
  Was n'er turned by the plough . . .

A stately house he did erect
  Upon his father's land . . .

The poem goes on to recount Kane's accidental
death:

A thick fog came o'er the place
  It was so very dark
The street lamps were of little use
  They shone just like a spark.

The Glen Head she was in port
  Tom Wilson was the mate
His brother Hill and Bob did go
  Upon him for to wait

As they were walking up the quay
  And Hill he was behind
He told them to be careful
  And of the way to mind

> But Bob he being confident
> Said, 'Leave it all to me'.
> In a short time they both stepped forth
> And plunged into the sea.

It would not be the last time that fog would determine the fate of those who lived in the old farmhouse.

Chapter 3

Undercover

(1979–82)

On 2 March 1979 Susan was surprised to receive a wedding-anniversary card from her husband. It was not like him to remember such dates. It had come from London, where he was undergoing training in covert operations in preparation for his new posting in the surveillance unit of the RUC Special Branch. The target he was following during a surveillance exercise had gone into a card shop, and Phoenix went after him. The trainee undercover cop was browsing among the merchandise trying to look inconspicuous. What could be more natural than to buy a card for his wife? By a happy coincidence it also happened to be their eleventh anniversary.

Phoenix had been promoted to detective inspector and transferred to the Special Branch on 29 January

1979. After undergoing the necessary training in London and Harrogate, he became operational at the beginning of April of that year. It was his last transfer within the police. He would remain a Branch man for the rest of his life.

The Branch started disrupting their family life straightaway, when the London training course ran on into the first week of the first foreign holiday the young family had taken. As a result, Susan had to take the children alone on the flight out and Ian joined them during their second week in Tunisia. They had chosen Tunisia because of their love of adventure and exotic destinations. It was still considered a 'cheapie' when Northern Ireland travel agents were just starting to encourage the package holidaymaker away from the Spanish islands.

Phoenix's love of different cultures and making new friends was evident when he almost immediately befriended the hotel gardener. Abdul was an elderly French-speaking Tunisian who used a small hut in the grounds to eat his wife's fennel-laden tomato and lamb stew. It was not long before Ian discovered that Abdul was a war veteran who was supplementing his pension by tending the flower-filled desert garden. Soon the whole family were spending part of every day sitting cross-legged outside the little hut dipping hunks of home-made bread into Abdul's aromatic pot of stew. In fact the children much preferred this fare to the more sedate French cuisine in the hotel dining-room. It was a source of sadness to Ian that the devout Muslim did not drink alcohol: he always carried a bottle of Blackbush whiskey for the cementing of holiday friendships or for repaying some local kindness. He had the solution, though, and before they left Tunisia all of the children's plastic pens, Susan's tights and unwanted clothes had been passed over as presents for Abdul's wife and family. Susan still treasures the little gold locket that Abdul presented to them on the last day. He had tears in his eyes as he thanked them for their friendship. With an arm round Ian's shoulders he said, '*Tu est vraiment mon camarade Irlandais.*'

Similar foreign friendships were to be made on family holidays all over the world in the years to come. Ian and Susan wanted to make sure that the children valued people from all forms and levels of society. However, their daughter was not so certain of the value of a Tunisian matron who shared her tea and nomad tent with them on that first holiday. Ian had impressed upon both children that it was considered bad manners to refuse local hospitality, so when the nomadic tribeswoman had brewed the little pot of thick sweet tea on her charcoal brazier the children prepared to accept the tiny glasses of brew. Unfortunately the pot ran out before the last glass was full, and the woman replenished the pot by adding a tasty blob of saliva from her mouth. The whole family giggled for days afterwards at the expression on the little girl's face as she 'remembered her manners' and drank the proffered glass.

After this relaxing break Phoenix was ready for his new job in Special Branch.

According to an officer who worked with Phoenix for many years, 'He went into the Special Branch for the excitement and because he wanted to take on the terrorists head to head.' At the time Phoenix joined the élite anti-terrorist branch of the force it was in the throes of a series of transformations.

Since the mid-1970s the RUC itself had been undergoing profound changes that were aimed at placing it in the centre of the struggle against the paramilitary organisations. British government policy was attempting to 'Ulsterise' the situation, gradually withdrawing the British army, including the SAS, from the front line by handing over the running of security to the police. This was part of the same process which had led to the abolition of internment without trial in 1975 and its replacement by special anti-terrorist courts, known as Diplock courts, where one judge presided without a jury. The strategy was to try to contain the terrorists as far as possible by means of ordinary legal procedures, rather than using military force and extrajudicial measures such as detention without trial, both of which fed into the Provisional IRA's propaganda that it was fighting a war of liberation against a foreign enemy on its soil.

Of course, juryless courts and the whole apparatus

of emergency legislation, which circumvented many of the legal rights customarily enjoyed in the United Kingdom, would continue to draw the fire of human-rights groups. But, as far as the government was concerned, they were an important step towards trying to normalise the situation and, whatever their faults, were less obnoxious than locking people up without trial for years on end. At any rate, the authorities had concluded that the threat from a highly organised and extremely violent group like the Provisionals could not be effectively dealt with through the normal criminal courts. As long as it existed, emergency measures in some shape or form would be necessary.

The RUC was to play a crucial role in the Ulsterisation process. If it was to take on the Provisionals and the loyalist terrorist groups, intelligence-gathering was of central importance. The failure of the internment operation in 1971 had been laid at the door of the Special Branch, which was blamed for having out-of-date and erroneous information, sometimes leading to the arrest of the wrong people. The Special Branch needed to improve its intelligence-gathering capacities, and up-to-date methods of surveillance and the recruitment and training of good operators were obviously vital to the success of its tasks.

There are two main ways that the Special Branch gathers intelligence. The first is through informers, and the second is via various types of surveillance, human- and technology-based. E3 is the Special

Branch department that specialises in running agents. E4 is responsible for surveillance. Phoenix would spend all his career as a Branchman in E4, but he had tremendous respect for the constables whose responsibility it was to handle informers. They often had to meet their sources in lonely, isolated spots – the perfect places for set-ups and ambushes. He recalled how one officer he worked with had a crisis one night as he sat in his car in the pitch black of a forest far from any main road, waiting for his source – a high-ranking member of the Provisionals – to arrive. Phoenix reported that the constable suddenly thought, 'I must be fuckin' mad sitting here like this, waiting for a fuckin' gunman!'

Shortly after E4A was set up, specializing in covert surveillance operations, Phoenix assessed the performance of its Belfast units and noted that there was a problem with the new 'handlers' of some sources (i.e. informers). They were not trained to the standard that he felt necessary for such a delicate role. He said they were 'unsure' of their role, whereas old handlers with well-established sources treated them like a 'broody hen' treats its chicks.

In relation to informers, Ian's chief responsibility was processing their information – he had to assess its value and how it might be put to use in monitoring counter-terrorist operations. However, as a senior officer, he would occasionally meet with highly placed sources – always in the company of another officer – to discuss the financial arrangements needed to ensure their cooperation. In the interest of security for all involved, he would never record any details of such meetings or identities. He found, and other officers confirm this, that the vast majority of paramilitary informers, like their counterparts in the 'ordinary' criminal organisations, do it for the money. They also tend to have criminal traits. They frequently begin their career as 'touts' after having been arrested for some petty offence.

Though informers remain the most powerful tool that the police have against illegal organisations, allowing them to anticipate crimes, as the years progressed technical surveillance would grow in importance as it grew in sophistication. By the 1980s the Special Branch arsenal included a range of the most up-to-date surveillance tools available.

In the mid and late 1980s, such surveillance equipment would lead to major intelligence break-throughs that enabled the security forces to thwart several large-scale PIRA and loyalist operations (see Chapters 6 and 7).

In 1976 the new unit, E4A, had been created. Its insignia was an eagle clutching a tourniquet – a reference to the fact that its first two operations were codenamed Eagle and Tourniquet. Possibly because of his army experience of operating behind enemy lines, Phoenix was assigned to the unit and became an

E4A team leader. E4A's aim was to provide province-wide coverage for various surveillance operations. It was meant to be a closely knit group, under a detective chief inspector. Secrecy was of the highest importance. Its standing orders stress, 'Aspects of a particular operation will only be discussed between those members involved. Operational matters will not be divulged by personnel to any persons outside the unit without express permission of D/Chief Inspector or above.'

Under the detective chief inspector in charge of each unit were two detective inspectors – one in charge of operational administration, the other of operations. The inspectors' duties were to ensure the smooth running of the team, and to deal with the personal problems of the team members if necessary. He had to assess future operations with the detective chief inspector, and made sure the equipment for them was available. He liaised with other units, and carried out routine inspections of equipment and vehicles.

A station sergeant, a training sergeant, a photography sergeant and a transport officer were under the control of the operational administration inspector.

The inspector responsible for operations had under him a sergeant in charge of intelligence, and a number of constables who made up the surveillance teams. The intelligence sergeant was responsible for preparing weekly reports, briefing teams, submitting daily logs within twenty-four hours or earlier, and preparing for operations themselves. The strength of each office was expected to consist of four sergeants and at least ten constables, plus two typists. But to maintain the efficiency of the unit these figures were increased when necessary.

The strength of the units also varied from area to area. As of December 1984, for instance, the unit based in RUC headquarters and covering the south-east of the province consisted of a superintendent, a chief inspector, four inspectors, ten sergeants and fifty-five constables. The unit covering Belfast was made up of one chief inspector, two inspectors, six sergeants and forty-two constables.

An earlier attempt to establish a surveillance unit, known as the Bronze Section, had failed, partly because the unit's role was not clearly defined. But E4A was modelled on 14 Intelligence Unit, a surveillance unit of the British army. Its members went through more intensive training, and took special weapons courses and courses in radio communication and covert surveillance. Like the SAS, they had to learn the most difficult discipline of all – to sit still. They would have to spend long periods of time in cramped conditions in covert observation posts (OPs) in damp ditches and hedgerows, or lying on the roofs of buildings with little protection from the weather, simply waiting and watching. While many men and women would be attracted to the idea of being an undercover cop, enjoying the 'macho' image (the medallion men, as Phoenix would later call them, because of their habit of wearing flashing neckchains), quite a few would find the conditions under which they had to operate too onerous.

After only seven months on the job, Ian was put in charge of organising and restructuring the whole E4A department. He wanted to put it on more of a 'military' footing, and set about providing it with the kind of equipment he judged it needed to carry out its tasks properly. In late November 1979 he set off to London with an E4A station sergeant to do a bit of pre-Christmas shopping. On their shopping list were 40 pairs of camouflage and windproof smocks (20 medium, 20 large), 40 pairs of camouflage and windproof trousers (20 medium, 20 large), 25 lightweight ponchos, 25 parkas and 25 parka hoods, 25 balaclava helmets, 40 face veils, 30 Bergen rucksacks, 40 sleeping-bags, 60 sleeping-bags with liners, 25 camp-beds, 2 woodland camouflage nets, 6 entrenching spades, 25 pneumatic mattresses, 20 quart-size vacuum flasks, 6 torches, 80 Amplivox ear-defenders, 6 plastic five-gallon water-cans, 25 mess tins, 80 first-aid kits, 18 packets of face paint (brown) for face camouflage, 80 pairs of thermal-underwear long johns, 80 pairs of thermal gloves, 80 pairs of thermal socks, 80 wet-weather suits, 2 tents with ridges, 20 putees, and 1 marquee. Some of the stuff would come from the RUC's own stores at Sprucefield, to the south of Belfast. Though the London store was unable to provide all the gear requested, it did supply the parkas, ponchos, face veils, balaclavas, mess tins, marquee, hoods, spades, camouflage nets, puttees, camp-beds and sleeping-bags and most but not all of the thermal underwear.

At the same time as the RUC was adapting itself to the new exigencies imposed on it by the policies of the British government, its main enemy, the Provisional IRA (PIRA), was undergoing a somewhat similar process. The Provisionals too were 'Ulsterising' their structures at both a political and a military level. They were also honing down their operational units into self-sustaining active-service units (ASUs). The men behind these moves were three northerners – Martin McGuinness from Derry City and Belfastmen Gerry Adams and Ivor Bell. They had witnessed the near-disastrous consequences of the prolonged cease-fire of 1974–5, when the Provisionals had become increasingly involved in feuding, sectarian killing and the running of drinking-clubs in the nationalist ghettos. In their eyes, the old southern-based leadership of men like Rauiri O Bradaigh and Daithi O Connail, with its strategy based on the belief that a British withdrawal was imminent, had become completely discredited. Adams and his supporters restructured the Provisionals so that the organisation was geared to fight a long, ruthless terrorist war. They established a Northern Command, which had the responsibility of running the campaign in Northern Ireland. Gradually, Northerners would be moved into top positions in both the IRA and Sinn Fein, the political wing. By the late 1980s Ulster men would control the Army Council, the seven-man ruling body of the organisation, and the twelve-member GHQ, which ran the day-to-day operations of the organisation. In the late 1970s a British army analysis of the structure and strength of the Provisional IRA said it had about 500 full-time terrorists, with thousands more passive supporters willing to hide a gunman on the run or to store a weapon. The report, drawn up by Brigadier General Glover, who was GOC of British forces in Northern Ireland, noted that 'The Provisional leadership is deeply committed to a long campaign of attrition . . . Even if "Peace" is restored, the motivation for politically inspired violence will remain. Arms will be readily available and there will be many who are able and willing to use them.' Unfortunately this assessment was to prove all too accurate, and the Provisionals would continue to absorb most of the attention and the resources of both the RUC and the army.

Of course, the Provisionals were not the only para-military organisation that the RUC and its surveillance units would be targeting. On the republican side, the Official IRA, which had been formed after the IRA split in 1969, was still intact but its armed campaign had been suspended since 1972. Most of its energies went into racketeering and robberies to fund the Workers' Party, its political wing. However, the Official IRA had itself split in December 1974 with the formation of the Irish National Liberation Army (INLA). By 1979 the INLA had developed into a small but potent force, and had carried out a 'spectacular' – the assassination of shadow Northern Ireland Secretary, Airey Neave, who was one of the architects of Tory leader Margaret Thatcher's rise to power. (The INLA had penetrated the security of the House of Commons and got into its underground car park. Using explosives which had come from sympathisers in Palestine Liberation Organisation, INLA operators had booby-trapped Neave's car.) The INLA never posed a threat comparable to that of the Provisionals, but its links to Middle Eastern and European groups and its recruitment of some exceptionally dangerous activists, including dissident Provisionals, made it a real threat – one that was enhanced by its unpredictability.

There were also two powerful loyalist paramilitary organisations – the Ulster Defence Association (UDA) and the Ulster Volunteer Force (UVF). The UDA was the larger, with several thousand members. It had grown out of a Belfast Protestant militia formed in 1971. Among its members there was a core of active assassins whose targets were mainly Catholics. It issued claims of responsibility under the fictitious name of the Ulster Freedom Fighters (UFF). The UDA itself was not outlawed until 1992.

The Ulster Volunteer Force was smaller, but had the reputation for being the more deadly of the two. Its main power base was in Belfast and in East Tyrone and Armagh. Among its most feared killers was Lennie Murphy – nicknamed the Shankill Road Butcher – whose gang hacked up its mainly Catholic victims before shooting them.

There was a third, much smaller, loyalist group, known as the Red Hand Commandos, active for a short time between 1972 and 1974, from when nothing was heard of it until the 1990s.

It was the web of violence and murder represented by the initials PIRA–INLA–UVF–UDA that Ian Phoenix as an undercover police officer would spend the rest of his life trying to break.

The Phoenix family were entering the shadowy world of undercover policing, which would change their lives for ever. They ran up against the reality of Ian's new posting when one day, shortly after they returned from their Tunisian holiday, he said to his wife, 'Susan, for goodness' sake, why did you make the car so bloody clean?' 'What do you mean?' she answered innocently. 'It looks lovely.' 'Lovely enough so that anyone can read the number plates,' he pointed out. 'From now on they're to be left dirty. It makes it more difficult for potential murderers to identify us.'

From then on, they had to follow a strict regime of security procedures:

- When answering the phone do not give your name or number, because it exposes you instantly to the caller who can check if they have found their target.
- When driving home, always check if there has been a car behind you for more than a usual length of time; if necessary, drive past your home and double back somewhere that would make it difficult for the suspect car to continue following you to your home.
- Write down car numbers of any vehicle that has passed the house too often or if it appears for any reason to be acting suspiciously.
- Vary the times of your trips. Ian himself would vary his times of departure and also take different routes as far as possible – irregularity was important both for work and for social life.
- Do not attend regular night classes. If the children made regular visits somewhere it was arranged that either of the parents would pick them up on an ad hoc basis. Joining clubs meant telling lies about your occupation.
- Always let the dogs out first at night – they would tell if there were any strangers about.
- When the doorbell rang it was Susan who answered it, after first checking who was there.
- Normally a gun was kept under the pillow. This became a way of life for Susan, who always needed a large handbag so that it could be concealed when they were visiting friends. When several policemen visited one house they would always ask for a safe

place to conceal their guns, away from the children and prying eyes.

- Fire extinguishers and torches should be kept in all rooms.
- Do not hang uniform shirts outside on the washing-line. Dry-cleaning uniforms could be a problem unless one found a friendly dry-cleaner who could be trusted.
- The car had to be checked after being left outside, whether it was parked at a supermarket or at a friend's house. Someone would casually drop keys next to the car to give them a chance to look under it to check for under-car booby traps (UCBTs). The engine would always be started with the door open, to dissipate any blast from a UCBT.
- The children had always to lie to strangers and passing acquaintances about what their father did for a living.

After a while the family carried out these measures automatically. They knew their enemy could be as cunning as it was ruthless. The one sure way to render it less effective was, of course, by good intelligence. And by 1979 the Special Branch had built up a picture of the Provisionals' Northern Command structure, concentrating on its membership from Belfast, one of the movement's most important power bases. E4A had a list of twenty-seven names of the city's top Provisionals, giving their names, their addresses, the registration number and colour of their car (if they had one), hair colour, and their position within the PIRA. Number 1 on the list was Gerry Adams, who later would become president of Sinn Fein, PIRA's political wing, and grow respectable enough to shake hands with the President of the United States. He was ranked 'Northern Command'. Number 2 was a thirty-eight-year-old man from Twinbrook in West Belfast, who was listed as 'Adj. N. Command PIRA' – that is, adjutant or second in command. Among the others named were Ivor Bell (Number 11), then a close confidant of Adams and regarded as an architect of the movement's restructuring, and Danny Morrison (number 23), listed as editor of *Republican News*, the Provisional's propaganda weekly, who later served a sentence for kidnapping. Number 19 was a member of GHQ staff, and later was put in charge of running the movement's finance-raising operations. As far as is known he remains active in PIRA to this day (see Chapter 9). Another prominent figure named was Robert Campbell, listed as Number 18. Like Number 19 he was a PIRA GHQ staff member, and police regarded him as a dangerous gunman. In May 1980 he was arrested after a gun battle which cost the life of an SAS man on the Antrim Road in North Belfast. James Burns (Number 5) held the crucial position of quartermaster for Northern Command – he controlled access to weapons and explosives. In February 1981 loyalist gunmen belonging to the UVF shot him dead in bed. Number 14 was of special interest to the police. As head of the so-called Civil Administration Team (CAT) he was responsible for unmasking informers within PIRA. Last but certainly not least on the list was Number 27. This thirty-three-year-old PIRA activist was identified as the 'IO Belfast Brigade' – Belfast PIRA's intelligence officer (IO) who was responsible for gathering information on possible targets.

Many of the individuals on the list became the object of E4A surveillance operations. Each operation had its own codename, chosen according to strict guidelines which have never been revealed before. The names are taken from a directory held at headquarters. To be selected, a name must never have been used before – even the fact that a name had been used for an MoD operation during the Second World War was enough to disqualify it from being employed again – and each name has to consist of only one word, which cannot be a proper name. Two words are used only when naming exercises, not operations.

The first operation that Phoenix undertook, code-named Hawk, was intended to mount surveillance on Number 27 and to monitor his movements with a view to establishing associates' addresses. The police were especially interested in a friend of Number 27 who they thought was his driver.

The surveillance operation had to be mounted in the Provisional IRA stronghold of Andersonstown. An observation post was set up near the suspect's house. The suspect was observed leaving the house at just after noon, and was then followed for the next hour by three E4A cars on a 'complicated journey' through

Andersonstown, during which four stops were made. The movements were precisely clocked in, and the suspect was seen to meet with two 'unknown males'. It was also noted that 'Suspect was alert to being followed.' The suspect returned home, and then some eight minutes later set off again in the car. This time it was on the move for only ten minutes. The route was similar to that taken a little earlier. Ten minutes after returning, the car set off for a third time, and was followed by a fourth surveillance car on more or less the same route again. This time, however, the surveillance operation may have been spotted. The police had parked in an adjacent street and one crew member had got out. The policeman saw a man answering to the description of the Belfast Provisional's intelligence chief. But Number 27 looked straight at the undercover policeman before getting into the other suspect's car and driving off. The policeman rejoined his car to follow Number 27 and the suspected driver. As he did so, they saw them driving towards them in the suspects' car.

The fact that two brown-coloured cars had been used may have aroused the suspicions of Number 27 and his driver. Phoenix later reported that it had been a mistake to use two cars of the same colour. But it was more likely that Number 27 became suspicious when he saw one of the operators on foot and then again in the brown surveillance car as it passed him. In any case, Phoenix concluded that the first drive round was 'an anti-surveillance run on the way out of the driver's home, and a clearing run on the way back'. He tried to never make the common mistake of underestimating the knowledge of the criminal, whether a terrorist or not.

Though Operation Hawk did not lead to any immediate breakthroughs, the next operation Ian was involved in did. It was codenamed Mistral, and it was unusual in that it exposed a traitor from within the ranks of the RUC. Mistral originally targeted Number 14, the head of PIRA's informer-busting team. He was 30 years old and based in Unity Flats, near the Loyalist Skankill Road. It was discovered that a renegade policeman was selling information to PIRA. The danger was that the policeman could betray vital information about informers to the Provisionals. Mistral began in August 1979, and Number 14 and his associates were under surveillance throughout the following month. The area under surveillance was near a large loyalist housing estate north of Belfast. It appeared that Number 14's police source, codenamed Fox, frequented a pub there.

By October, Phoenix's team suspected who Fox was and wanted to confirm his identity. The police knew that Fox had a list of ten names of police informers which he was willing to sell for £200, which in 1979 was a not inconsiderable sum. He was, in effect, signing their death warrants at the rate of twenty pounds each. Once the CAT got their hands on the suspected touts they would be tortured and almost certainly 'executed'.* Phoenix learned that an exchange between the rogue policeman and PIRA was scheduled for 15 October at around 7.30 p.m. A courier was to be used to bring the money to Fox. Police observed them in advance. Three OPs were established in the area of the pub. Phoenix's team prepared for the night of the 15th. They knew at what time the courier planned to reach the rendezvous. Phoenix warned the team on the ground 'assume that he knows our identities and will have a knowledge of surveillance/counter-surveillance. He will already be in the area and will most likely be doing dummy runs along that stretch of road. He may not make contact.'

The drop was made and the money handed over to a suspect who drove off. The driver was not initially recognized until he entered a housing estate where a checkpoint of uniformed S. B. men identified him as the rogue policeman Fox. When searched he was found with incriminating material and money in a white envelope, and then handed over for questioning.

* Among those 'executed' by the CAT (Civil Administration Team) was Maurice Gilvary, a member of PIRA's third battalion in North Belfast. PIRA accused Gilvary of betraying an operation in 1978 that led to the deaths of three of its 'volunteers' who were ambushed by the SAS. A republican source revealed that at the time Gilvary was taken away by PIRA for interrogation he was living with the widow of one of the PIRA members killed in the ambush he is accused of having helped set up.

E4A in Belfast was running a dozen simultaneous operations throughout Ian's first year in surveillance. As well as Operations Hawk and Mistral, there were operations such as Concorde, Dupont, Cohort, Entrance, Iona, Eagle, Ragtime, Eusteace, Sundog and Kinslow – all running between the early summer of 1979 and early 1980.

Concorde was directed against high-ranking members of the Provisional IRA. It involved the establishing of OPs in the Castle Street area at the foot of the Falls Road, which Phoenix visited on 16 August. He looked over several abandoned buildings (all now demolished), including an old RUC station, trying to spot a good site to place an OP. The targets were a high-ranking female PIRA member and several male associates. This operation led to her arrest after Phoenix himself followed her through Belfast, watching as she met her PIRA contacts.

In 1979 Ian had encouraged Susan to go back to university to obtain qualifications which they felt would be useful when the children grew up. Her voluntary projects had grown since the Glengormley days, and she was now taking an interest in the deaf population as a result of conversations with a new deaf neighbour. The Phoenix family did not do things by half measures, of course, and the whole family applied themselves to learn sign language to be able to communicate with Mum's new friends.

Ian's rapid and narrow lip patterns, acquired in Co. Tyrone, were as impossible for deaf people to lip-read as his speech often was incomprehensible for his Belfast- or London-born colleagues, so signs became very useful for all concerned. He even mooted the idea that surveillance operators should learn sign language for silent communication, but this was not greeted with any enthusiasm.

It was during Susan's second year of her honours degree in Psychology that Ian became very ill during a team meeting at work. He had already moved to sit beside the radiator with a cuppa in his shaking hands; he was clammy, weak and feeling pains in his chest, when his colleagues suggested that he should go home. It was unusual for him to report his symptoms in work, but it looked as though he had the flu. He later stated that he really thought that he was dying. He therefore did what he always did in times of stress – he went looking for Susan. As he searched the university corridors he became increasingly ill and abandoned his search, deciding he'd rather die at home. When Susan eventually found a note on the seminar-room door she rushed home with fear mounting. Ian was lying on the sofa looking very ill indeed. The doctor was not able to make a diagnosis, only repeating, 'Don't worry – it's not a heart attack.' Whatever it *wasn't*, it certainly terrified Susan to watch her usually fit and healthy husband crawling in pain along the bedroom floor later that night calling plaintively to her, 'For

God's sake do something.' She was eventually to beg the doctor to 'do *something*' to make a diagnosis. It was necessary to hospitalise Ian to gain a tentative diagnosis of left lobar pneumonia with a query of legionnaire's disease (they had recently returned from holiday). On hindsight, Susan feels the illness may have been symptomatic of an anti-trypsin deficiency syndrome that causes lung and liver problems, later to be diagnosed within Ian's family.

After two weeks in hospital Ian was on sick leave for five months, until November 1980. Those five months were relaxing and therapeutic for the whole family. Ian was able to indulge all of his outdoor hobbies almost simultaneously. He had evaluated and discussed many changes in their life as he had been lying in his hospital bed – possibly the longest he had been in one position for many years. The first thing he did was to buy a petrol-driven rotovator – to save his wife digging, he said! This meant that they could continue to grow all of their own vegetables with less effort. He vowed to lose his temper less often – he had already mellowed considerably from the fiery young paratrooper of earlier years. His springer spaniel gun dogs were in ecstasy with daily walks to search for pheasant, pigeon and woodcock and to cool off with swims in the Irish Sea. There was scarcely a Northern Irish hill or beach not explored with family picnics and rambles. He started the first of his small building projects. Garden walls, later to be destroyed by the wild coastal winds, were erected and admired by all of the many visitors. The extensions to these DIY projects were later to be labelled as 'Dad's follies', after the Victorian follies found around Britain and Ireland's country estates. In fact Phoenix revelled in this fresh air and relaxation and was noticeably disappointed when the doctor pronounced him fit enough to go back to work. His favourite expression at the time was 'I really don't have *time* to go to work.'

However, in spite of growing their own vegetables and feeding their chickens to produce eggs, they had found their meagre savings totally eaten away without the usual overtime pay to supplement the wage packet. The family had continued to offer the hospitality of their home to friends and acquaintances. It was always important to Ian that interesting people were invited to dinner on a regular basis, and the family budget always had to stretch to feed countless visitors. Ian's philosophy of life included sharing whatever he had, and he would also judge others on their ability to share. He would give to whomever sought his help, and he continued to support Susan's work with the deaf community throughout Ireland. This philosophy extended to ideas as well as hospitality, and Phoenix never understood colleagues who would not share their ideas in meetings. He disliked secretive tendencies among friends and colleagues. He could have noisy arguments in meetings over serious matters of policy, but he was instantly convivial and friends with everyone when business was over. His habit of confronting hypocrisy or what he termed 'sleeked' behaviour in any rank was not always appreciated by senior colleagues – especially when he decided to express his feelings openly, often with a bluntness to which senior officers were not accustomed. But many of the men he worked with enjoyed his directness and ability to shock. He was cheekiest, they say, when admitting he was wrong – which he usually did with a wry smile and a shrug of the shoulders.

When he eventually returned to work he felt much more relaxed but also more determined to eradicate the 'back-stabbing' and internal politics which he so detested. He felt that such behaviour inhibited efficient crime detection and only aided the terrorists' campaign. His spell in hospital had reinforced one of his favourite expressions: 'Life's too short to piss about.' Notwithstanding his senior officers' sensitivities, many of his colleagues thought that had always been his policy.

In late 1980, shortly after Ian had gone back on the job with E4A, he was moved to the Tasking and Coordination Group (TCG) Belfast. TCG Belfast had come into existence in the late 1970s to allocate responsibilities between the various intelligence-gathering agencies – the Special Branch, Army Intelligence and MI5 (or BOX as it is known to the police, because its address, as well as that of MI6, was then a simple box number in Curzon Street in London). It was not only inefficient to have them all running separately but dangerous as well. These agencies were finding that on more and more occasions they were coming into contact with each other while following some target, thus jeopardising their whole operation. On a few occasions situations occurred which are known as 'blue on blue' in security-forces parlance. These are situations when, especially where people are working in plain clothes, friendly forces can easily be mistaken for enemies and a shoot-out could occur.

TCG was created as an agency which would task the right surveillance or undercover unit to carry out a specific operation and at the same time monitor the day-to-day running of that operation. In other words, undercover units could no longer run around acting independently on their own behalf to their own agendas: they were now answerable to a centrally based unit. TCG would also coordinate other units to work together where different areas of an operation required different skills. This coordination would also minimise the danger of a 'blue on blue' situation ever arising again. Because of police supremacy in Northern Ireland, TCGs were commanded by a detective superintendent from Special Branch. The rest of the staff under him were experienced Special Branch officers ranging in rank from detective constable to detective inspector.

An army officer and an NCO – usually men who

have served with SAS or army surveillance 'Det' units – act as liaison between TCG and the army, both with the regular army units seen every day on the ground and with specialist units such as the SAS and close observation platoons (COPs). COPs are regular army units trained especially to carry out covert observation of specific targets and always work in uniform, unlike Det. Other units of the armed services will assist a TCG operation, when required, for example to provide helicopter support, either to carry men or to be the eyes in the sky of a surveillance operation. Some of the helicopters are fitted with long-range cameras and also infra-red cameras which can distinguish the heat from a human body – maybe lying in hiding – from that of an animal.

MI5 works with TCG, with backup from specially trained SB and army undercover units. The regional heads of SB are the conduit to the head of TCG, providing him with all the intelligence for any operation to be mounted.

TCG Belfast was the first TCG unit, but after it came TCG South, based in Gough Barracks, Armagh, and TCG North, headquartered in Derry. The TCG areas fitted in with the military brigade boundaries, which made it easier to coordinate operations. TCG officers typically set up their offices and control rooms in Portakabins erected within the base. At the beginning a posting to a TCG was considered a siding for a Special Branch officer, because he was no longer out in the field handling agents. However, by 1981 that view had changed. According to Mark Urban, 'The TCGs attained a critical role in what security chiefs called 'executive action' – locking together intelligence from informers with the surveillance and ambushing activities of undercover units.'*

In TCG Belfast, Phoenix was responsible for the organisation, planning and running of operations, as well as upgrading and collating information. He had to decide on manning levels and maintain the communications system. The pattern set by Ian in each of his new jobs was to reorganise and restructure to develop and use resources for greater efficiency. Generally this meant that he tipped everything upside down and started from scratch, thus earning his new nickname of 'Captain Chaos'. His team-building skills did not need management courses at Bramshill (the English police staff college) to be able to get men to work around the clock for him. He actually had more problems in stopping them from working. He did not believe in massive overtime hours for family men. He insisted that the most important factor in the life of a successful policeman was a strong home life. He advocated working hard in the allotted time and playing equally hard at home during rest days.

An officer who worked with him at different periods

---

* *Big Boys' Rules: The SAS and the Secret Struggle Against the IRA* (Faber, 1992)

in TCGs recalls, 'One of Ian's ways of starting the day would be when he came in he would say, "OK, what's happening and what the fuck are you doing about it?" This would scare the life out of anyone who didn't know him. Those of us who did know him would laugh and give a stupid answer such as "We're winning the war. What more do you want?" He would then say, "We're not, you know."'

Throughout 1981 it must have seemed that Phoenix was right. It was a tense time. On 1 March the whole province was in the grip of a crisis brought about by the hunger strikes started that month by Bobby Sands, the officer commanding the Provisional IRA in the Maze Prison, who had refused food in an attempt to force the authorities to restore certain privileges that paramilitary prisoners had enjoyed up until 1976, such as the right to wear their own clothes. Both PIRA and INLA used the frustration and anger in nationalist areas to step up their campaign of terror. The motivation of most of the hunger strikers was regarded with scepticism by Phoenix. He felt that they were being manipulated by their PIRA godfathers from outside. He often said that it was more likely this pressure which killed them in a more cruel way than any bullet. At any rate, as Sands's condition worsened, violence began to escalate. Soon it was approaching levels not seen since the early 1970s. By the year's end there would be 1,141 shootings and 530 bombs planted, of which 398 exploded, resulting in 101 deaths. The figures for the same categories of violence for 1980 were, respectively, 645, 400, 280 and 76.

By late 1980 and early 1981 there were three major Special Branch operations running in Belfast that would prove especially fruitful in the months and years to come. Two of these were codenamed Lectern and Campaign. Operation Lectern was directed against leading figures in Belfast PIRA, two of whom were gaining reputations as among the city's most dangerous gunmen and operated out of the Lenadoon estate in West Belfast. Operation Campaign began when the police recruited an informer. It seems mainly to have been aimed at explosives dumps and supply routes used by the Provisionals to move material into the city (see Chapter 5).

The RUC came under tremendous pressure to hold the line against the surging violence. And in the front of that line were the undercover surveillance units.

Information from Operation Lectern had led to the identification of an arms dump at a house in West Belfast. At 8.10 p.m. one Monday evening the police knew that a gun was being taken out of the dump. At 8.27 p.m. a police unit was immediately tasked. According to Phoenix, 'They located a suspect vehicle outside [. . .]'s house. It was confirmed a short time later that two men were involved in the movement of weapons from [. . .].'

For an interception of armed and dangerous men special support units (SSU) were usually deployed. These were highly trained police squads, heavily armed and protected, employed as backup to surveillance units. But on the day the weapons were being moved from their hide no SSU units were available in B Division in West Belfast. Also, according to Phoenix, an 'ongoing operation was taking place in East Belfast. E4A and two SSU vehicles were involved in this' – which meant they could not be deployed for use in West Belfast.

Phoenix noted, 'Firstly, the two operational crews were involved in East Belfast operations. Secondly, they had no Hotspurs (Land Rovers) to carry out operations in B Division.' To use Cortinas in a road stop in that area would have obviously pointed to a source. Because of the insecurity of the open net, it was not possible to task ordinary police or army to execute what would appear to have been a casual road stop.

Phoenix decided to let the two suspects move the weapon to another location without attempting to intercept them at that time. Interception could have compromised lives, and 'an open net' tactic, whereby casual checkpoints would be used with ordinary troops, in an area like West Belfast would have exposed them to PIRA attack.

One of those suspected of carrying the weapons was a well-known Provisional IRA gunman. He

March 2, 1968. This was the first of many photos of Mr and Mrs Phoenix looking fondly into each other's eyes.

Ian's paternal grandfather (nearest camera) meeting the Queen. A veteran of the Boer War, he inspired Ian to embark on a military career.

Ian's parents, Maggie and Willie Phoenix, in Granville 1970.

Ian's birthplace in Granville, near Dungannon, County Tyrone.

Libya airfield
1968. Ian and his
friend waiting for
the flight home.

Ian and friends
from D Company
3 Para in the
jungle in 1967.
This was one of
his favourite
environments.

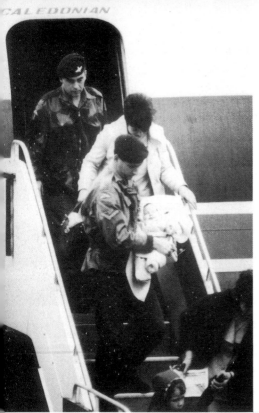

Ian and Susan with baby daughter arriving at LUQA airport, Malta in December 1968. Families travelled together. Baby Phoenix had just escaped 'near death' as the plane landed.

Below Ian and Susan and baby daughter in Malta 1969, where they were stationed for 18 months.

Below right 'Cap and Boots'. Newly recruited Constable Phoenix at RUC depot Enniskillen with his daughter, there to watch the passing out parade.

The first and last full military funeral in Belfast. Sgt Michael Willetts was killed by an IRA bomb as he started duty with his colleague from the RUC – Constable Ian Phoenix. Ian is standing directly above the end of the coffin. Springfield Road Police Barracks, 1971.

Mug-shots used by the RUC in B Division Belfast in the 1970s to spot potential troublemakers when on duty.

Joseph Cahill   Geräld Adams (Snr.)   Gerald Adams (Jnr.)

Ian on duty after the Oxford Road Bus Station explosion in 1972. He was helping to pick up debris of bodies.

Lieutenant-Colonel Peter Chiswell and Constable John Phoenix.

Friends turn back the clock

By Joe Oliver

An Army chief and a young police constable shook hands yesterday and turned the clock back five years.

For it took the troubles in Ulster to renew a warm friendship between Constable John Phoenix and Lieutenant-Colonel Peter Chiswell.

Five years ago Colonel Chiswell, then a Major, was in charge of the 3rd Bn, Parachute Regiment fighting provoca... in the ...

"I was in the Army for nine years and served under Colonel Chiswell for six months in Borneo," recalled John at the reunion yesterday.

"And I joined the RUC last May after being demobbed from the Army and you can imagine my surprise when Colonel Chiswell and the 3rd Parand turned ...

Front page of the *Belfast Newsletter*.

Ian with new sergeant's stripes outside his house in Glengormley.

The young Sgt. Phoenix having a tea break in the Belfast sunshine.

Belfast Telegraph, Tuesday, December 18, 1973   11

BID TO KILL RUC MAN: 3 ACCUSED

By Belfast Telegraph Reporter

THREE YOUNG Belfast men appeared at the Magistrate's Court today charged with the attempted murder of an RUC sergeant yesterday.

Francis Gerard Goodall (21), unemployed, of Carlisle Road; Francis Joseph Collins (18), unemployed, of North Queen Street, and Michael Joseph Reeves (17), van boy, of Artillery House, all refused to recognise the court.

They are jointly charged with attempting to murder Sergeant John Phoenix in the Duncairn Gardens area.

A detective said that each of the accused made written voluntary statements.

In reply to the charge, Reeves said: "No." Collins: "I wasn't there," and Goodall: "I second that. He wasn't there."

They were remanded in custody until December 21.

At the same court a 27-year-old Belfastman appeared, accused of the attempted murder of Gerard Ignatius McCann on

the Crumlin Road, on December 12.

He is Arthur James Bettice, unemployed, of Oldpark Road, and he is charged with trying to murder the man with another person as yet unknown.

A detective told the court that Bettice refused to make a written statement, but made verbal statements.

When charged, Bettice replied: "No. Just not guilty."

He was remanded in custody until December 31.

The *Belfast Telegraph*, 18 December 1973.

Ian and his children returning from a fishing trip in their old ferry boat.

Ian with his toddler daughter on the beach in Douglas on the Isle of Man, 1972.

Ian and a beekeeping friend during his 'beekeeping phase'. Susan had bought a hive at an auction. Unfortunately it was full of bees and Ian applied himself to becoming a beekeeper for several years until he found he was allergic to their stings.

was arrested but released a few months later, in May 1981, without charge. But he was kept under surveillance. During July the police were led to believe that other leading Provisionals who were part of an active-service unit were planning to ambush an army patrol.

OPs were set up to monitor increased activity. However, problems evolved between the surveillance operators and regular army units on the streets of Belfast, causing some confusion in the surveillance operation. This lack of cooperative liaison between the regular RUC and green (regular army units) became something that Ian vowed to alter during his years in Special Branch. However, in spite of these frustrations, the operation eventually led to the arrest of three PIRA gunmen. They were sentenced to eighteen years each.

Two years later, in September 1983, two of them were involved in a mass break-out from the Maze Prison. Bobby Storey, who led the escape, was arrested a few hours later, lying in a stream and sucking in air through reeds, but the other managed to reach the South – where he remains to this day, a leading member of the Provisional IRA's Southern Command.

Simultaneously with operations Lectern and Campaign, TCG Belfast was running another operation, targeting INLA and its leading gunman, Gerard Steenson. Steenson – nicknamed 'Dr Death' – was more feared as a hitman than almost any figure in the city's paramilitary underworld. He had established his reputation as a ruthless operator in 1975, when, at the age of sixteen, he had gunned down the leader of the Official IRA in Belfast, Billy McMillen, during the feud which followed the formation of INLA. He was later arrested, charged with possession, and spent the next four and a half years in jail. He was released from prison in April 1980. Steenson was to prove a slippery operator, successfully eluding the police for well over a year before he was finally trapped. Steenson was not the typical gunman. He dressed well, and was extremely fussy about his appearance. Said one police officer, 'He looked like an off-duty policeman.' He was also a model of politeness when stopped at checkpoints. And under the cool exterior he was determined and organised. To Phoenix he was a cunning killer with something of a psychopathic strain. The police who searched his house found that he slept with a bayonet under his pillow and a crossbow hanging on the wall. They believed that he was high on amphetamines, and would discuss with their colleagues and friends how many bullets it would take to stop him if he came gunning for them. But to both his friends and his enemies in the republican movement (and he had many enemies, because of the various feuds in which INLA got involved) he was compared to Michael Collins, the legendary IRA leader of the 1919–21 Irish War of Independence.*

In the end, whatever the truth about Steenson, what is undeniable is that the police were having problems catching him. Though intelligence was coming in about INLA, thanks to this operation, the Special Branch proved unable to act on it with any great success. This meant that often the security forces were made aware of pending INLA operations but were unable to arrest the terrorists involved.

An example of this occurred on 9 January 1981, when Phoenix learned that two pistols – one a Czechoslovakian-made VZOR, the other a Browning – had been handed to an INLA hit team. Tragically, the police did not know who was to be the intended target. Unfortunately Reserve Constable Lindsay McDougal and a colleague were on the beat in Great Victoria Street, a busy shopping area of Belfast, and the footpath was thronged with shoppers. Steenson and another gunman walked up behind the two policemen. Steenson was armed with the VZOR and shot McDougal in the back of the head, fatally

* Steenson, in spite of his nickname, was actually responsible for only a handful of killings in 1980–81. He was involved in the shooting of Colin Quinn, an off-duty UDR man in December 1980. A few weeks later he and two other INLA gunmen, Harry Kirkpatrick and Roddy Carroll, went to the home of Hugh McGinn, an off-duty member of the Territorial Army in Armagh, and shot him dead. In early 1981 he was one of two gunmen who murdered Constable Lindsay McDougal. See *INLA: Deadly Divisions* by Jack Holland and Henry McDonald (Poolbeg Press, 1996).

wounding him. The second gunman had only let off one round when the Browning's magazine fell out, saving the life of the second constable. The attack illustrated the callous disregard of the gunmen for their fellow citizens, who were forced to dive for cover while out for a day's shopping in Belfast.

Steenson targeted an off-duty policeman a few weeks later. Unknown to the police, Alexander Scott was to be the victim. Frustratingly, a checkpoint intercepted an INLA car containing Steenson and several other INLA members, but none was armed, having obviously been on a reconnaissance mission, and they were not detained. A few days later an INLA hit squad murdered Scott as he got into a car outside his shop. Two killers gunned him down in the presence of his young daughter. One of them was Jim Power from the Markets area of the city, where INLA was especially strong. Three months later, Power was decapitated when a bomb he had planted exploded prematurely.

Throughout the first half of 1981 police did not have much success against INLA. However, they had a minor victory on 11 February, when they arrested the wife of a leading INLA man as she carried two Browning pistols through the Markets area of Belfast. On 23 February the surveillance team were watching the trains coming into Belfast from Dublin, awaiting a courier who was expected to transfer arms to the Belfast INLA. But the courier either did not show or managed to get past the police.

Throughout February, March and April INLA occupied much of Phoenix's time – not surprisingly, given the murderous reputation that Steenson had acquired.

In spite of inside information and forewarnings about possible INLA murder attempts, the police were still largely unable to intercept the INLA active-service units. In April, Steenson's men attempted to murder a leading civil servant, Kenneth Schimeld, at his home in the wealthy Malone Road area of the city. INLA operators planted an under-car booby-trap bomb similar to that which had been used in 1979 to assassinate Airey Neave. It fell off Schimeld's car and was defused by the army. But the would-be assassins escaped.

A possible attack by Gerard Steenson was marked down for 14 April, but nothing happened. However, INLA continued to claim more victims. On 27 April it booby-trapped a hijacked lorry. The explosion killed Constable Gary Martin. In July a van with an INLA bomb in it exploded in the car park of a local brewery where a member of the UDR worked. The target escaped, but several workers were injured.

The police's streak of bad luck in hunting INLA continued throughout the year. Information came to Phoenix that 'Sparky' Barkley, a small-time criminal who had been recruited into the INLA through his friendship with INLA gunman Harry Kirkpatrick, was to carry out a robbery on 28 August. The day before, Phoenix briefed the surveillance team. However, once more INLA slipped through their fingers. On the day of the robbery Phoenix noted, 'E4A failed to understand the briefing and did not cover OP. Aborted by SSU.' It was another example of inadequate communication and cooperation between departments, the politics of which he would discuss at home.

Phoenix often shared his frustrations with Susan when he failed to gain cooperation from fellow officers in departments which were designed to work in tandem. On these occasions it would be her task to suggest that perhaps he was making his requests too aggressively – she felt his manner may have appeared to threaten his colleagues' positions. The couple had long worked reciprocally in advising each other on how to communicate appropriately with colleagues in their respective projects. Susan had often witnessed people's reactions to Ian's abrupt manner and knew that he was sometimes misunderstood because he could be so blunt. He in turn would advise her that she was 'too soft' and needed to be more assertive in her presentations. Thus slowly they internalised aspects of each others' personality.

Shortly after this problem with Barkley being allowed to escape the net, Phoenix went to RUC headquarters to meet with the team leaders. He was concerned by what he perceived as a lack of cooperation, and aimed to give them a 'morale booster'. They were certainly going to need it.

The most serious failure of all occurred the following month. Throughout the first weeks of September Ian was sick with a chest infection and unable to work. Operations continued to run, but always with negative results. Following a particularly gruesome murder in Belfast, Steenson had once again managed to avoid arrest. His known accomplices were picked up and questioned, but the police could not offer concrete evidence and, with nothing on them, they were released. This lack of indictable evidence was always a source of frustration to Phoenix and his men in their quest to defeat terrorism.

This failure prompted a rethink of TCG strategy involving the SSUs and HMSUs (headquarters mobile support units, which derived from the old SSUs). Phoenix had always argued in favour of deploying SAS units in such situations, rather than police, however well-trained. He often discussed the lack of support for policemen if jobs went wrong when they were trying to 'do their duty'. He did not want to see a policeman in the witness-box charged with murder for any of his jobs. He would argue that, if the SAS were called to court, like other soldiers they could retreat to their safer homes in England in between the legal proceedings. Their families were not exposed to the same pressures as those of a local policeman, who had his home and family in the area to protect. From late 1983 onwards the SAS were reintroduced to fulfil this role, though the chief constable continued to resist their deployment in built-up areas like Belfast, where there was always the high risk of civilian casualties. Ian often stated that all security forces should be answerable to the rule of law, but that they should be supported by the government when they were being asked to act legally for the protection of society. He was not always convinced that civil servants in positions of power would not 'throw an innocent soldier to the lions' in order to further some misplaced political initiative.

Throughout the rest of 1981 the current operation continued, but so did Steenson's hit squads. By then he had ousted the old leadership of the organisation in Belfast and had taken the reins of power into his own hands, giving his supporters such as Harry Kirkpatrick all the key roles. On 16 October his men assassinated a member of the UDA, William 'Bucky' McCullough, outside his home on the Shankill Road – the very heart of loyalist West Belfast.

The surveillance operation went on into the new year, still without getting the breakthrough the police sought. It was not until the beginning of February that this occurred. Information led to the arrest of an INLA member who was charged with arms possession. He made several statements to the police, incriminating many of his colleagues. Among those he named was

Rabbie McAllister, an INLA gunman. McAllister in turn began naming names, foremost among which was that of 'Dr Death'.

On February 1982 Phoenix noted in his diary, 'Steenson, Kirkpatrick, and Barkley arrested.' Two days later there followed a series of early-morning lifts and searches. A large part of the Belfast INLA's most active killers were scooped up and held, including 'Rook' O'Prey and Thomas Power, the brother of Jim Power.

However, things took an unusual turn when on 8 March McAllister withdrew his statements. He made another one. It said, 'Towards the end of 1981 as a result of constant arrests and psychological pressure I was trapped into working as an informant for the RUC Special Branch.' Fortunately for the police, others being held began making statements of their own. As Steenson and Kirkpatrick were walking free, McAllister having retracted his statement, they were rearrested on the word of another accomplice, Jackie Goodman. Eventually, Steenson's henchman Harry Kirkpatrick, at whose wedding a few months before Dr Death had been the best man, began to cooperate with the police. Between 24 March 1982 and 15 May 1984 he would make sixty-six statements, implicating dozens of INLA members. After a trial in 1985, at which Kirkpatrick was the main witness for the prosecution, Steenson and twenty-four others were found guilty of a series of serious crimes, including several counts of murder and attempted murder. Steenson, whom the judge called 'an enemy of society', got life.*

McAllister meanwhile was convicted of having been involved in five murders and was sentenced to a total of 766 years in prison. His activities as an informer did not save him. Kirkpatrick was more fortunate. Though convicted in 1984 of five murders, and given life, the Judge did not impose any minimum sentence. It is believed he was released within five years.

In these years Ian managed to find some relaxation in a new hobby which he insisted the whole family share: peat-digging on the high bogland of Co. Antrim, above the coastal village of Glenarm. Here the family would spend whole days digging the sticky black peat from the bog before drying it in the traditional way. The wet turfs were first laid out in the sun, turned regularly for several days, and then stacked into 'castles' to complete the drying process.

Much to his annoyance, one of his major operations interfered with his peat-digging pleasures. This was

---

* However, the full consequences of this operation had not yet manifested themselves. In 1986 an appeal court overturned Steenson's conviction and that of the others. Within a month of their release, the bitterness and suspicion that had been created by the arrests in 1982 exploded into a bloody feud. INLA tore itself apart. A new splinter group, calling itself the Irish People's Liberation Organisation (IPLO), emerged. The feud ended only with the murder of Gerard Steenson on 14 March 1987, when he was shot dead by some of his former comrades. With his death, one of Northern Ireland's most deadly operators was removed from the scene. The INLA was permanently weakened, but it still represented an unpredictable threat that could at times result in terrible bloodshed.

operation Campaign, begun in March 1980 and aimed at disrupting the flow of PIRA explosives into Belfast. The police had identified the town of Antrim as a staging-post for moving explosives into the city. For the next six weeks Phoenix would spend most of his time shuttling between Belfast, his home and Antrim, where the police had located the house which was being used to store the bomb materials. On 30 May he was alerted that 600 lb of explosives had been moved into the 'transit house' in Antrim. He immediately went back to work, completing the first of several fifteen-hour days which were to follow on this operation. The police were expecting a move soon, and units of E4A and the SSU were tasked. It did not occur.

In the meantime he arranged for four bottles of whiskey to be given to the army staff involved in the operation. He always made sure that everyone involved in such operations was made aware of his appreciation for their work towards peace. The watch continued into June, but on 5 June Phoenix took a day's leave to get back to turning his peat on the Star Bog, from where he could almost see Antrim, given a bit of imagination. His mind would have been on the Antrim job as he worked away with the family, his turf spade flying into the wet bog and his arm muscles flexing as he threw the turf across to the heather bank at Susan's feet where it landed with a 'plop'. As the family sat around the small camp-stove for their favourite alfresco lunch of bacon and eggs, which always smelled far better in the mountain air, he would suddenly look worried, wondering if all was well with each of the operations he was then controlling.

Then in July the police were put on standby as information had come in indicating that explosives were to be moved the next day. They were – at 3.20 p.m. They were taken to Belfast and housed. At that point, the police struck, arresting three leading Provisionals from the city and recovering over 500 lb of explosives and detonators for bombs. Countless lives were saved.

The Provisionals had another defeat a month later when Phoenix learned that a leading member of the organisation from North Belfast was planning to move explosives to the west of the city. The move was covered, and fifty pounds of explosives were recovered in a DIY store on Springfield Avenue.

Another operation was reactivated later that August. Undeterred by the set-backs of July, the Provisionals were determined to resupply their Belfast units with explosives. In August came word of an impending attempt. It was carried out on 10 September. The Provisionals' Transit van was stopped on the Andersonstown Road and a leading member of the Belfast Brigade, Anthony Cahill, was arrested. The store used to house the material was also located.

Another leading IRA operator from the city, was arrested on 26 October. Yet, in spite of Special Branch successes, the Provisionals were still able to mount deadly attacks. On 14 November they assassinated the Revd Robert Bradford, the Unionist MP for South Belfast, who was also a Methodist minister. He was shot dead at a community centre where he had been advising his constituents. The caretaker of the premises, twenty-nine-year-old Kenneth Campbell, was killed with him. The Provisionals had targeted the MP because he had opposed giving concessions to the hunger strikers and had called for the reintroduction of the death penalty for terrorist murders. They issued a statement accusing Bradford of being 'one of the key people responsible for winding up the loyalist paramilitary sectarian machine in the North'.

Ironically, it was the actions of the IRA which wound up the loyalist death squads more than anything else. Within a few days of Bradford's murder three Catholics had been shot in retaliation by the UDA and UVF.

With the following month came a lull. After a bloody eleven months, December 1981 was the first in twelve years during which there were no deaths due to the Troubles. Ian spent Christmas Day on duty at TGG, but he did not mind too much – he was going to have his annual Boxing Day 'shoot' at home. It had become a custom for the Phoenix family to invite friends and lonely soldiers stationed in Northern Ireland to his home on that day. Originally Ian had enjoyed coarse shooting with a walk along the brush- and whin-covered braes of Co. Antrim to hunt pheasant and woodcock. The bag was then cooked for a game supper in front of a roaring turf fire, with mulled wine to wash it all down. As the years went by, however, with more and more friends joining the hunting group, and birds becoming fewer, in the interests of conservation Boxing Day became devoted to claypigeon shooting. As a lot of SAS men would show up for these shoots, it sometimes sounded as if the Third World War had broken out among the quiet braes of Antrim. Game donated from far and wide made up the supper afterwards (roast clay pigeons, they defined it as), with pigeon pie, braised duck, venison in port and salmi of pheasant on the menu.

As 1981 turned into 1982, Ian took a few days' holiday to see in the new year in true Phoenix style. As ever, long mountain rambles in the crisp winter air were the prescription for recovery from the excesses of the festive season. However, it was but a brief breathing-space.

Chapter 4

The Cap'n Takes Command

(1982–85)

On 1 November 1982 Phoenix received news that he was being promoted to chief inspector. In his new position he was now in charge of E4A operations throughout Belfast. His experience may have been missed on the ground, when so many of the operations, particularly against INLA, had gone awry the year before. But Ian, though happy about his promotion, suspected that his return to operations was a sign that certain senior officers were uneasy about his role at TCG Belfast. Throughout his career he had tended to view sideways moves without promotion as attempts to neutralise his influence in the decision-making process that determined broader aspects of security policy. He had many strong views on policy that he hoped to 'pass up the line' by report writing.

However, he sometimes felt that such reports were neutralised as they went through the recognised chain of command.

His 'Captain Chaos' nickname was to stay with him. He moved from RUC headquarters to the outskirts of Belfast. It was to an RUC complex where some specialist units are based and trained. E4A Belfast operated from there, as did HMSU squads. Ian would occupy his new position for three years. It gave him the opportunity to assess individual surveillance operations, their strengths and weaknesses, and to recommend how improvements might be instituted so that flaws and failures could be avoided in the future. Ian's analyses give a remarkable insight into how such operations work. These three years would see him undertake several important operations against loyalists, and E4A in Belfast also delivered major blows against the Provisional IRA, including the arrest of one of their master bombers, the man held responsible for almost killing Margaret Thatcher and wiping out her entire Cabinet.

Within weeks of assuming his new post, Operation Furlong which had been allowed to lapse became active again. It had originally been targeted at PIRA. Its aims were to confirm and identify PIRA targets, establish the make-up of the ASUs which carry out the killings, prevent the attacks from taking place and apprehend those involved – using both human and technical sources. Technical attacks involve the planting of various devices which help the police to monitor movements and activities within targeted buildings. For these operations, E4A employed BOX agents – that is, MI5 personnel.

During the summer of 1982 police intelligence discovered an unusual conjunction of forces. James Pratt Craig, a leading member of the UDA – the largest of the loyalist groups – was proposing to meet with the Provisional IRA. Craig, a former boxer, had been released from jail a few years earlier, and was known as a tough, rather flamboyant character with a taste for luxury. E4A learned that Craig was meeting with one of the PIRA members who was on their list of leading members of the Belfast Brigade of the Provisionals as Number 9 – he was in fact the OC (officer commanding) of the Belfast Brigade at that time. The police were naturally curious as to what it was these two supposed enemies had to talk about. Soon it became clear that Craig was passing information to the PIRA leadership in Belfast about some of his rivals in the loyalist paramilitary underworld whom he would like to see eliminated.

Lennie Murphy, a notorious loyalist killer, also came under police notice at about this time. Murphy was a cut-throat and gunman, the leader of a UVF gang in the late 1970s that became known as the Shankill Road Butchers. Their favourite mode of operation was to kidnap Catholics late at night, drive them to some lonely spot, beat them with hammers, then cut their throats with a butcher's knife. The wounds were so severe that the throats of the victims were frequently sliced through to the spine.

Murphy had served a short prison sentence for weapons possession, but he was released in 1982. The police watched him when it was reported he was planning a bombing attack, but this did not materialise. On 24 October, however, when surveillance had been lifted, he kidnapped, tortured and killed a Catholic, Joseph Donnegan.

By the beginning of November an E4A operation indicated that the IRA were targeting leading loyalists. The first victim was Lennie Murphy who was gunned down as he went to meet his girlfriend on 16 November.

Six days after the killing of Murphy, Craig was due to meet with a leading Belfast Brigade member of PIRA. The police are not certain if the meeting went ahead. On 18 February 1983 Craig held what the police called 'an important meeting' with Andy Tyrie, the chairman of the UDA. Tyrie had been UDA chairman since 1973, but his relationship with Craig would eventually cost him his position. Over the next four years, a series of loyalist leaders would be assassinated by the Provisionals or INLA, and the UDA eventually concluded that Craig had been responsible for passing on intelligence to their enemies. However, he was not the only prominent member of the UDA involved in this game. Phoenix felt it would have been useful for the security services' press agencies to release some evidence of such collaboration. 'If only the man in the street realised that the so-called politically motivated terrorists are often just criminals masquerading as defenders of the people, it could bring peace closer,' he said to Susan at around this time. 'Some of these gougers would sell their granny. They certainly are not interested in the country or its economy – just whatever's in their own pocket!' Ian liked to use the term 'gouger' to describe the thugs and gangsters whom he often considered to be acting in their own idealised gangster movies.

Police suspected that three other UDA men were in contact with the Provisionals. In September one of them met the Belfast Brigade member Number 9 on the E4A list (see Chapter 3). 'Mutual assistance was discussed', according to Phoenix, whose men monitored the discussions. The UDA men were among the organisation's leading gunmen. In the early 1970s they had been involved in some particularly brutal murders of Catholics in the East Belfast area. At one time they were close to Tommy Herron, a vice-chairman of the UDA who was found murdered in a ditch south of the city in September 1973. His killing was an internal UDA job, and one of this group was suspected of being the assassin.

The Provisional leadership, however, did not seem to mind associating with loyalist killers if they thought they might extract help or information from them.

Number 9 and a UDA man met again on 28 September 1983, in a bar in downtown Belfast. The undercover police team watched as the UDA man handed over a piece of paper to the PIRA member. Two further meetings were monitored at the beginning of October. On the 10th of that month Number 9 had a series of meetings. At 1.30 p.m. he spoke with another leading member of the Belfast Provisional IRA, a man who would later become its commanding officer. One and a half hours later, Number 9 met with the UDA man. Something was observed being passed between the two paramilitaries. When the meeting broke up, the UDA man was stopped by a police patrol and searched. He was found to be carrying a custard tin, inside which were six phials of cyanide. Phoenix speculated that the cyanide was 'obviously for poisoning supergrasses [informers] in Crumlin Road prison'. It is speculated that the UDA man had agreed to smuggle it in for the PIRA.

The UDA man did not stay in custody very long. The UDA and PIRA meetings were resumed again in early 1984. There was a meeting at a dog race on 4 January, then again on the 20th. E4A followed Number 9 closely, and observed him meeting three days later with the current commanding officer of the Provisionals' Belfast Brigade, as well as another active member. After one such meeting the following month Phoenix noted, 'Interesting day's work and confirmed tie-up between all concerned.' His unit was building up a picture of the Provisionals' intelligence-gathering cell, and its links. Jim Craig met Number 9 on 23 March at 3.p.m. The police observed them 'in deep conversation until 16.30 hrs'. Two months later there was an attempt to arrest Number 9 and Craig, but it failed due to poor communications. Two new E4A operators were slow in identifying Craig as he sat in the lounge of a city-centre bar.

It is believed that the information passed between Craig, a colleague called Tommy McCreery and Number 9 has been linked not only to the murder of Lennie Murphy but to several other killings of loyalists. Craig is also believed to have exchanged information with INLA, which resulted in the deaths of several other loyalist activists in the 1980s. The UDA finally got wise to Craig and McCreery's double-game. Craig was shot dead by UDA gunmen on 15 October 1988. The UDA shot dead Ned McCreery, Tommy's brother, on 15 April 1992, after he arrived home from the pub he owned in East Belfast. They accused him of having been an informer. After his death, he was described in one report as 'one of Northern Ireland's most brutal loyalist assassins'.*

* *Independent*, 16 April 1992

Tommy McCreery was accused of drug dealing and was wounded in a UDA shooting. He then fled to England.*

Though the surveillance on Craig and McCreery petered out in mid-1984, Operation Furlong continued to monitor PIRA members very closely.

There was another major operation mounted in 1983 against the loyalists. It was codenamed Morrisdance, and its target was the Ulster Volunteer Force, the oldest of the Protestant terrorist groups. Morrisdance began on 1 February 1983. The resources of the undercover teams were called in to protect innocent Catholics who were being targeted by the UVF.

For Ian, home provided a welcome escape from death and destruction. There were two major projects in his personal life in 1983. One was an extension to his house, which he had applied for a higher mortgage to build. He took a few days' leave for a break from the long hours which operations Furlong and Morrisdance had been necessitating and enjoyed his discussions with the builders and joiners who were working on the extension. The good-natured banter included chat about wildfowling and wine-making,

---

* In May 1993, he was named in a London court during the trial of four men accused of a gangland murder. McCreery was said to have acted as a go-between for London-based mobsters who sought to hire former Ulster paramilitaries as hitmen. He was believed to be on the run in Spain.

and he liked to make sure that everyone who came to work on the house shared meals with the family. It would have been difficult for those tradesmen who enjoyed the conviviality of the Phoenix household to imagine that their relaxed employer and host was involved in some of their country's most crucial security operations.

The second of his major personal concerns at that time was to support Susan through her final month of examinations and assignments for her degree. He took over the housekeeping quite happily. Ever the keen chef, he would make one of his infamous curries for the family dinner and open a good bottle of wine at just the right time when Susan needed to relax from her studies. Ian himself had gone back to night school to study a course in sociology the year before. When he started to apply what he had learned to her psychology course, Susan sometimes wished he had not bothered. He had little patience for some of the more abstruse aspects of psychological theorising, which seemed to him to hold little insight into why people behave as they do. Phoenix family discussions around these theories would have made a great *Monty Python* series. Their combined sense of humour helped them both to keep things in perspective.

Life went on normally, with the children working hard at school and bringing home as many friends as they could cram into the house at any one time. Thus early 1983 found a busy household full of builders, teenagers, Susan's student friends helping with revision, and the occasional deaf person wanting help with a variety of problems. Susan's diary for 20 January reports, 'a heavy frost, roofers, plasterers and electrician here. Meeting 11.30 Rev George Grindle at Kingham Mission for the deaf. The two Ians away to auction. Arrange deaf trip to Edinburgh.' Ian and his old friend 'Scottish Ian' were off to investigate farm tools in a local auction. Most of them would never be used, but Phoenix could never resist bargaining and loved the banter and excitement of a country auction. There was a favourite story of when he had arrived home with pig-feeders which they did not need, bought 'accidentally' while bidding for some fine mirrors which they did need. He would continue to hoard 'things which may come in useful one day', culminating in the rescuing of a rusting 1939 American Dodge truck. Its renovation developed into a major operation in the garden shed.

The major operation which kept Phoenix himself 'on the ground' thoughout 1983 remained Furlong. Not only did it provide information about UDA–PIRA links, but it led to a series of successful strikes against the IRA's most dangerous ASUs in Belfast. Thanks to intelligence gathered through Operation Furlong, the police knew that the Provisionals were targeting prominent Northern Ireland judges. Among them was Judge William Doyle, a fifty-five-year-old Catholic. Doyle lived in the prosperous Malone Road area of

South Belfast. This had once been a predominantly Protestant district, but throughout the 1980s as more and more Catholics moved into the middle-classes many of them bought homes along its leafy avenues. It was worlds away from the working-class streets where the paramilitaries flourished, though the physical distance between them was not so great. Andersonstown, for instance, one of PIRA's chief strongholds, is not more than ten minutes' drive from the Malone Road.

On Sunday 16 January 1983 Judge Doyle attended mass at St Brigid's Catholic church on Derryvolgie Avenue, just off the Malone Road. Though he had been warned that he was on a death list, he had refused to accept a police escort other than when he was going from his home to the court. As a result, he was not protected as he went to and from mass. He walked out of the chapel with a seventy-two-year-old woman to whom he had offered a lift home. They had both got into the judge's green Mercedes when two men walked over to the car and rapped on the window. As he rolled it down, they drew their guns and shot him five times, seriously wounding the old lady next to him. The shooting sent the other worshippers scattering in terror. It was a yet another cold-blooded, ruthless murder.

Judge Doyle was not the first member of Northern Ireland's judiciary to be murdered by the Provisionals, who especially wanted to target Catholic members of

163

the courts. Nor would he be the last.* But his shooting outside a church was particularly shocking to a devout community, and his funeral united both Unionists and Nationalists in a display of solidarity forged by grief and outrage. James Molyneaux, then leader of the Ulster Unionist Party, attended, as did prominent members of the moderate nationalist party, the Social Democratic and Labour Party.

When Phoenix arrived home on the night of 17 January he received a call in connection with Furlong. He was informed of a possible link between the murder of Judge Doyle and a Queen's University lecturer. The police had identified a house used by the lecturer that they suspected had been put at the disposal of the Provisional IRA hit squad. As it happened their suspicions were confirmed. The lecturer was a spy for PIRA.

Phoenix returned to work at once, and that night began a complex surveillance operation under the aegis of Furlong. As a result of Judge Doyle's death Ian was even more determined to ensure that PIRA's next target in this campaign against the Northern Ireland judiciary would be saved, whoever he was. It was not long before he learned that it was to be another judge – Judge K. This time PIRA were planning an assassination that was as cunning as it was brutal.

---

* Over the period of the IRA's campaign against the judiciary, eight were to die at their hands, including three judges, four magistrates and one official working at the office of the Director of Public Prosecutions.

One of those involved in the plan was Danny McCann, the explosives officer for the Belfast Brigade and an active gunman. McCann already had a long record of PIRA involvement by 1983. He had been charged with riotous behaviour in 1973, and in 1977 he had been arrested a number of times for questioning. In 1979 he was arrested again, under Section 12 of the Prevention of Terrorism Act. Two years later he was sentenced for possession of explosive substances and sentenced to two years. His conviction had little deterrent effect, however.

On 28 June two members of PIRA were observed in an area, east of Belfast, where Judge K lived. The two men videoed the area and left. Information led the police to believe that the murder bid would come near the home. Two days later, two well-known members of the Provisionals, one of them a woman, rented a flat in a nearby village, possibly to use it as a safe base for the ASU to hide out in after the attack. At the beginning of July Phoenix's information led him to think the attack was imminent. On 7 July an SSU came across an unknown male who was acting suspiciously around the judge's house. He was followed back to the city.

However, the attack did not come. For several weeks the house was watched, but no further activity was noticed. Then, at the beginning of August, Phoenix learned that Danny McCann was trying to obtain an ambulance for use in the area east of Belfast, within easy range of the judge's home. At first it was not clear why. Then, shortly afterwards, intelligence reached Ian and his unit that the killing was going ahead.

The plan was to drive a bomb into the judge's home on the back of a milk float and detonate it. An ambulance carrying three PIRA members would be the first at the scene. It was obvious that they planned to check if the judge was dead. If the judge had survived the explosion, it was surmised that their task would be to take him away in the ambulance to be 'executed', in Phoenix's own words. That is, the Provisionals were prepared if necessary to take a badly wounded man and murder him in the guise of providing him with aid.

The disruption of the ghoulish murder plot against the Judge was only one of several major successes linked to Operation Furlong and an operation which ran alongside it, codenamed Entrance. Operation Entrance involved the use by PIRA of the Beechall Health Centre as an explosives hide. An E4A team had observed a leading PIRA member go there to check out its suitability. The Provisionals began constructing a hide under the watchful gaze of Phoenix's operators. The fact that it was in a public building frequented by women and children made it a critical target for police protection.

The first stage of the assassination plot against Judge K had involved the moving of explosives from PIRA's major arms dump in West Belfast, the Health Centre, a former convent set in parkland near the Beechmount area of West Belfast. Phoenix had tasked two teams to cover this stage of the operation. Team A would cover the garage where the explosives were to be taken; team B would cover Beechall.

At 8.40 p.m. a van drove to Beechall. At 9.20 p.m., it left carrying eleven gas cylinders packed with explosives. It drove to an address about two miles away and reversed into a garage there. Surveillance was covering the garage, and reported activity. The Provisionals were transferring the explosives from the cylinders into four beer kegs. A police OP observed a light on in the garage until midnight. At that time, a milk float appeared and drove into the garage, the van having left. The bomb in the beer kegs was loaded on to the back of the float. An hour later a woman went into the house next to the garage.

At seven that morning a young boy going to chapel compromised the OP. It had to be withdrawn, but a second car was quickly sent to replace it. At 8 a.m. an ambulance was observed behaving suspiciously nearby. Thirty minutes later the milk float trundled out of the garage and headed east. It was followed by the ambulance, on board which were two of the Provisionals' leading members in Belfast, Alex Murphy and Harry Fitzsimmons. The convoy was completed by a Granada driven by an unidentified woman who, Phoenix observed, 'was very nervous as she nearly had a crash at a roundabout'. She retreated very quickly into West Belfast when she realised something was wrong. She was last seen going into a shop visibly shaking in fright.

According to Phoenix, writing in his usual tongue-in-cheek manner, 'the driver of the milk float was obviously inexperienced as milk began falling off the float'. However, this was merely the excuse the police gave for stopping the float at a vehicle checkpoint. The car and the ambulance were allowed through. Both did a U-turn a little further up the road. Meanwhile the police began what seemed like a very casual search of the milk float, at one point almost allowing it to proceed. But the driver's look of relief vanished when, before he could restart, the police changed their minds after seeing something 'suspicious' they just happened to have noticed. The police enjoy straining the nerves of PIRA operators when they know they have them red-handed. The ambulance and the car were stopped, and arrests followed. Among those detained in the follow-up raid at the home of the milk float's owner was Danny McCann, the Provisionals' Belfast Brigade bomb-maker.

Murphy and his ambulance companion, Harry Fitzsimmons, were arrested and charged with terrorist offences. Both were later acquitted on the grounds of insufficient evidence. (Five years afterwards, however, Murphy was convicted of the murder of two off-duty soldiers after they had been brutalised by a mob in Casement Park in West Belfast.) When this happened Ian would often share his frustrations with Susan. 'My hardworking men and women risk their lives to arrest would-be murderers, and then the court system lets them go free. Is it any wonder people leave the police for jobs where they get more support?'

He was to repeat these thoughts several times in the coming months. At 7.10 a.m. on 31 May the police surveillance was alerted, having observed a known PIRA member and another unidentified man move eleven canisters from the Beechall hide. They loaded them into a red Escort van which was followed to a glass factory where the Provisionals had their main bomb-making facility in West Belfast. Phoenix took no chances: a decision was taken to act at once. An SSU squad raided the factory, arresting Gerard Dunlop and Brendan McLaughlin at the scene, along with the security man. The next day a follow-up search uncovered another man who had been hiding in a roof space in the factory.

The bomb contained 400 lb of explosives. A hole had been cut in the base of each cylinder, the explosives had been packed in, and a metal plate painted the same colour as the cylinder had been put in place. One cylinder contained cortex and detonators. Intelligence suggested that the Provisionals had intended to bomb an RUC station in Dunmurry, South Belfast. All three men were later acquitted due to lack of evidence in court. Ian's frustration at the lack of credibility given to police evidence continued.

The Provisionals still had no idea that their Beechall

hide had been compromised and continued to use it throughout 1983. Late in the year the police learned that the hide was going to be emptied to make way for a fresh supply of explosives coming into the city. The police were alerted at 8 p.m. on 1 December as Liam McCotter, a member of the Provisionals' Belfast Brigade, along with two others, began moving the explosives-packed cylinders. They had intended taking them to a house in Andersonstown, but because of the presence of army patrols they delayed making the drop. They eventually succeeded after three runs. E4A observed a lot of activity around the house, where a total of three cars, including a Cortina and a Lada, were on the move.

The surveillance teams remained in place throughout the night. Next day, at 8.40 a.m., the Lada drove off with three unidentified males on board, followed twenty minutes later by the Cortina. The Cortina was halted by an SSU a mile away on Finaghy Road North, with a bomb on board. The Lada was stopped in Andersonstown, and in the car police found Sean Savage and 100 lb of explosives in a beer keg. Savage had long held a reputation in Belfast as an active gunman and bomber. The year before he had been charged with attempting to blow up an RUC band.

Earlier in the year, Phoenix had drawn up an assessment of Operation Furlong and the role of E4A. He concluded that success, which depended as ever on the reliability of sources, had been 'varied'.

But they had acquired 'a very good idea of the make up of the Intelligence cell of the Belfast Brigade'. He believed that E4A in Belfast still did not have enough backup, resources and money to achieve its full potential. But he concluded that 'our reputation has greatly improved throughout the SB in Belfast. There is still the odd hiccup and reluctance to show flexibility, but given time this will soon disappear.'

Among the uncertainties that still remained in regard to Furlong was the role of the Queen's University academic suspected of having Provisional IRA connections. As 1983 drew to a close, another murder occurred in the university area which again drew E4A's attention to that location. Edgar Graham, a Unionist Party member of the Northern Ireland Assembly and chairman of its Finance and Personnel Committee, was a barrister and a lecturer in the law faculty at Queen's. He was responsible for legal submissions to the European Commission on Human Rights, arguing on behalf of the widows of terrorist victims. On 7 December he himself became a victim of terrorism. The Provisional IRA shot him dead as he left his office in University Square. Phoenix immediately ordered surveillance to be placed on the suspect lecturer's house.

A series of connections began to emerge between certain staff and students within the university faculty and members of PIRA. PIRA's intelligence officer (IO) for the university/South Belfast area and his superior, Number 9, were linked to both a student and a lecturer at the university. A third man with university connections was also identified – Phelim Hamill. He would later play a key role in the Provisionals' campaign in England in the early 1990s.

Another associate of the South Belfast IO was Basil Henry, who was also a student and who lived near the university. The IO was under steady surveillance, and on 24 January 1984 was observed with someone later identified as Henry. On 15 March, two months after this initial contact, Henry was again identified visiting the IO's home address.

Apart from his meetings with the IO, Basil Henry was not known as a PIRA player. However, the following June he was seen on several occasions in a Belfast café talking with Number 9 of the PIRA's Belfast Brigade staff. The café was a favourite meeting-place for Number 9. At first Henry was not identified, simply listed as a 'u.k. [unknown] male'. His identity was established on 28 June, and a surveillance operation was mounted to monitor his movements. By late June it was established that Henry rented a flat in an apartment building in South Belfast.

Between 9 June and 27 July Number 9 and Henry had seven meetings. Phoenix's team concluded that 'Henry was now no. 9's replacement for the IO and his pattern of behaviour indicated the conducting of recces within a mile radius of his address.' Among the places Henry visited either on foot or by bicycle was a former residence of a police superintendent. There were another five locations he seemed especially interested in, most of them quiet, tree-lined avenues typical of South Belfast, but the police never did establish the identify of any possible targets associated with the places visited.

Phoenix observed that 'Henry was a loner and did not appear to have many friends, male or female' – a rather sad note, indicating an isolated and unhappy individual. But the police were sufficiently interested in this 'loner' to install an OP near to his flat. At the beginning of July, Henry might or might not have become aware that he had new neighbours – a group of 'shipyard workers' who were renting a flat near his. They were in fact a surveillance team, equipped with a camera lens which gave them coverage of Henry's front door.

The first positive surveillance breakthrough occurred on 26 July when Ms M – a known associate of Number 9 – arrived at the flat. Meanwhile, Number 9 was observed meeting two unknown males at Ms M's address in West Belfast. Phoenix concluded that an attack was to take place within the next twenty-four hours. As yet the target of that attack was unknown, but the police went into action. The OP team was instructed to provide full twenty-four-hour coverage of Henry's flat. At 10.10 p.m. on 26 July an unknown male arrived at the flat. A short time later another unidentified man arrived. Between then and 3 a.m.

on 27 July Henry was observed carrying out five separate recces of the area, about a mile down the Ormeau Road from his address. At 3 a.m. Henry and his two visitors left the flat, Henry in front. The second male was carrying a white plastic bag, with the third bringing up the rear. The three proceeded in convoy down the Ormeau Road.

At Ardmore Avenue the police swooped. When they searched the three men, they found in the plastic bag a bomb made up of eleven pounds of commercial explosives and a .38 Smith & Wesson revolver. The three were arrested. Henry's visitors were later identified as James Henry and Dominic Adams, an unemployed bricklayer and brother of the Sinn Fein leader Gerry Adams. Henry's brief career as an IO for the Provisional IRA had come to a sudden end.

It was never established whose life was saved in the early hours of that July morning, but the operation was a fine example of the quiet, painstaking police work that goes on behind the scenes, usually unacknowledged and uncelebrated but often a matter of life and death in the war against the paramilitary groups.

Phoenix's work did, however, enjoy an unusual recognition in the form of a social visit of the sort that chief inspectors of the RUC do not normally receive. On 20 August the commander of land forces, Northern Ireland, came to supper. He was

Ian's former Para commander Peter Chiswell, who came with his wife, Felicity, to the Phoenix home. A security helicopter was tasked to recce the area and various strange cars roamed around the vicinity of the farmhouse to check out the suitability for such an unorthodox gathering. As a result a very successful evening was enjoyed by several ex-members of D Company 3 Para and some civilian friends who were amused by Susan's attempts to feed her guest with her latest home-made goat's cheese. This event took place during Ian's annual leave, the rest of which he spent on one of his favourite tasks – 'clearing up about the place'. The family could not afford a holiday that year, because of the house extension and the expense of Susan's research trips to investigate services for the deaf in England and Scotland. They devoted the break to gardening, milking the goats, cheese- and wine-making, and taking the children for bike rides on the rickety bikes recently acquired at yet another auction.

The killings in Belfast and Londonderry continued. Though Gerard Steenson was locked up in the Crumlin Road Prison, INLA remained active throughout 1982, 1983 and 1984. Indeed, in December 1982 it had carried out one of the worst bombings in the history of the Northern Ireland Troubles – seventeen people, eleven of them off-duty soldiers, were killed when an INLA bomb exploded at the Droppin' Well disco in

Co. Derry. Five of the other six fatalities were young women who INLA in its statement claiming responsibility for the massacre described contemptuously as 'consorts' of the dead soldiers. Several of these innocent young women had gone to the disco after attending the seventeenth-birthday party of Barbara Dixon, who was killed in the blast. INLA operations in Belfast, where the group was badly hit thanks to Harry Kirkpatrick's revelations, were on a reduced scale. However, between 1982 and 1984 E4A kept the organisation in its sights, knowing well its capacity to surprise. Among those kept under surveillance were Gino Gallagher, 'Ginger', Paul 'Bonanza' McCann, Hugh Torney and Jimmy Brown, as well as Brown's girlfriend. McCann was an up-and-coming gunman, who was close to 'Mad Dog' McGlinchey and Hugh Torney. Torney had been involved in the Official IRA from 1970, and then joined the INLA while in jail.

During the latter part of July, the police became aware that 'Ginger' was to pass a quantity of explosives to McCann and Gallagher. Four days later the police observed a transaction occur outside a social club in the Markets area – one of INLA's principle strongholds. Involved were 'Ginger', Gallagher and a third INLA member who was later seen leaving on a bicycle. The cyclist was followed and raised a chuckle among his police observers when he fell off his bike crossing a stretch of waste ground. A couple of weeks later, on 2 August, Gallagher and

McCann were again under surveillance because of the expected explosives handover. It was seen to occur at 3.05 p.m. Gallagher took possession of four sticks of gelignite, and was followed by E4A operators. An SSU was alerted to make an arrest. Gallagher spotted the uniformed police approach. He took to his heels, throwing away the gelignite as he ran. A detective constable who had been following him gave chase and caught him. He was held until the SSU men came on the scene. The explosives, weighing three pounds were recovered.*

Jimmy Brown was one of Steenson's most devoted followers, and, with his mentor in jail, he came to the fore as intelligence officer for Belfast. In truth, Brown was not taken seriously by many of his fellow terrorists

---

* This did not end Gallagher's paramilitary career, however. In the early 1990s he became OC of the Belfast INLA. Over a period of two years (1993–5) he was involved in about six murders. He was trigger man in the killings of Samuel Rock and former RUC man Jack Murphy. He played a leading role in the deaths of Jack Smyth, a doorman whom the INLA accused of being a loyalist, and three other Protestants, David Hamilton, Colin Craig and Trevor King, on the Shankill Road. Hamilton and Craig were prominent UVF members. After the arrest of Hugh Torney in 1995, Gallagher became INLA chief of staff. He steadfastly refused to commit his group to supporting the Provisional IRA cease-fire and the peace process, which the IRSP has condemned. On 30 January 1996 he was shot dead, apparently by an INLA gunman as part of a feud within the organisation.

'Bonanza' McCann was killed in a shoot-out with the police in June 1984, during which Constable William Todd also died. McCann was responsible for several murders, including that of fellow INLA member 'Sparky' Barkley, killed it is suspected because of his friendship with 'supergrass' Harry Kirkpatrick. See *INLA: Deadly Divisions*, by Jack Holland and Henry McDonald (Poolbeg Press, 1996).

as he tried to live up to the reputation of his leader. He was nicknamed 'Brown the Clown' by some of them. He aspired to be a revolutionary, only to end up a drug-runner.

Information coming through the long-running Belfast E4A operation was keeping the police up to date on INLA's Belfast operations. INLA had over the years developed contacts with left-wing terrorist groups on the Continent. In April 1983 Brown, as a publicity stunt, arranged a weapons display for a group of left-wing Spaniards who were visiting Belfast and staying at its best hotel, The Forum (previously The Europa, to which name it later reverted). Phoenix requested that the visitors be placed under observation, but permission was refused. A few months later, on 10 August, the police learned that one of Brown's girlfriends was meeting with a Dutch member of the Red Brigade, from whom she was hoping to buy a SAM-7 missile for £7,000. However, nothing came of this.

Nor did anything come of the couple of schemes Brown hatched to murder Harry Kirkpatrick and staunch the flow of information that was coming from him. One plan involved picking off the 'supergrass' with a sniper. When Brown was imprisoned in 1983, on Kirkpatrick's word, Kirkpatrick was to be 'sprung', then shot. This too fell through. But the movements of Brown's girlfriend were kept under close watch, though she was never actually convicted of any crime and later went on to become a social worker. Brown himself was eventually convicted of terrorist offences and remained in jail until 1986, when his conviction was overturned.*

While the informers who provided so much of the information for these operations were an essential part of the Special Branch's network of intelligence, they were far from the only means of acquiring details about the paramilitaries' plans. Technical attacks became more and more sophisticated, and developed into a crucial arm in the weaponry of surveillance units. Some of E4A's targets for such technical attacks were also of interest to BOX. In the area of technical attack it is essential that all agencies work collaboratively, and Phoenix spent considerable time writing reports spelling out the need for cross-agency cooperation. When he met BOX agents with whom he could establish rapport he always felt that the operations ran more smoothly. Unfortunately this was not always the case, and he lamented the ignorance of Northern Ireland's culture exhibited by some young BOX agents.

Whatever the successes and setbacks of E4A's Belfast operations in 1984, they were all overshadowed

---

* When the INLA splintered in 1986, Brown became a leader of the IPLO faction, which grew notorious for its drug-running activities. Brown, like Steenson and so many of his INLA colleagues, would die in a feud with fellow republicans. On 18 August 1992 he was shot dead by an IPLO gunman.

by events in Brighton. Since the ending of the hunger strikes, Prime Minister Margaret Thatcher had become one of the most hated figures for PIRA, and the organisation sought to wreak revenge on her for the loss of the hunger strikers' lives. She had quickly risen to the top of the Provisionals' hit list. On Friday 12 October, the Conservative Party was getting ready for its annual conference. Many of its members, including the Prime Minister herself, were staying at the Grand Hotel. At 2.54 a.m. a bomb exploded in room 629. Containing between twenty and thirty pounds of explosives, it collapsed four floors, caving in the centre of the hotel. Jennifer Taylor, who was staying in the hotel with her husband, Eric, testified:

> I remember going to sleep about 2 a.m. We were both terribly tired and I fell asleep very quickly. The next thing I remember is a loud bang. I was lifted upwards and then had the sensation of falling and falling. When I had finished falling I opened my eyes believing I had been dreaming but I couldn't see anything. My eyes slowly cleared and I found myself sitting on the ground. I saw a wall and a light to my left about four feet away. There was debris all around me – a stainless steel sink, girders, bricks and water, and lots of smoke and dust.*

Her husband had been killed in his sleep.

---

* Quoted in *The Provisional IRA*, by Patrick Bishop and Eamonn Mallie

Also killed were Sir Anthony Berry MP, Roberta Wakeham, the wife of the government chief whip, Jeanne Shattock, and Muriel MacLean, the wife of Donald MacLean, a senior figure in the Scottish Conservative Party. Among the thirty injured in the blast was Sir Norman Tebbit, Thatcher's Trade and Industry Secretary. Thatcher herself narrowly escaped death and serious injury. The Provisionals later issued a statement claiming responsibility for the attack against what it termed the 'British Cabinet and Tory warmongers. Thatcher will now realise that Britain cannot occupy our country, torture our prisoners and shoot our people on their own streets and get away with it.' It closed with a warning: 'Today, we were unlucky, but remember, we only have to be lucky once – you will have to be lucky always. Give Ireland peace and there will be no war.'

It was discovered later that the bomb had been planted in the middle of September. It had been equipped with a timing device of the sort found on video recorders, which allows people to pre-set weeks in advance the recording time of programmes they want to tape. The bomb had been hidden behind wall panelling in the bathroom of room 629, heavily wrapped in Cellophane so that search teams which scanned the hotel before the conference would not detect any smell from the explosives.

A fingerprint found on the hotel registration card, signed in the name of Roy Walsh on 15 September, was identified as belonging to Patrick Magee, a known member of PIRA. Magee was wanted in connection with an arms find in England in 1983, as was Evelyn Glenholmes. Glenholmes was a suspect in several operations, including that to assassinate Judge K. But six months after he had been linked to the Brighton bombing Magee was still at large.

The trail which led to the capture of the Brighton Bomber began in the second week of May 1985, in what was codenamed Operation Drain. Police had intimations that another English bombing campaign was in preparation. Ian learnt that a major PIRA operator had been identified on the mainland. It was Peter Sherry, O/C of the East Tyrone Brigade of Provisional IRA. A Dungannon man, like Ian, he was also a prominent member of Sinn Fein.

Sherry had stood for election to the local town council and been defeated. According to authors Mallie and King, he had the reputation as a marksman. A few months after his election failure, he was believed to have been part of an ASU which had planned to murder an-off duty UDR man but had been intercepted by an SAS unit. Sherry and the other IRA men engaged in a brief exchange of fire with the undercover troops and managed to escape. In the confusion, an innocent passer-by was killed.

On 20 May Phoenix along with five others – an E4A sergeant and four of his unit's detective constables – hurriedly prepared to leave for Scotland. Because of the urgency of the situation, he did not go through the ordinary RUC channels for providing transport, and hired two cars himself. He called into his home on the way to the boat, hastily grabbed an overnight bag, kissed Susan, patted the dogs, and left his wife standing somewhat bemusedly at the door. She waved goodbye to the retreating cars as the tyres spun on the drive. The air of excitement, although not explained to her at the time, was plain to see. The five men took the 6.30 p.m. ferry and arrived in Scotland at 10.30 p.m. They contacted the CID in Strathclyde and briefed them and a surveillance team from the London Metropolitan Police. However, two local detective constables, one armed with a revolver as big as a cannon, wanted to intercept the suspect at once. 'They were acting as if they were in *Miami Vice*, perhaps looking for medals and glory or maybe just wanting to get home to have their supper,' recorded Ian in his diary. Phoenix and his unit insisted that the suspect should not be arrested yet, only to be informed by the local detectives that they could handle it. Phoenix sent his sergeant to talk to a detective inspector, who saw the wisdom of the RUC men's advice. Peter Sherry was allowed to leave the area unhindered. The police followed him to the railway station, where he purchased a ticket to Carlisle.

Sherry waited at a bookstall on the platform at Carlisle station, where he was observed by local police who had been briefed. Before long, he was approached by another man. The RUC quickly identified the newcomer as Patrick Magee – the suspected Brighton bomber. The two took a train to Glasgow, where they were followed to a flat at 236 Landside Road. The police judged that they were about to launch their campaign and struck. At 7.40 p.m. twenty-two officers, most of them armed, surrounded the flat. A detective inspector of the Glasgow police rapped on the door. It was opened by a man recognised as Patrick Magee. The police rushed in, to find that the occupants were about to sit down to eat. Along with Magee and Peter Sherry was Gerry McDonald, who had escaped from the Maze Prison in a mass breakout in September 1983. McDonald had a Browning automatic pistol in his waistband and a money belt containing £5,000. There were two young women there as well. One of them, Martina Anderson from Derry, was a former beauty queen; the other was Ella O'Dwyer, a student from Dublin.

The police reported back to Phoenix that they had found McDonald, who was OC of the English unit, in possession of plans for a bombing campaign. PIRA had planned a bomb blitz on eleven seaside and holiday resorts. The plans showed that one of the bombs had already been planted in the Rubens Hotel near Buckingham Palace. Like the Brighton bomb, it had a delayed mechanism – in this case programmed to go off on 29 July at 1 p.m. PIRA had intended setting off small bombs in Brighton, Ramsgate, Dover, Southend, Southampton, Margate, Folkestone, Blackpool, Torquay, Great Yarmouth and Eastbourne, between 12 July and 5 August. A follow-up raid at a cellar some distance away from the Landside Road flat uncovered an arms and explosives hide, which included rifles, booby-trap devices, detonators, ammunition, maps, batteries, and twenty-five packets of explosives – everything, in fact, that terrorists required to conduct a long and deadly operation.

Sherry's presence in the ASU suggested that PIRA had intended to do more than just set off bombs, however. He was known to have marksman's skills, which might have been used against security-forces personnel when they arrived to deal with the explosions.

All the suspects were later convicted of conspiracy to cause explosions. Magee was also convicted of the murders of the five people who had died in the Brighton bombing.

For Phoenix, the aftermath of Operation Drain proved anything but satisfactory. He had funded the ferry crossings himself, because the operation had to be done in a hurry and there had not been time to go through the proper channels. When he tried to claim the costs back, senior officers refused to authorise payment on the grounds that he had not used the correct procedures. Phoenix never did receive back the money he had spent on helping to prevent one of the worst bombing campaigns that PIRA had ever planned in England. And, what was even more galling, the senior officers who had denied him the refund went on in a report to claim credit for the whole operation – 'Notwithstanding', Phoenix noted drily, 'their commitment [had been] of little consequence in comparison to our men.'

This would not be the last time that Phoenix would find himself in conflict with the RUC hierarchy. As time passed, it was a conflict that would become more intense.

Chapter 5

Discord Within

(1985–87)

The aftermath of the capture of the Brighton bomber and the arrest of PIRA's entire mainland ASU had left a bitter taste in the mouth of Chief Inspector Phoenix. Conflicts within E4A and with senior officers now began to take on a sharper edge. Ian was becoming increasingly impatient with what he saw as bureaucratic obstacles, inefficiency and the failure of some senior ranks to take decisions. In particular, he believed that the SAS was not being deployed in situations where its training made it more effective than the police.

Within a month of the successful conclusion of Operation Drain, there was in Phoenix's words 'a concerted semi-mutiny' within a section of E4A. As part of Operation Ramsey, which involved BOX in the targeting of leading members of Belfast PIRA, a surveillance team was ordered to occupy an OP. Three detective constables refused to go into the post and on 23 July they refused to obey their inspector's orders. Ian felt that they could be partly what he termed 'medallion men' – the kind of surveillance officers who liked the glamour of undercover work when it was clean and warm but did not like freezing their balls off in hedgerows, which might be detrimental to their health and hairstyles. Phoenix spoke with them after his inspector, and they again refused. He told them that if they continued to disobey the order he would ask for their transfer out of E4A. The next day they applied for transfer. In another confrontation, Phoenix told them that those who wished to go would be accommodated at his discretion, and where possible moved back into the uniform branch of the service. The three dissident officers then withdrew their requests for transfer in writing.

Possibly as a result of this dispute, BOX informed E4A that it was aborting Operation Ramsey. During 1985 PIRA had been improving its mortar-bomb technology in an attempt to overcome the elaborate security arrangements protecting police stations and army bases, most of them now impenetrable to all but the most gigantic of bombs. It had now developed a massive mortar, the so-called Mark 10, capable of hurling forty pounds of explosives from the back of a truck over a station's high perimeter walls. On 28 February one such bomb struck a lightly constructed canteen inside Newry RUC base as a crowd of officers were having their evening meal. The resulting explosion killed nine constables, two of them women. It was the worst single case of loss of life in the history of the force. Police resources were stretched to maximum with the aim of frustrating similar attacks against Belfast security-force bases.

In September 1985, Phoenix found himself posted back to RUC headquarters, where he was made deputy head of the E4A department and given responsibilities for province-wide operations. He had not long settled into his new situation when he was faced with another row. One of the detectives who had refused to go into the OP in July was again causing problems. On 5 October Phoenix found out that this detective had not fully deployed the team of which he was in charge. Their job was to cover an OP, but the sergeant told him that his men were on 'standby', awaiting reaction from the OP. According to Phoenix:

I then ordered him to deploy his team on the ground to cover the OP, especially as rest days were cancelled to allow him full coverage on the target. On entering the HQ operations room I was told by the D/Sgt that he had extracted the OP and stood the team down without first consulting me. He further stated that he had taken himself off duty and was not working today. I asked the D/Sgt to come to my office and he stated he would not discuss anything with me until he saw the superintendent on Monday morning. I again asked him to step outside and discuss the matter; again he refused. I then told him to go home to which he retorted, 'You will have to carry me out of here'. I then stood the remainder of the team down. The D/Sgt refusing to discuss or obey any order given to him, I informed the superintendent.

The detective sergeant was informed that he would be reported with a view to disciplinary proceedings. Phoenix, however, felt he needed to go to his senior officer, the superintendent, to clarify his own position. The officer assured him that he was in control of operations. However, Phoenix was not happy. He felt that he had made enemies within E4 (surveillance) department, particularly among some senior officers who resented his approach to operations, which always derived from his military experience. Among the things that this experience had taught him was the need to share information. According to McStash, an old friend and former para who had served with Phoenix in the 1960s, his principle was 'keep information broad and across all ranks', so that everybody has enough of the facts to know what is going on and what his role is in it. However, Phoenix discovered that this principle was not applied within many areas of the police, where people built up little fiefdoms, which they jealously guarded.

Soon after the dispute with the detective sergeant,

Phoenix was shocked to learn that his senior officer, the superintendent, had been holding briefings from which he was being excluded. These meetings concerned operational matters, and since Phoenix was in charge of E4A operations he assumed that he would be automatically included. On 3 February 1986 he went to the superintendent to complain. He expressed his 'concern' about his position within E4 and noted, 'the conversation was useful but as usual he [the superintendent] will not openly admit his mismanagement'. Phoenix added, 'The matter will not rest.'

The occasion for another internal conflict was not long in arising, and it came in connection with the deployment of SAS units to support the police. The SAS had been used in the province from the late 1970s, but with the increasing role of the police, under the so-called 'Ulsterisation' programme, their operations had been reduced. Indeed, between November 1978 and December 1983 the SAS were not responsible for the deaths of any republicans in Northern Ireland. (Two PIRA members were shot dead in Derry by a plain-clothes soldier in 1981, but he belonged to an army surveillance unit.) Things began to change, however. SSU squads killed five republicans in late 1982, as well as one innocent civilian, in a series of incidents that provoked the Stalker inquiry and led to allegations of a deliberate shoot-to-kill policy being pursued by the RUC. Police officers insist (both publicly and privately) that there was no such policy, and the rarity of incidents such as those that led to the Stalker inquiry would suggest that they are right.* But the shootings and the subsequent trials exposed the RUC as never before and helped influence policy-makers towards a decision to strengthen the SAS's role in counter-terror operations.

Phoenix had long been in favour of a more aggressive counter-terror policy, both by the police and by the SAS. In September 1983 he had planned a police operation which he had personally felt to be a way of saving more lives. He had wanted the RUC to leak information to PIRA that an important 'supergrass' was being held in a safe house. He would then use the bogus supergrass to lure a PIRA active-service unit into a trap and, in his own words, 'capture them'. He did a series of recces on suitable houses in the Antrim and Ballymena areas, but this was as far as the plan went – it was scratched by senior officers as being far too risky.

At the same time Ian was reluctant to use police officers for such operations, for several reasons besides the superior training of SAS units. He recognised the

---

* Statistics show that in the years between 1969 and 1993 the RUC was responsible for the deaths of 53 people, including 18 paramilitaries. This compares with the British army's total of 294, including 136 paramilitaries. During the same period Republican paramilitaries have killed 749 civilians, the majority of them in accidental bombings and shootings. Loyalist groups in those years claimed the lives of 899 civilians.

additional dangers for RUC personnel in that they were Ulstermen for the most part, and had to live in the community. If they were involved in fatal shootings, they, like the soldiers, might end up on trial, as did four police officers who had been involved in the shooting incidents investigated by John Stalker. They then ran a grave risk of being targeted by paramilitaries thirsting for revenge. SAS men, on the other hand, were in Northern Ireland for only a fixed period of time. They could return for court appearances, but they did not have to make their lives there.

In 1986 an operation developed which was aimed at aborting a planned bombing attack by several of PIRA's most dangerous activists. It was a case in which Phoenix would argue strongly for SAS deployment.

One of those involved was Laurence Marley, a PIRA operative from the Ardoyne in North Belfast. Marley – known as the 'Wee Devil' – was perhaps most renowned for having planned the massive breakout from the Maze Prison which took place on 25 September 1983. He had originally been arrested in 1973 and convicted of armed robbery. In prison he distinguished himself by his fierce determination to escape, which earned him his other nickname – 'Papillon'. Two years later he succeeded in breaking out of Newry courthouse, where he was being tried for a previous escape attempt. Along with B he escaped from an army patrol the following year, but was rearrested in 1977 riding a motorcycle. His passenger was Francis Collins (see Chapter 2). In prison he took part in various protests and remained tireless in his quest to escape.

Ironically, though he eventually planned the most successful PIRA escape plan of all, Marley himself was not among those who broke out. He had only just over two years to serve in 1983, and relinquished his place on the team to another. He was released in November 1985, and police information shows that, like his friend Collins, he became involved in ordinary crime as well as terrorist activities. Said one officer, 'Marley was an out-and-out hood.' Once released he was watched closely by the police, and before long they knew he had resumed his activities with PIRA. From around the beginning of May 1986 he and other leading Provisionals were the focus of several surveillance operations. Marley's career did not go too far. On 2 April 1987, UVF gunmen went to his home and shot him dead.

During this period when Phoenix was at Belfast headquarters, Special Branch operations faced a number of set-backs. Many problems were associated with the recruitment and support of informers. Information from a top-ranking source had been fed steadily to the police in Operation Campaign throughout 1981 and the first half of 1982. Many Special Branch successes were attributed to a number of different 'sources'. During this period, police received a fright when they thought the Provisionals might have their high-ranking informer under suspicion. Phoenix and his team stayed on duty all night covering the house where they feared he was being held for questioning by PIRA, but he returned safely. He seems to have curtailed his activities at this point, as Operation Campaign was shelved for a few years.

Operation Campaign reappears in the records three years later, on 19 June 1985, when it seems that the source was back in contact with the police. He obviously had begun supplying information again, because on 23 July he told the police of an ASU meeting. Three days later Phoenix assumed that the ASU's operation was still on, as they had 'received no signals from our source'. A year goes by before the same source is active once more. He was in contact with his Special Branch handler again, this time about a bombing that was planned in Belfast city centre for Friday 15 August 1986.

Other informers and suspected informers linked to different operations run by Phoenix had been taken away for questioning by the Provisionals' security squad, which PIRA euphemistically refers to as the Civil Administration Team. Frequently the suspected tout was taken to the border area of South Armagh for questioning.

The Tyrone Provisionals were among the most dangerous in Northern Ireland, with a long history of sectarian killings, as well as attacks upon the security forces. They obviously did not think twice about torturing their own people. Among the not-very-civil methods they are known to use is burning the suspect's genitals with cigarettes. It can easily be imagined what must run through the mind of an informer when he is brought in for questioning by such people. However, PIRA's tout-hunters don't always get their man. Highly placed informers linked to operations against PIRA, INLA and the UVF remained active. One of the Special Branch's most important informers in those early years was questioned by the PIRA security team. Phoenix said 'he expected the worse' and had his source covered from 9 p.m. to 11.10 p.m., to rescue him if it seemed he was going to be 'executed'. But he was released without harm, and lived to tell a tale – or two.

Unfortunately, another alleged source was not so lucky. PIRA's security team broke him, and his body was found among the garbage in an entry near Clonard Street, in the Lower Falls. He was thirty years old. According to press reports, some informers have been paid a total of £10,000 for information given over the years.

Throughout 1986 and 1987 there was a noticeable increase in the level of PIRA violence. Unknown to the police, between 1985 and 1987 the organisation had received four huge shipments of weapons from Libya, amounting to some 120 tonnes. These Libyan supplies were a result of the worsening relations between Libya and Great Britain and the US which culminated in the American bombing of Tripoli using F1–11 aircraft based in England. It was Colonel Gaddafi's intention to punish Margaret Thatcher for her support of the American operations. As usual it was the innocents who were to suffer. A fourth shipment, comprising 150 tonnes, was seized by French authorities on 1 November 1987.* It was revealed that the hauls that had been landed on the south-east coast of Ireland safely had included 1000 or more AKM rifles, a million rounds of ammunition, a dozen surface-to-air missiles, and four tonnes of the plastic explosive Semtex. Colourless, odourless and very malleable, Semtex would become the Provisionals' most important weapon in its drive to force the British government to the bargaining table. The violent death rate rose inexorably between 1986 and 1987, as did the number of bombings and shooting incidents.

Among those in the Belfast Brigade who no doubt welcomed the new explosives was Danny McCann, its chief bomb-maker. He had been released in 1987 after serving only two years on a possession charge (see Chapter 4), but his movements were then monitored as part of Operation Sedative, which had begun on 18 October the previous year. The operation led to several police successes – most spectacularly on 16 June 1987, when a bombing mission was intercepted and eleven pounds of explosives and two detonators

---

* Libya had originally approached the more left-wing INLA asking if it was interested. But INLA did not have the resources to absorb the amount of weapons that was on offer. See *INLA: Deadly Divisions*, by Jack Holland and Henry McDonald (Poolbeg Press 1996).

were recovered. However, the police could not always keep McCann under surveillance, and as a result of his becoming increasingly adept at giving police the slip two RUC officers were to lose their lives.

During the evening of 26 August 1987 three Special Branch detective constables who were assigned to watch Belfast's port area were in the Liverpool Bar, a dockside pub. At 10.30 p.m. Danny McCann and Sean Savage, accompanied by a third gunman, walked into the bar and opened fire on them. Detective Constables Ernest Carson (fifty) and Michael Malone (thirty-five) died in the hail of bullets. Their colleague escaped serious injury, but several customers were wounded. The gunmen fled.

The police had discovered earlier (thanks to Operation Sedative, perhaps) that McCann and Savage were to be involved in an even bigger operation – a bombing attack in Gibraltar using a massive quantity of the Semtex that PIRA had so recently acquired from Colonel Gaddafi. Also involved in the plot were two women members of the Provisionals – Mairead Farrell and another who had been under surveillance by the police since about 1983. She was suspected of being a member of a six-woman team which was planning an incendiary blitz in Belfast city centre, scheduled for 14 July that year; the team was monitored until it became clear to the police that the planned attacks had been aborted. Farrell had served a sentence for a bombing attack in the late 1970s.

On 5 March 1988 the second woman was observed in Gibraltar by an SAS unit. She was seen reconnoitring the area around the governor's palace, where, it was thought, the Provisionals were going to target a changing-of-the-guard ceremony. She was followed into a nearby Catholic chapel, where she was observed lighting a candle before leaving. It is unknown whether this was for the bombing team or for the hundreds of potential innocent victims.

The next day, as Farrell, McCann and Savage met near a car which one of them had just parked, the SAS struck, shooting dead all three. The undercover soldiers had thought that the team were about to detonate a bomb, which they thought was in the car. As it turned out, no explosives were found in the vehicle, and the three were unarmed. Two days later, on 8 March, a car was found in an underground car park across the Gibraltar–Spain border in Marbella. It contained three false passports, detonating equipment and 140 lb of Semtex – the largest Semtex bomb ever uncovered in the history of the Troubles.*

The woman who did the original recce was the only member of the ASU to escape. Currently, she is on the Ard Chomhairle, or Central Committee, of Sinn Fein.

* Eight years on, the shootings continue to provoke controversy. In 1995 the European Court of Human Rights ruled that, though the three were killed unlawfully, the soldiers involved were not to blame. British intelligence was faulted for providing them with inadequate information, but lives were saved regardless.

The fact that the Provisionals used activists like McCann, who was known to the police as a key player, for such an important operation was an indication that they did not know the extent of police surveillance. Of course, this was never thorough enough to halt every PIRA operation, as Ian Phoenix was all too aware – lapses due to inefficiency or poor decision-making, or just sheer bad luck, always meant that the paramilitaries could slip through the net. But it was thorough enough to give the police an accurate profile of PIRA's main activists, and a forewarning of many of their plans.

An operation of an entirely different kind – Operation Ike – was launched in early 1987. Like an earlier Operation Narcissus an operation with horses, it involved animals – though this time they were dogs, and this time the animals were central to the plot. In a way, it was typical of the kinds of incident that frequently occur involving loyalists – indeed, such incidents almost constitute a genre of their own in the annals of terrorism, the chief characteristic of which is a thorough-going incompetence.

At the end of the first week of January 1987 the owner of a greyhound bitch reported to the RUC that his dog and its two pups had been stolen. He had then received a call from the Loyalist Prisoners Association. The LPA is an organisation which raises money to help support the families of jailed loyalist paramilitaries. Usually, it does this by making collections at pubs in working-class Protestant areas. However, callers told the astonished dog-owner that they had his bitch and her pups. He could have them back for £7,000. He talked them down to £1,000. They changed their minds and upped their demand to £4,500.

The next day, according to Phoenix, the owner received a stream of further calls which 'developed into a haggling match with the dog-nappers raising and lowering the price from £1,000 pounds to £3,000'. The owner thought that a deal had finally been reached when the loyalists agreed to return the dogs for £1,000 pounds cash and a cheque for £2,000, but after some discussion the LPA rejected the offer. The owner then told the LPA to 'stick the dogs up their arse'. However, the LPA was not easily discouraged. It came back with yet another deal – it told the increasingly impatient owner that one dog could be found at a certain place for £1,000. This final call was traced by the police, and a search operation was instigated. The dogs were recovered in a derelict shed, and two loyalist brothers were arrested. Dog-napping did not prove to be a fruitful source of funds for the LPA.

Another favourite in the genre of 'Prod stories' that Ian and his colleagues enjoyed hearing in the office when there was time on their hands concerned how a UDA man from Ballymena got the nickname 'Walking Dead'. One night he had a row with his father and walked out of the house. He went to his girlfriend's. He had a row with her, and said he was going home. He got home to find everyone was in bed, so he quietly let himself in, stole up to his bed, and fell asleep.

As the story goes, at about 3 a.m. a car containing four 'Prods' and a bomb blew up. Police thought that one of the disfigured bodies might be 'Walking Dead', so they went to his house, knocked at the door, and asked the father where his son was. The father replied, 'At his girlfriend's.' The police went to the girlfriend's, but she said he was not there – he had gone home. Police went back to the father's and explained their concern. They took the father to the morgue, where he identified the remains of a scalp with long straggly hair as his son's and made a statement to that effect. Next morning everyone was sitting around the breakfast crying and consoling each other when the son walked down the stairs and wished them all 'Good morning'. Hence the name 'Walking Dead'.

Phoenix had spent much of the 1970s and the 1980s in Belfast. But in September 1987 he was called for an interview at headquarters to do with a possible promotion that would take him out of the city for three years. After four years as chief inspector, he was being considered for promotion to superintendent. It would mean a move to Tasking and Coordination Group (South), based in Gough barracks in Armagh. It would also mean tackling some of the most dangerous and violent PIRA units in Northern Ireland – those that control East Tyrone and the so-called 'bandit country' of South Armagh.

However, Ian had already been involved with an operation in May 1987 that was to inflict the worst casualties on the Provisionals that they had suffered since the outbreak of political violence in Northern Ireland. In the history of the Troubles it is known as the Loughgall Massacre.

Chapter 6

In Bandit Country – Loughgall

(8 May 1987)

The appearance of the countryside of East Tyrone and Armagh belies the area's reputation as one of Northern Ireland's worst killing-zones. It is a landscape of fields and laneways that merge imperceptibly with the low, flat shoreline of Lough Neagh, of rolling hills covered with orchards, and, further south, towards the border with Co. Monaghan in the Irish Republic, of barren mountains and bleak stony pastures which seem entirely given over to the monotonous rhythms of sheep and cattle farming. Other than the cathedral city of Armagh, its towns offer nothing to the visitor's eye but the drab perspectives of Irish provincial life. It is only the military helicopters darting about in the sky, and the occasional glimpse of massive and elaborate fortifications encircling the police stations, that indicate to the casual passer-by that behind the dull façade of everyday rural life something else is happening. That something has earned the East Tyrone–North Armagh zone the nickname 'the Murder Triangle', just as it has led people to refer to South Armagh and its borderlands as 'Bandit Country'.

Many of the acts committed among these fields or in the lonely laneways and streets of counties Armagh and Tyrone rank among the worst in the annals of Northern Ireland's violent history. Two Catholic brothers and their pregnant sister dismembered by a loyalist bomb; ten Protestant workmen taken out of a bus, lined up, and shot; a hand-grenade thrown into the midst of a group of women prison officers as they lay wounded after being mown down crossing the street in their lunch-break – these are just a handful of the crimes that over the years have earned the area its grim reputation for violent death and destruction.

In late 1985, with the first batch of Libyan arms and explosives flowing into the Provisionals' hides, East Tyrone PIRA came under the command of Paddy Kelly, who replaced Peter Sherry, caught along with the Brighton bomber in England that summer (see Chapter 4). On 7 December Kelly launched a daring attack on the police station at Ballygawley, killing two officers – Reserve Constable William Clements and Constable George Gilliland.

The Provisionals broke into the station, planting a bomb and using a flame-thrower to destroy anything and everything they came across. A year later Kelly again attacked a small rural RUC station, at the Birches, near Portadown. This time PIRA activists used a mechanical digger with a bomb in its bucket to plough through the station's wire defences. The bomb was then detonated against the wall of the building, destroying it. According to Mark Urban, over thirty-five PIRA members were involved in what was a complex, well-coordinated operation.*

However, it was not just the attacks on police stations which were worrying and embarrassing the authorities. In August 1985 the Provisionals had begun murdering contractors whose companies were involved in repairing the stations. In a particularly brutal killing, on 21 April 1987, Harold Henry, who helped run a building contractor's which had worked for the security forces, was taken into the backyard of his home, put up against a wall, and shot. It was a cold-blooded 'execution', meant to strike terror into building contractors and their workers, and make the work of repairing damaged bases ever more difficult. Four days after Henry's death, Chief Justice Maurice Gibson, aged seventy-four, and his sixty-seven-year-old wife, Cecily, were blown apart by a massive bomb

* *Big Boys' Rules: The SAS and the Secret War against the IRA* (Faber, 1992)

as they drove along over the main border crossing into Northern Ireland at Killeen, Co. Armagh.

A Special Branch officer who worked closely with Phoenix over the years said that at the time 'we were under pressure from the government to get results'. He said the firing-squad-type murder of Henry was a turning-point. They knew after that that strong counter-measures would have to be taken.

The opportunity came sixteen days after the death of Henry. Information gathered from a variety of surveillance sources disclosed that the Provisionals were planning another 'spectacular' along the lines of the Ballygawley and Birches attacks. According to police, thirty-one-year-old Jim Lynagh was PIRA's commanding officer in charge of all cross-border operations in the Monaghan–Armagh zone. Lynagh has been described as a 'hardened, dedicated' PIRA member, involved in dozens of killings in the border areas of Armagh and Fermanagh. He had served two prison terms, north and south of the border, and was at one time elected to Monaghan county council for Sinn Fein. He was known to the gardai in Monaghan town, his base, as 'the Executioner'. On 7 May the police, had been informed of an impending attack and had already identified its target as the small police station in the hamlet of Loughgall in North Armagh. It was a place of almost no security importance, being open only during daylight hours and staffed by a handful of country policemen. But its political importance was of mythic proportions for Ulster Protestants: Loughgall was the spot where the Orange Order had been founded in 1795, to counter the growing republicanism that led to the United Irishmen's rebellion three years later.

After consultation with the Northern Ireland Secretary of State, Tom King, Operation Judy was launched to counter the expected attack. Phoenix was in charge of coordinating the HMSU response in line with the Headquarter's remit to support actions province-wide. The regional head of Special Branch in Armagh was a well-respected and highly experienced officer with a legendary hatred of republicans – they had almost taken his life on one occasion. Both he and Phoenix were forceful characters, and they would later clash over operational policy when they worked together. But these clashes, although appearing hostile, would usually end in hearty banter. Ian was to find himself in the unusual position of seeking to restrain his more senior officer's at times unbridled eagerness to hit back at PIRA.

On this operation, which Ian joined to oversee his team from HMSU, he noted that there was a 'large, complicated operation planned' involving local police, E4A, HMSU units, the UDR and the SAS. Intelligence indicated that:

'Lynagh and other Tyrone OTR [on the run] terrorists

were to execute a similar attack to that on the Birches RUC station a couple of months ago. It became apparent that they had planned to travel to Loughgall in a hijacked van, then hijack a JCB on the outskirts, load a bomb into the JCB bucket, roll it over the station fence and after the explosion assault the station wiping out any surviving policemen.'

Unfortunately for them [Phoenix observed], SB had four cut-off ambush groups of SAS outside the station, and one group in the station. The commander of the SAS units was also inside the building, along with three policemen who had volunteered for the dangerous duty. They were all on the first floor. There were also other observation groups and surveillance covering approaches into the area. HMSU cut-off patrols were also secreted in a laneway outside the village and two local policemen had volunteered to remain in the station to give an air of normality. They had been made fully aware of the personal risk involved.

Operation Judy was run out of the Tasking and Coordination Group (South) base in Gough Barracks, Armagh, where, along with Ian and the rest of the operations team, an SAS NCO was manning the radios waiting for news of the 'contact'.

As the day developed, different sightings and snippets of intelligence provided the final parts of the intelligence jigsaw. A surveillance team spotted a van acting suspiciously at around 7 p.m. going into Loughgall village. It was then lost for twenty minutes when it reappeared followed by a JCB with two men on board and a forty-gallon drum in its bucket.

Back in the operations room at Gough Barracks, everyone waited for news of contact. As usual at such times of tension, the room was enveloped in a deathly silence, broken only by the crackle coming over the radio from the operators on the ground.

A few miles away in Loughgall, as the Provisionals' van neared the station, it slowed down, then went some twenty yards past it. At the same time, according to Phoenix, 'a terrorist on the JCB lit a fuse. The bomb and the JCB were driven through the fence and covering fire from the van was directed at the station.'

In Gough, the waiting officers heard the words 'Go, go, go' coming over the radio, meaning contact had been made. It was to be one of the most traumatic encounters in the history of the Troubles. At times like that, as the operation began, people in the room could only imagine the scene, but each knew that, whatever the result, the lives of security forces personnel and terrorists would be dramatically changed.

The JCB bomb, estimated to have been between 300 and 400 lb, exploded with a deafening roar. One of the SAS men later said that it was one of the loudest explosions he had ever heard. He thought that it had killed everyone in the station, one wall of which completely collapsed. Part of the roof was lifted off. Inside, one of the two constables was blown off his feet. The others were buried under the rubble, one of them suffering a fractured skull and the other a broken nose and facial lacerations. The SAS officer picked himself up after the explosion, grabbed his weapon, and ran for the stairs, intending to join in the action, only to find the stairs had gone and he was peering over a rubble-strewn precipice.

Said Phoenix, 'After the explosion, the van reversed and its occupants began to disembark.' Five PIRA activists, heavily armed, scrambled out, wearing blue boiler suits, flak jackets and Balaclava helmets. They were Jim Lynagh, Paddy Kelly, Padraig McKearney – who had escaped from the Maze Prison in September 1983 – Declan Arthurs and Eugene Kelly. Seamus Donnelly, the driver, remained in the van. Two others, Tony Gormley and Gerard O'Callaghan, were still in the JCB digger. Phoenix continues that as the five got out, 'they came under fire from the troops in the station and from the other ambush groups on either side of the station. They were totally shocked at such a reception. Lynagh attempted to get back into the van. Three made for a nearby field, but were forced back because of SAS fire from the woods bordering it.'

Their situation was hopeless. The SAS were firing from all sides with general-purpose machine-guns (GPMGs), Heckler & Koch high-velocity rifles and Browning pistols. Donnelly was hit and killed at the wheel of the van. Paddy Kelly returned fire furiously. His weapon had two magazines taped into a double deadly package by Elastoplast, and he was into his second magazine when he was cut down near the door of the van, from where he had begun firing furiously at the station. McKearney and Lynagh appear to have dived back into the van in a desperate attempt to find cover. One soldier manning a GPMG said in a statement read out at the inquest in June 1995 that he fired into the van 'until there was no more movement from that target'. Another SAS man, also in a written statement, told how he saw one of the men lying in the back of the van 'make a sudden movement' whereupon he 'fired one more shot into him'. Eugene Kelly and Declan Arthurs were shot trying to take cover at the side of the van. Meanwhile, Gormley and O'Callaghan, who had set off the bomb in the digger, fled when the shooting started, and for a few moments they seemed to have escaped the attention of the SAS. Then Gormley was shot by a soldier who had seen him set off the bomb and thought that he was holding what appeared to be a detonator in his hand.

Elsewhere, two brothers, Anthony and Oliver Hughes, had driven into the village just as the shooting started. Unfortunately they were wearing overalls. As their car reversed, first slowly, then violently zigzagging to escape the bloody mêlée, they came under fire from other SAS troops, who mistook them for late-arriving members of the PIRA ASU. Forty shots were aimed at their vehicle. Oliver Hughes tried to get out of the car. One soldier, in a statement read out before the inquest, told how he shouted at him not to move and, when his warning was ignored, fired three shots at him. Soldiers then went over to the car and found Anthony Hughes dead, but his brother still alive. They dressed his wounds before he was taken to a nearby hospital, where he later recovered.

Another innocent civilian was caught up in the ambush. He was a Guinness representative whose car was hit by fire from a GPMG as he drove through the village. Said Phoenix:

> He managed to outrun the pursuing fire towards a nearby house with a man standing inside it. Just as he approached the door with bullets chasing him and another trooper coming round the side to cut him off, the man closed the door and in desperation the Guinness rep. fell to the floor. Fortunately, he was well dressed and the cut-off trooper hesitated in shooting him. When I spoke to him some twenty minutes later, he was handcuffed and sitting at an HMSU VCP [vehicle checkpoint], obviously in a state of delirium at managing to survive.

Back in the Gough Barracks TCG operations room there was silence as they waited for a situation report from the commanding officer at Loughgall. An SAS officer was at the radio receiver when it crackled into life with the first news of the ambush. Colleagues were gathered round him.

'How many?' he asked the commander on the ground. What he was told startled him. He paused, then looked up at the officers around him in the operations room. 'Eight,' he told them. 'Eight arrested?' someone asked, delighted. He shook his head, then, with his free hand, turned his thumb down and gave the ancient Roman amphitheatre sign for death.

Twenty-four heavily armed soldiers had carried out the ambush on the eight-man PIRA ASU, inflicting the worst fatalities on a republican organisation since the Irish War of Independence in 1919–21. The exact number of shots they fired has never been established, but it was well in excess of 200. For the soldiers, the morality of the ambush was clear. The Provisionals had gone on the attack, raking the police station with fire without warning, and detonating a huge bomb against one wall. They would certainly have slain without mercy any policeman unfortunate enough to have fallen into their hands. Any attempt at that stage to make arrests would undoubtedly have resulted in army fatalities. From the point of view of the soldiers, confronting a large group of heavily armed, highly motivated gunmen, there was but one course of action open to them.

The funerals of the eight Provisionals who were killed were a chance for the group's spokesmen to indulge in the usual rhetoric which seeks to turn defeats into propaganda victories. Gerry Adams predicted, 'Loughgall will become a tombstone for British policy in Ireland and a bloody milestone in the struggle for freedom, justice and peace.'

215

Eight years on, the Loughgall ambush and the sub-sequent massacre are still a matter of controversy. To PIRA, the eight dead men are known as the Loughgall Martyrs, and their memory is still celebrated. Every year in the Republic of Ireland's high-security prison at Portlaoise, where republican paramilitary prisoners are held, the inmates hold a 'Volunteer Jim Lynagh Week' at the beginning of May in commemoration of the man who led the ASU into the jaws of death. According to Brendan O'Brien, this takes the form of 'a series of political lectures dedicated to a man whose "total commitment to every aspect of the national struggle for national liberation was a powerful inspiration to everyone"'.*

Needless to say, others have different view, however. They point to the weapons that the police recovered from the bodies of the dead paramilitaries. Subse-quent forensic tests linked them to seven murders and twelve attempted murders, nearly all of them in the mid-Tyrone area. One of the guns had belonged to Reserve Constable Clements, who had been killed during the raid on Ballygawley RUC station, and had been subsequently used to murder three other people. Another of the weapons recovered had been used a few weeks earlier to murder Harold Henry, the building contractor. Had it not been for Loughall, undoubtedly those same guns would have been used to wreak

---

* *The Long War: The IRA and Sinn Fein* (O'Brien Press, 1993)

further misery and human destruction throughout mid-Tyrone.

Seven years later, just after the inquests were held, the Committee on the Administration of Justice – a Belfast-based human-rights group – announced that it was taking the cases of the eight dead PIRA members to the European Human Rights Commission, in an attempt to get the European Court of Human Rights to rule on the matter.

For Phoenix the events at Loughgall were traumatic. As he walked around the ambush scene, the crumpled bodies strewn about him, the words of Wellington after the Battle of Waterloo would doubtless have seemed appropriate: 'There is only one sight worse than a battle lost, and that is a battle won.' To close friends who met him later on the evening of the ambush he was unusually reflective. John, a friend of Phoenix's for twenty years, recalled that he had never seen him so subdued. He lamented the waste of young Irish men who, the pity was, were so determined to murder other good young Irish men. It was heart-wrenching for him to see young men so dedicated to destroying their fellow countrymen. If only they had redirected their enthusiasm away from the path of violence into helping their fellow countrymen, what goals they could attain. At home, he sat in a chair in front of Susan and cried at the waste of life he had witnessed. 'Young Irishmen should not be throwing their lives away like that,' he repeated again and again. Later that night, his son found him in the garden, in the dark, staring out across the cold Irish Sea shaking his head. John commented, 'I saw for the first time the impact that deaths like that had on him.'

A few days after the shooting Susan accompanied her husband to Musgrave Park Hospital to visit two of the young policemen, of whom Ian had been so proud, who had been wounded in the explosion. They were sitting up in bed, Susan remembers, smiling through bandages which covered their bruised and battered faces. Ian just said, 'Thanks lads. Well done.' On the way out they bumped into the chief constable, John Hermon. 'I doubt if Hermon even knew who Ian was,' Susan says. 'Ian hated going up and introducing himself to senior ranks. He thought that was a form of crawling.' They merely nodded politely, and went their separate ways.

Four months after Operation Judy, Phoenix received word that he had been promoted to the rank of superintendent. He was also told that he would be in charge of Tasking and Coordination Group (South), where he would be responsible for running all covert operations in the Armagh and Tyrone area. He was to coordinate SAS, police and M15 operations.

Ian's promotion was confirmed on September. The week before, he had gone to Bramshill police staff college for a course entitled 'The Carousel of Terrorism'. It was designed to encourage senior officers to discuss the subject of international terrorism. Phoenix enjoyed the opportunity of talking to fellow officers about operational techniques and methodology. He was well-read on the issues relating to the international political situation, and over the years he had followed keenly the different crises that had shaken the world. He also admired the tranquility of the place, so different from the real world of violent death, and enjoyed the quiet walks around the wooded grounds, with lakes visited by grey geese and khaki Campbell ducks. But he was decidedly not impressed by the English academic 'experts' on terrorism, nor by their approach to the subject of political violence. He would often say to Susan that he thought the academics learned far more from talking to the police than the police ever learned from them. He maintained that they were, for the most part, a bunch of pseudo-experts. He often wondered how many of the university-trained 'experts' had ever actually met a real terrorist. No doubt as he listened to them lecture with their flow charts and diagrams he wondered what they would make of a 'Mad Dog' McGlinchey or a 'Bonanza' McCann. 'You can't be an "expert" on terrorism without operational experience,' he would say. 'You may as well have teetotallers talking about the joys of wine.'

Wine was very much on his mind that autumn as the course ended and he met his wife in the pretty village of Hartley Wintney near Bramshill. She had driven

138 miles from her parents' home in Peterborough to pick him up to begin the first leg of their trip to the Loire Valley for their annual vacation. Phoenix's Bible at the time was Arthur Eperon's *French Wine Tours* book, and he intended to visit every area mentioned in the guide. He was going to be as thorough about his pleasures as he was about his work. Susan had brought with her a bottle of wine, fresh pâté and crusty bread, and they picnicked on these while crossing the Channel to Le Havre.

After spending the night in Le Havre, they drove south until they reached the valley of the Loire at Langeais. For almost a week, they followed the river's sinuous course, down to Saumur. 'We picnicked on goat's cheese and olives, washed down with local wine,' Susan recalls. 'Early one morning we arrived at Saumur's Ackerman–Laurence vineyard. At the same time, a group of English schoolteachers came in to visit the cellars. The owners were extremely generous with their samples so we had a pleasant conclusion to the tour, with all the teachers enjoying the sparkling wine. We didn't realise how potent it was until we got in the car and tried to drive. We found ourselves wobbling along the road singing hymns and Ian's favourite Irish folk songs, and swiftly concluded it was time to stop – best have lunch and sober up. Unfortunately, at the little country café we stopped at the first thing they plonked on the table was a litre of local wine – free. We hadn't noticed the "vin compris" sign.'

Ian was nonchalant about the matter. He just said, 'what the hell' and booked into a local hotel, where they slept it off.

The couple returned home via Dublin, where Susan attended a conference on the deaf. Her husband still liked to advise her about being more assertive in her quest to improve the services available to deaf children and their families. Susan still countered by suggesting that Phoenix might help his own position a little if he was more subtle in his approach to disagreements with senior officers. In his new job as controller of TCG(S) he would have ample opportunity to test her advice. In fact those who worked with him say they did see a gradual change in his approach, as he sought to deal with authority that he often believed was out of touch with the realities of political violence.

Chapter 7

The Champagne Briefing

(1987–90)

In spite of a series of further successes against the paramilitaries, in which he played a key role, Phoenix's promotion to superintendent would be his last promotion within the RUC. Some saw his being moved to TCG(S) as a kind of punishment. Mainly because of the problems of operating in East Tyrone and South Armagh – areas notoriously dangerous and dominated by some of the Provisional IRA's deadliest units – it was not a posting that many RUC officers would have sought. The additional drive of almost 100 miles to reach his office each day was a pressure that he became accustomed to in his usual resilient manner.

TCG(S) originally had its headquarters in Gough Barracks, Armagh, but later was run out of temporary

Portakabins in the Mahon Road base, Portadown, a nondescript conglomeration of army and police offices protected by a grey concrete wall surmounted by a high metal fence.

Basically, Phoenix's task was to take in raw intelligence and produce a covert operation out of it. During this period, he impressed many of the SAS men with whom he worked as being unusually direct and forthcoming. An SAS non-commissioned officer who served under him said, 'He was different from the other policemen, because he actually spoke to the troops when briefing them. Other SB men would often just pass on their instructions. He tempered all of his briefings with a unique humour and style.'

A colleague recalls how he adjusted to his new position in charge of TCG(S): 'Ian immediately settled in. He was a natural leader of men who used the art of delegation [of authority] to great effect. He knew that the men and women below him and in the agencies working for TCG were all experienced and highly trained personnel. To get the best out of them Ian knew he had to have their respect. This he earned quickly. His own past record and experience helped, of course, but his ability to get to the root of a problem rapidly, using only the right people to do a specific job, working closely with them throughout, then giving praise where it was due, ensured that respect.'

Each weekday morning Ian attended an intelligence

briefing in the Special Branch regional headquarters office, to be updated on any intelligence from which operations were to be mounted. He then held a briefing in his office to discuss the current situation and any present or forthcoming operations. He would update his own officers at this meeting, usually attended by a detective chief inspector, a chief inspector, a detective sergeant, and one or both the military liaison officers. After discussion with his officers and listening to their views, Ian would decide on which agencies were required to carry out the operations. The officers present would then be detailed by him to get on with the plan agreed.

These officers would then ask the agency required to come to the TCG(S) office for a formal briefing. If the importance of the operation warranted it, Ian would chair the briefing of the agencies to be used. Always at these briefings he would use his sense of humour for two purposes. One was to help the men relax, to take their minds off the possible dangers in the task ahead. The other was to get his way in difficult times when a commander of an agency to be used didn't want to do the operation. According to colleagues, Phoenix was able to make people think that he 'was so happy with his plan that it must be the right one'.

Phoenix knew that the officers involved were all highly trained and highly experienced men. 'He listened to their arguments,' said a colleague, 'then formulated a plan that everyone was happy with. On many occasions, more than one agency was used in a specific operation and close, detailed coordination was required. At any time in TCG(S) eight or more operations could be running, so Ian had to be able to balance many plans and ideas in his head at one time to ensure that they were all as successful as possible.

'Ian's greatest qualities were courage to make decisions that needed to be made, to delegate authority when required, to keep up morale in his unit with his wit and humour, to understand his men's needs, and to listen – to admit he didn't know it all. He was able to mix and relax with his men when times were quiet, yet he never became too familiar – he was still the boss. After every operation he was there to thank and congratulate the men involved.' According to colleagues, 'Morale was always a priority to him and he would ensure that the people involved in the job always had his backing throughout. The next day there would be another debriefing and another operation with different problems. There was no time to dwell on the past.'

An SAS officer who served with Phoenix during this time recalls, 'In 1988, when I was reacquainted with Ian, I was on the training build-up phase for returning to duty in Northern Ireland. This would be my seventh tour. We met in a pub in Hereford, as Ian was over to brief us the following day. Some of us had a lot, some a little, and some no experience at all of the

North. We were going over for a long tour of duty. He briefed us on who we would be working with in support of the RUC – mainly with his department, TCG(S), as well as HMSU, E4, DMSU and HQ. He covered the ops, the good and the bad, and how we fitted in to the overall aim, how we tied in with the above-mentioned units and the rest of the military and other security services TCG(S) was responsible for. The main thing he always put across was who was in control. He always stressed that we were there to work within the law, regardless – the law applied to everyone – and as long as we did he would back us up. He was never heavy-handed about it – as with everything, he put it across with charm and a smile.

'The troop would often see Ian in the location we worked from, so all got to know him in the first few vital weeks. Myself and others had contact with him every day. I had taken over as ops officer for the troop. When TCG(S) had something in mind that could involve us, Ian would give us the heads-up. If time allowed, we would meet Ian in his small office – sometimes up to twenty people crammed into it – and discuss the situation before we were officially tasked. Ian gave us an outline, tasked the organisation, and asked if anyone had any questions, then he would send us away to come up with a plan. We would do all we could on the information he gave us. If we had time, he would listen and hear (others listened without hearing) what we thought about the use of the troop on any given task, and how from our point of view it would be best achieved. But most of the time he knew what we would say, how we would carry out the job, such was his vast experience with the troop, and his knowledge and understanding of the North, and all the agencies involved on both sides – it showed. When there was not time, he deployed us with most of our requirements already arranged and in motion. There was never any doubt where Ian stood on the task – it had to be done right, within the law and by the right people whoever they were and whether they agreed or not.'

All who worked with Phoenix agree that one of his main strengths was his ability to take decisions and accept responsibility. This is perhaps best illustrated in an incident which took place when he *wasn't* there to fulfil that role. The SAS troop had been tasked to cover an arms hide in South Armagh. They had been watching it for two weeks. One night when they moved forward to eyeball the hide they were unable to get a safe access. The following day the team found themselves watching the routes into the cache area but were unable actually to monitor the hide itself. At this point Phoenix was at home catching up on a long-overdue night's sleep.

The team on the ground reported seeing a car moving towards the arms hide, which was at the end of a track. The SAS men could see no reason why the car, and the two people in it, would be in such a location other than for sinister purposes. The team leader called TCG(S) and explained the situation, as he was required to do. He said that he thought that if the car was unsighted for more than ten minutes he should order the observation team to react to the target. But he told TCG(S), 'It's your call.' However, the officer on the telephone could not find the officer who was in charge in Ian's absence, and refused to take a decision himself. The team leader said, 'Get Ian at home. He told me he would be there.' The officer on the telephone said no, he would find his superior and get him to make the decision.

'If I don't hear from you by the time the car gets back,' said the team leader, 'I'm going to order the unit to stop and check the car. Tell [your senior officer] or call Ian.' He then put the telephone down and waited. If he did not stop the car he would risk a number of automatic weapons getting out, but if he did stop it and it turned out to be an innocent intruder he would alert the Provisionals to the fact that the security forces were in the area. The Provisionals might then send along someone uninvolved to the cache to check it for them, thus forcing the OP (who would have to react) into the open; or they might even decide that that was too risky and abandon the hide altogether.

Nearly ten minutes went by and there was no word from TCG(S). The team leader was about to call them and tell them to get him Ian at once when the car began to move. He ordered his team to react. They stopped the car, searched it, and the result was – nothing. There were no weapons in the car and the people had no form. The team leader called TCG(S) back with the bad news.

Suddenly the senior officer had turned up. 'Who ordered the stop?' he asked. 'I did,' the team leader replied. 'Do you realise you have blown weeks of work?' he was told. 'I felt like a shit,' said the officer who had taken the decision. 'I'd made the wrong call.' His only hope was that the Provisional IRA would think that the car had been stopped at a casual road check and that the patrol had then been airlifted out of the area.

He was not looking forward to the next day. Phoenix was back on duty and ordered everyone involved in the previous night's operation to gather in his office. The SAS man who had taken the decision found that the chairs on either side of him were empty. 'All the people who had been involved in the operation were sitting as far away from me as they could get in that room,' he observed later. 'Ian entered the room and they looked at me as if to say, "You've had it now, lad."' No one breathed.

Ian looked at the men. 'Last night,' he began, 'that was the right call. We could not risk on any account weapons getting out of our control and into the hands of PIRA to kill people who we are here to protect. Good call, Gaz.' 'All of a sudden,' said the soldier who had made the decision, 'I've no spare room around me. "Nice one, Gaz. Well done, lad," they were saying. "Good call Gaz."' 'Well, it's a shame no one at TCG(S) had the balls to make it,' Phoenix interrupted them. He looked each of them in the eye, and as he did so their gaze dropped away from his. 'But back to priorities. What do we do now?' he asked.

However, he wasn't finished. Later that day he made each of those at TCG(S) who had failed to shoulder their responsibilities aware of his displeasure. 'People had their ear to the wall, to hear what was befalling their fellow officers,' said the vindicated SAS commander.

There was one more incident that showed the mettle of the man, in which the same SAS officer was also involved. A Provisional IRA sniper was operating in the South Armagh area. After he had picked off a member of an army foot patrol, the SAS troop was sent down to brigade HQ. The local RUC wanted the military to patrol the area as normal while the SAS unit went undercover, ready to react if the sniper struck again. The trouble was that the commanders did not necessarily want the soldiers to know that they would be a decoy, and the SAS could not guarantee that they could detect the sniper in time to stop him firing and perhaps killing a member of the patrol.

Both the SAS officer and Phoenix disagreed with this plan. They wanted to inform the brigade in enough detail so that the patrol members would know the risks they were taking. However, senior officers said the brigade would be told only a limited amount.

During the briefing, according to the SAS man, 'I could see the concern in Ian's eyes. As questions were asked, he knew the whole truth was not being told. He looked at me and just nodded. Without a word being said, I knew what he wanted me to do. When it came to my part, I gave the outline of the plan and mentioned the fact that the patrol was a decoy and that we could not guarantee to stop the shoot in time. I said the patrol must fully understand this. Before the others could play down what I was saying, Ian came in to fully support me, emphasising the risk. He said only the brigade could make the final choice. The others could say nothing. The truth was out. They knew that had been his intention all along. I had thought it strange that he had said nothing stronger before. After, I understood why. If he had pushed it before, knowing the others as well as he did, they would not have let him do as he wished. It had to happen at the right point.' Everything was then worked out and everyone was deployed, but no sniper was in fact encountered.

Another colleague who worked with Phoenix on most of the major operations at TCG(S) recollects, 'Ian's time at TCG(S) was marked by many successful operations. He knew this was not just down to him but to a great extent the team he had gathered around him, all dedicated to one purpose – the defeat of terrorism.'

After Loughgall, the two most successful operations he organised struck powerful blows against both loyalist and republican paramilitaries.

Though cracking the Provisional IRA's units in the Tyrone–Armagh area remained the highest priority, the first operation he undertook in his new post was directed at the Ulster Defence Association – the largest of the loyalist paramilitary groups.

Unionism had been undergoing a trauma since 1985 – one which fuelled the militancy of the Protestant paramilitary organisations. On 15 November that year the British and Irish governments signed the Anglo-Irish Agreement, which broke new political ground in two ways. First, it recognised the role that the Irish government could play in Northern Ireland, establishing a secretariat at Maryfield, Co. Down, near Belfast, staffed by Irish government officials which would oversee certain aspects of the running of the state. Second, as a return for this gesture, the Irish government for the first time recognised the existence of Northern Ireland and that its legitimacy was based on the will of the majority of its population to remain within the United Kingdom. However, this important concession from Irish nationalists was not enough for the Protestants, who were enraged that Dublin was now permitted to have a say in Northern Ireland affairs. Massive protest demonstrations were held throughout the province, and there were attacks on the homes of RUC men by angry loyalists, further alienating the police force from those sections of the community which had traditionally identified with it. An 'Ulster Says No' campaign began, which would last for years.

What was especially bitter for Unionists was that it was Margaret Thatcher who had signed the deal with Irish leader Garret Fitzgerald. Thatcher had been much admired by Unionists, particularly for her tough law-and-order stance. She espoused the kind of conservative values that they held dear. However, that changed with the signing of the agreement, and during a fiery sermon in his Martyrs Memorial Church on the following Sunday the Revd Ian Paisley thundered, 'We pray this night that thou wouldst deal with the Prime Minister of our country. We remember the Apostle Paul handed over the enemies of truth to the Devil that they might learn not to blaspheme. O God, in wrath take vengeance upon this wicked, treacherous, lying woman. Take vengeance upon her, O Lord, and grant that we shall see a demonstration of thy power.'*

Unfortunately for Paisley, God declined to accomplish what the Provisional IRA had failed to achieve, and Mrs Thatcher continued to stand by the agreement, the implementation of which led to a new era in Anglo-Irish relations and paved the way for future

* Quoted in *Northern Ireland: A Chronology of the Troubles 1968–1993*, by Paul Brew and Gordon Gillespie (Gill & Macmillan, 1993).

initiatives. However, as usual in Northern Ireland politics, the words of passionate sermons are often translated into action at the paramilitary level. Loyalist killings had reached a low point in 1985, with only four sectarian murders. Over the next decade they were to steadily rise, until the UDA and UVF were killing more people than the Provisional IRA. But this was not just because of a backlash against the Anglo-Irish Agreement. It had as much to do with the fact that two years after the agreement the loyalists had succeeded in rearming themselves.

Davy Payne gained notoriety in 1972, when he was a member of a UDA gang which kidnapped and tortured Catholics. Before the advent of the Shankill Road Butchers, Payne and his gang wielded the knife on their victims. He was nicknamed 'the Joker' by some, because he liked to laugh as he 'questioned' the gang's captives. Among his victims were several women, including Irene Andrews, who, along with a nationalist politician, Paddy Wilson, was stabbed to death in June 1973 after being taken by the UDA gang to a lonely spot outside Belfast. Wilson was stabbed thirty times, and Ms Andrews twenty. Both had their throats cut.

Payne first came to Phoenix's attention in 1987. Payne and his associates were planning to move a large consignment of weapons. An elaborate counter-operation – Operation Fremitus – was launched by TCG(S). Unfortunately the UDA succeeded in lifting a stack of UDR weapons. Though the arms were recaptured immediately afterwards at a vehicle checkpoint, Payne and the major players slipped through the fingers of the police. A year later they went on to take part in another major arms-running venture, this time involving arms dealers from South Africa.

South African arms dealers were interested in obtaining missile parts from the Shorts aircraft factory in Belfast, in return for which they supplied a huge arms cache. The shipment was divided into three parts. One was due to go to the UVF, one to the UDA and one to an organisation which had sprung up to fight the Anglo-Irish Agreement and was known as Ulster Resistance. On 7 January 1988 Phoenix learned that a 'Prod. resupply was in the Province and due for dispersal tomorrow.' Surveillance was carried out on one of the suspects, N, who met twice with UDA leader Andy Tyrie on that date to discuss arrangements to get the UDA's share into the city. A watch was kept on N all night.

The following day, two Granada cars were seen acting suspiciously and were followed in the Tandragee area. A VCP was mounted and the cars were stopped. Inside was Davy Payne, plus approximately fifty AK-47s, fifty 9-mm pistols, 150 Russian grenades and 11,000 rounds of ammunition. Two other UDA men were arrested with Payne.

While the police were in Payne's car, his mobile telephone rang. A constable picked it up. 'Where the fuck are you, Davy?' a voice asked. 'Where the fuck are you?' the policeman replied. 'We're here at the garage in [. . .] Street – where do you think?' So Payne's confederates obligingly gave the location of the lock-up garage where they were awaiting the weapons. The police arrived soon after and arrested them.

The next day follow-up searches were carried out in the Tandragee–Markethill area. The searches continued, and on 3 February the police uncovered another loyalist arms hide containing rocket-launchers, a sub-machine-gun, rifles, revolvers and 12,000 rounds of ammunition.

The double blow hit the UDA and the UVF. The only group successfully to get its hands on the South African weapons was Ulster Resistance. However, it later reached an agreement with the other two organisations and shared its portion of the haul with them, ensuring that the loyalist escalation of violence would take place over the coming years. But Payne at least was not able to play a part in it. At his trial, much to everyone's surprise, he did not contest the case and pleaded guilty. However, he made a speech from the dock claiming that he was not a member of the UDA. He said that he had no idea that the weapons had been in the car. The judge did not believe him, and on 1

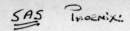
November 1988 he was sentenced to nineteen years in prison.*

Phoenix threw himself with enthusiasm into working with the SAS. He got on well with soldiers. They recall that on their return to the North he always greeted them with his usual easygoing manner. 'They were always chuffed that Ian remembered them and shook their hands as soon as he saw them, irrespective of rank,' said an SAS NCO. It would be the first thing he said to Susan later that night: 'Guess who's back?' His house became a home from home for many of the troop stationed in Northern Ireland. He was re-creating his days in the Parachute Regiment, when Susan and he were always ready to provide a good dinner and a drink for men who were eager to enjoy the conviviality and relaxed hospitality of the Phoenix household. During the long summer evenings, when weather permitted, there would be barbecues on the Phoenixes' patio, overlooking the sea, or trips down to the beach at the foot of the garden for picnics – always accompanied by generous quantities of good wine and champagne. It was a temporary escape from the business of terror and counter-terror which otherwise absorbed their mental and emotional energies.

---

* Just over six months later, three loyalists were arrested in a hotel in Paris as they passed on missile weapons parts to a South African diplomat who was accompanied by an arms dealer. It was established that the parts came from a display model used in Shorts aircraft factory that had gone missing earlier.

Susan was always impressed by the calibre of these men, who proved to be good friends to her husband and family. She felt that it surprised many of their civilian friends that the stereotypical reputation of 'the SAS' was not always true. The men who became their friends were a mixture of interesting people from a variety of cultures, backgrounds and education. The unexpected intermeshing of former public-school boys, self-taught school dropouts and a few ex-villains had produced a group of men with a high code of conduct who enjoyed wide conversation and good food. About one thing she was certain: she would trust such special-forces operatives, who were trained to a high level of self discipline, over and above any of the civil servants and politicians who were responsible for sending these dedicated men to the world's troublespots.

'The troop knew we had a friend, and a friend is what he, his family and his home would turn out to be,' according to Gary, who spent the years from 1988 to 1993 working with him.

'The hours were long,' testified another colleague, 'and many times he couldn't leave the office until late in the evening – sometimes returning to run an operation into the early hours of the morning. It was the same for all of his men, and so when the times were quiet Ian ensured that the men could relax – usually by sending out for a half-dozen bottles of quality wine and a carry-out from the local Chinese. Those quiet times with a drink and a chat were Ian's way of letting the men and women of his unit unwind, and, after a few glasses, more operations, problems and plans for the future were worked out and solved than ever were at a dry briefing.'

One such briefing became something of a legend in TCG(S). It was known as the Champagne Briefing. One of the SAS men was leaving and a police officer had been promoted, so Phoenix decided to send them off in style. He sent one of his officers out to get five bottles of champagne at 10.30 in the morning. On his return he, Phoenix, two SAS men and five other Special Branch officers settled down for an impromptu farewell party. Unknown to them, the regional head of the Special Branch had a group of visitors from Scotland Yard who had come to see how the RUC was running the war against terrorism. He decided to pop down the corridor and introduce the English policemen to the head of TCG(S). Recalls one of the participants, 'They arrived dressed in three-piece suits, with cups of tea in their hands. We were toasting each other with our glasses of champagne. Ian greeted them with, "Glad you could come. It's our champagne briefing, you know. Would you care to join us?" They looked completely gob-smacked.' By the time it was over, eighteen empty bottles of champagne had accumulated, and the English visitors went away with a perhaps unusual view of how the war in Northern Ireland was being conducted.

Loughgall had delivered a stunning blow to East Tyrone PIRA, but it did not put it out of business. Phoenix knew, perhaps better than anyone, that no single blow could do that, and that they were involved in a war of attrition during which the Provisionals would adapt to meet whatever new security measures they had to face. This became apparent as 1988 progressed. With their arms dumps replenished thanks to Libya, the Provisionals were expecting to make a 'big push'. Semtex was playing an increasingly important role in the PIRA campaign. During 1988 twelve people would die because of booby-trap car bombs made from that explosive. It was also employed as a booster for larger bombs manufactured from home-made explosives. It was one of these which, on 20 August 1988, the Provisionals planted on the road between Ballygawley and Omagh, along a stretch known as 'Bomb Alley'.

This had been the scene of several major PIRA killings. In July 1983 four UDR men had lost their lives in a bomb attack there. Then in December 1986 came the attack on Ballygawley RUC station which had claimed the lives of two constables. The RUC warned the Ministry of Defence never to use the route. When on missions, the SAS always avoided that area – even if it meant going miles out of their way to do so. However, in August 1988 the advice was for some reason ignored or forgotten – with tragic consequences. A coach carrying soldiers back to their base in Omagh took that road on the night of the 20th. Just beyond Ballygawley a huge bomb exploded, ripping the vehicle apart and hurling bodies and parts of bodies everywhere. Eight soldiers died in the blast, and dozens were injured.

Before the attack, Ian had already identified through intelligence three of the main PIRA operators in East Tyrone, and at the time of the bombing he was in the last stages of setting up an operation against them. They were two brothers, Gerard and Martin Harte, and Brian Mullin.

Seemingly the Harte brothers and Mullin were going to ambush a lorry driver who was a part-time member of the UDR. They planned to murder him as he drove through the small, rather lonely town of Drumnakilly, near Carrickmore. An SAS officer – G – who bore a resemblance to the UDR man began to drive the same route a few days in advance of the date of the planned attack. On 30 August, just ten days after the Ballygawley bombing, G followed the usual route. This time he pretended to have a flat tyre. His lorry came to a halt at a prearranged spot in Drumnakilly. Directly opposite to where the lorry came to a halt an SAS unit was waiting, among whom was a little Scotsman famous for his rather unlovely appearance.

As the make-believe lorry driver knelt at the side of the road, fiddling with his tyre while keeping an anxious eye on what was going on around him, the assassination team drove by. They continued up the road without stopping. The SAS men waited. Suddenly a different car, a white Sierra, came down the road with 'two up' – two men in the front. The SAS watched, slightly puzzled, until the Sierra braked near the immobilised lorry. G looked round in time to see a masked figure rise up from the back seat with an AK-47. The soldiers suddenly realised that the PIRA ASU had changed cars. As bullets smashed into the road around him, G took to his heels, heading towards a wall over which he bounded in one go. Gerard Harte jumped out, intending to follow his victim and finish him off. The SAS ambush team in the hedges opened fire. Brian Mullin was struck in the head by a 7.62-mm bullet. Martin Harte was also killed while still in the car. When the SAS shooting started, Gerard Harte had turned round and caught a glimpse of the Scottish SAS man sitting in the hedge staring at him. According to one who was involved in the operation, 'The last thing Gerard Harte saw before he died was this really ugly little Scotsman in the hedge aiming a gun at him. What a way to go, poor bastard!' He was cut down in a hail of bullets, a few feet from the car.

According to a Special Branch officer, 'None of these operations were set up with a deliberate aim of killing anyone, but because of the firepower in the hands of the terrorists and their willingness to use it their deaths were unavoidable. Ian did not celebrate after these deaths. He regretted that anyone had to die. But he knew as commander of TCG(S) it was his job to coordinate an operation on the intelligence provided and, using the right agencies, thwart the terrorists' plans.'*

Such operations, however, were the exception rather than the rule, in that they actually resulted in action. A non-commissioned SAS officer who worked with Phoenix for two years at TCG(S) estimates that roughly '85 per cent of ops did not come off'. This was mainly because the Provisionals did not appear on the scene, for whatever reason.

Another SAS officer who served with Phoenix at TCG(S) recalls, 'There were many occasions that Ian deployed us with good information, using all sorts of major assets, without any result. The IRA may have sussed us out for whatever reason. You have to remember also that the IRA's basic thought is that if there was any chance they would not get away they would not attempt it. Fifty per cent of their planning is their escape. Or they just could not be bothered showing up. Sometimes Ian would be forced to take the option of just recovering equipment without making an arrest. But he knew none of this was wasted. He and his teams must

---

* At the inquest into the deaths of the three PIRA gunmen, held in March 1993, the coroner commented that the pictures from the scene of the shooting were 'quite horrifying'. He found that the army had fired 220 shots. One PIRA rifle recovered belonging to Gerard Harte had fired sixteen rounds. The army's rate of fire was ten rounds a second. The inquest did not reach any conclusions about who opened fire first.

have saved hundreds of lives on both sides over the years.'

During this period a number of operations were planned with RUC and SAS liaison. When the initial intelligence would arrive, Ian would call his team together and discuss the format. He would then call in the SAS group to be deployed. He would present the potential job to the SAS and ask them to formulate the plan of operation. Ian would be walking up and down as the SAS men were in a huddle discussing how to avoid the pitfalls with the troop commander. If a problem with tactics arose they would consult Ian. He would often say, 'If there's a problem, I'll sort it out after. I'll back you all the way.' According to the NCO, the sceptics gave him a doubting look – they'd had experience of senior officers promising support only to deny all knowledge of an operation when it went wrong. But the SAS men who knew Phoenix and had worked with him before declared, 'That'll do for us.' The jobs went ahead with the SAS knowing that Ian Phoenix was a man of his word.

There was always a feeling of let-down when nothing happened – particularly if the operation was a big one. This was the case in two of Phoenix's most ambitious schemes, both of which had the potential to make Loughgall look like a picnic. The first came about as a result of information that PIRA was planning to assassinate a leading member of the Ulster Unionist Party, Ken Maginnis.

Maginnis was a former member of the B-Specials, the part-time militia abolished in 1970, and then of the UDR which replaced them. He entered politics and won a seat on the Dungannon town council. He was always an outspoken and credible opponent of terrorism. In the general election of June 1983 he contested the seat for Fermanagh–South Tyrone, formerly held by hunger-strike leader Bobby Sands and later by Owen Carron for Provisional Sinn Fein. The entry of an SDLP candidate into the contest split the nationalist vote and Maginnis won. He held on to the seat four years later, and again in the general election of 1992. He is a well-liked MP, on the liberal wing of his party, and regarded by both Protestants and Catholics as a fair and decent man. Indeed, as a local journalist put it, 'He is one of the few Unionists that you can imagine enjoying a pint with in the pub.' However, his jolly reputation did not impress the Provisional IRA. Perhaps the fact that Maginnis had taken the seat that had been formerly occupied by Sands, whose memory the Provisionals revered, made them feel especially bitter towards him. Whatever the reason, they hatched several plots to murder him. The most ambitious and brutal were planned in 1988.

Originally, the Provisionals planned to ambush Maginnis between the offices of Dungannon town council, of which he remained a member, and his home. A member of the SAS troop posing as the MP took the route on several nights to act as a decoy. Maginnis and his family were taken out of their home on several occasions for their protection. At other times they remained in their house under the protection of the security forces and nothing happened. It was then feared that the PIRA might be planning a full-frontal assault on Maginnis's well-protected house outside Dungannon.

Rehearsals to counter a suspected attack took place and security was increased in and around the Maginnis's home for a number of weeks. Mrs Maginnis impressed Ian by very bravely insisting that, should the occasion arrive, she would be staying at home that day, carrying out her regular household work, to make sure everything looked as normal as possible.

Had the planned assault on the MP's house gone ahead, with PIRA willing to attack innocent unarmed civilians, Loughgall could well have lost its pre-eminence in the history of the Troubles as PIRA's single most costly defeat. However, though the men on the ground were frustrated that their rehearsals did not lead to the opportunity to strike a major blow against the Provisionals, they were very relieved that two brave people lived to continue their work for the community.

During this period of intense protection for the Maginnis family the police actually recovered a large cache of weapons not far from the Maginnis home. It was speculated that they could have been earmarked for use in a particularly nasty assassination attempt.

The cache included a number of high-powered weapons, including rifles and an RPG-7 rocket. Ian remarked at the time that if he were Maginnis he would get himself some really vicious dogs to keep his home a little safer.

Dogs were among the greatest threats that undercover operators had to confront in Northern Ireland. Among the first thing that surveillance teams had to establish before doing a CTR was whether or not there was a dog on the premises. If there was, then it was necessary to bring along food treated with sedatives. Enough was needed to put the dog asleep for a short period of time. It had to be awake before the owner returned if suspicions were not to be aroused. On one occasion the plan went badly wrong when the SAS unit involved used too much sedative. The result was that by the time they had CTRed the house and were ready to depart the dog was still unconscious, showing no signs of waking in spite of a lot of shouting and shaking. The men reluctantly decided that there was only one thing to do to save their operation from being compromised. They dragged the unfortunate animal into the laneway next to the house and ran over it with their car, making it look as if it had been killed in a hit-and-run accident. Fortunately for the SAS, autopsies are not normally performed on animals.

Perhaps the most ambitious of all the operations that in the end never materialised was to involve a massive counter-strike by airborne forces, codenamed

Operation Cruise. Two things had happened that pre-cipitated the planning of the job that never was. On 23 June 1988 a helicopter had been shot down by fire from several heavy machine-guns. Following this, in the spring of 1990, security forces on both sides of the border were horrified by a near-successful attempt to wipe out a border checkpoint during which the Provisionals had employed a reinforced lorry, a DHSK machine-gun and a flame-thrower. The 12.7mm machine gun fires tracer incendiary rounds which burst into flame on impact making it a deadly weapon capable of doing damage even to a heavily protected position. The lorry had crashed into the checkpoint, resisting rifle fire from the soldiers. The massive machine-gun was used to pin them down while PIRA members burst into the checkpoint with a flame-thrower, intending to burn alive anyone they encountered. Fortunately only one soldier was on the ground floor at the time, and he managed to hide behind a fridge where he had gone to get a sandwich. The three members of the ASU swept past the terrified young squaddie, not noticing his rifle sitting beside a sandwich on the worktop. A returning army patrol forced the Provisionals to abandon their attack, but they had come uncomfortably close to inflicting major damage and scoring a massive propaganda victory.

To decide how to counteract this style of attack, Ian and his team had a brain-storming session. They came up with the idea of using a helicopter assault force equipped with general-purpose machine-guns manned by the SAS airborne troop. The plan was to sweep down on an identified target and simply obliterate it.

In June 1990 Superintendent Phoenix went to discuss the potential of such an operation with the commander of land forces (CLF). The CLF at first refused to consider such an outrageous idea as using the SAS in an airborne assault, but after a further briefing at British army headquarters in Lisburn he relented and allowed training to go ahead. The helicopter pilots and the proposed assault team used an old boat on a lake for target practice, swooping on it from the air, guns blazing. The helicopters were rather makeshift gun platforms, with the heavy 50 calibre Browning machine guns being weighted down with sandbags for extra stability.

The helicopters that would be needed for such an exercise consisted of four Lynxes, two Gazelles and two Pumas. The day that all of the airborne force was in place, Phoenix and the other members of the Special Branch involved in the operation sat around on the fringe of the helicopter landing-pad drinking coffee and admiring their helicopters. He took a break from this less than taxing day to give Susan a ring.

'Guess what I've got in my garden?'

'I haven't a clue. What?'

'Eight helicopters. And they look great. Only problem is I have to keep stopping [. . .] from taking all the pilot's phone numbers – you know how he's always looking for free flights!'

'You've never been the same since I allowed you to watch that *Whirly Birds* programme with the kids!'

Ian's mischievous sense of humour caused some consternation when, according to one of the SAS NCOs, he enquired about the possibility of mounting Tannoys on the helicopters with Wagner's 'The Ride of the Valkyries' playing! He thought it would be a nice idea to blast the music out at full volume as the helicopters swooped down on their target – like a scene from the Vietnam War movie *Apocalypse Now*. It was his bit of fantasy to lighten the operational side of life. However the analogies did not end there, for had it ever been necessary for the operation to go ahead it would have been one of the largest helicopter assaults by a Western democracy since the end of the Vietnam conflict.

Susan remembers that almost two years later, in February 1992, when the East Tyrone Brigade of the Provisional IRA used a DHSK machine-gun in a reckless attack on Coalisland RUC station, Ian watching it on the TV news muttered to himself, 'Now *that's* where they could have used my helicopters!' The machine-gun was mounted on the back of a lorry and driven up to the target, which stands in the middle of the town. After a burst of fire which hit the station's perimeter wall, the lorry drove off, eventually stopping at a church car park, where the ASU had intended to dismantle the big gun and make their getaway. Instead they encountered an SAS unit, which opened up on the Provisionals, killing four of them. This would be the last SAS action which resulted in fatalities before the PIRA cease-fire of August 1994.

If the Provisionals had several close calls because of Phoenix's operations, then so had he because of them. Most notably, on 26 April 1989, a PIRA ASU drove a lorry containing sixteen mortars to a location near the Mahon Road base. Three of the mortars exploded together prematurely, destroying and scattering the others. Fortunately, as the scattered debris was raining down on his office Phoenix was caught in a traffic jam. He arrived for work just as the area around the base was being sealed off by the security forces. Unfazed, he went to the local station and made arrangements to run all operations from elsewhere until his office was repaired.

Much less fortunate were Chief Superintendent Harry Breen and Superintendent Robert Buchanan. Breen was commander of H Division, and he and Buchanan made regular trips across the border to meet with the gardai in Dundalk. The two men always took one of three routes back into Northern Ireland. On 20 March 1989 their car was followed from Dundalk as they took the road to Jonesborough in South Armagh. Unknown to them, the Provisionals had had ambush teams waiting along each of the three routes. Breen and Buchanan drove into an ambush outside Jonesborough. At least four gunmen raked their car with gunfire, killing both men. Breen was the highest-ranking RUC officer to die at the hands of republican paramilitaries during the troubles.

Given the nature of the war of attrition in which the police were engaged, there were bound to be set-backs and losses, regardless of their efforts. But Ian felt that often these could have been avoided. During his period at TCG(S) he was as ever frustrated and occasionally angry at the restrictions which he felt were placed on operational capabilities by some senior ranks. In the first month of 1990 there was a series of attacks on off-duty members of the security forces which claimed several lives. On 9 January Oliver Kilpatrick, an off-duty UDR man, had been shot working in his shop in Castelderg, Co. Tyrone, and thirteen days later an off-duty policeman, Inspector Derek Monteith, was gunned down in the kitchen of his home in Armagh. Around this time the police were aware of a PIRA assassination plan, but they could not identify the target. Operation Leonora was launched to counter the PIRA plot. Phoenix noted, 'Restrictions imposed on operational plan which will undoubtedly hinder full exploitation of intelligence and in the long run cost us lives.' The exact details which led him to record these intense feelings are uncertain.

Three weeks later, however, his words came tragically true. A forty-year-old off-duty sergeant in the UDR, Thomas Jamison, was driving his lorry when an ASU ambushed it from a garden at the roadside, near Donaghmore, Co. Tyrone. The killers first threw a grenade in front of the lorry, then, when it pulled to a halt, raked it with high-velocity rifle fire. The unarmed man inside never had a chance.

However, such sad incidents had to be balanced against the breakthroughs that came about through patient work, good intelligence and sheer luck. The results rarely made the headlines, but they were important in the struggle to defeat the paramilitaries. In the summer of 1988, for instance, the police seriously disrupted the flow of explosives from Draperstown, Co. Tyrone, into Belfast, capturing three containers full of nitrobenzene, used in the manufacture of home-made bombs.

One of the last successful operations in which Phoenix became involved while still at TCG(S) was that codenamed Askew. It focused on the Irish People's Liberation Organisation. Since its formation following a split within the INLA in 1986, the organisation had only rarely attempted to attack the security forces. In November 1986 it had murdered an off-duty policeman, Derek Patterson, in Belfast, and later that same month it had attacked a police station with grenades. But it had concentrated most of its energies on sectarian killings and drug-related murders.

In the Armagh area a young man called Martin Corrigan who was a member of the Provisional IRA abandoned that organisation and joined the IPLO. He intended to establish the IPLO's paramilitary 'credentials' by killing members of the security forces. No doubt he was partly motivated by a desire for revenge. Eight years earlier his father, Peter Corrigan, an active member of Sinn Fein, had been shot dead from a passing car as he walked along a street in Armagh. The UVF claimed responsibility. An ex-UDR man had been arrested and convicted of Corrigan's murder.

In early April SAS men were deployed in the area of an off-duty member of the security forces who was a possible target. However, the IPLO attack did not take place. It was another eleven days before the ASU launched its murder bid. On 18 April, the Special Branch learned that two police reservists were possible targets. Both were watched. At eight o'clock that evening, the IPLO approached the garden of one of the policemen. Corrigan led the gang, armed with a carbine rifle, and his two fellow operators carried shotguns. The SAS opened fire, killing Corrigan. The two others escaped. Corrigan has the dubious distinction of being the only member of the IPLO to die in an attack on the security forces.*

---

* The IPLO had been declared an illegal organisation by the Northern Ireland Secretary of State only a month before Corrigan was shot. As such, it did not last long. In October 1992 the Provisional IRA moved against the IPLO, after accusing it of being a criminal gang. Several of its members had been involved in the brutal rape of a young woman in

Phoenix's period at TCG(S) had been forma-
tive, and exhausting – among other things, it had
necessitated a daily journey from home to job and
back of over a hundred miles. But the posting had
taught him to think strategically, in operational terms.
Those who knew him before and after say that he
lost something of his abrasiveness as he grew into
his new role. But when he was faced with the old
problems that he had encountered before – lack of
decisiveness, restrictions on capabilities, and often
the withholding of information – he always met them
head on. After one briefing in September 1988 he
had noted, 'Still unaware of what [A] and [M] were
talking about. Had to contact HQ to find out what
briefing was about.' He always insisted that military
principles held good in the policing situations the
RUC faced – that is, information had to be kept
broad and across all ranks for effective deployment of
resources. Nothing angered him more than the refusal
to share vital facts – he saw it as power-building and
a type of influence-peddling. He complained, in his
notes, that the individuals named – senior Special
Branch officers – had never given him the kind of
information that was essential in making operational

Belfast, and the organisation's drug-running activities were well-known
in the Catholic areas. On 31 October the Provisionals shot dead one
of the IPLO's leaders and wounded dozens of its members in a series
of raids throughout the city. Others were ordered out of the country.
The group then disbanded.

decisions. He only resorted to going above the people concerned if he felt his own teams were being left in a dangerous position because of a lack of information. He normally managed to get the information that he needed by using humour and good-hearted banter. However, when the other officer's personality did not lend itself to such negotiations he felt it necessary to resort to other means.

On one occasion, after a particularly frustrating briefing, involving an SAS officer and the RUC, Phoenix followed the officer to the helicopter in which he was travelling. It was what the officer later related as an odd sight, as Ian ran across the heli-pad doubled up to avoid the blades, shouting, 'Come back, you bastard, and tell me what the hell's going on.' Meanwhile the SAS officer was grinning down at him and calling to the pilot to 'Get me out of here.' As eventually happened in this case, Ian much preferred to call into the SAS billets and drag men out of bed to gain his information over a cup of coffee, or something stronger.

In the summer of 1990 Phoenix was told he was being moved back to Belfast, to headquarters. Over the next three years he would learn about the politics of power. His gruffness might have been mollified by experience in TCG(S), but in his new posting his indignation at what he saw as mistaken policy would find ample new targets. In November 1989 the new Secretary of State for Northern Ireland, Peter Brooke, had made a speech in which he had said that the government had to accept that the Provisional IRA could not be militarily defeated, only contained. He went on to say that if the Provisionals abandoned violence the British would be 'flexible and imaginative' in their response. Shortly after this speech, the operational restrictions that Phoenix had complained about were tightened, limiting the use of HMSU and SAS units. After Loughgall and Drumnakilly, the government had become cautious, worried about 'shoot-to-kill' accusations. But there were other, more expedient, reasons for the changing political climate. The British government had started making behind-the-scenes moves in an effort to reach an accommodation with the Provisional IRA.

At the same time, elements in the intelligence services were attempting to implement a strategy aimed at giving BOX a new dominance in counter-terror operations, bypassing the RUC. It was a strategy that Phoenix believed could threaten the integrity of police operations.

Chapter 8

Battles for Belfast

(1990–1992)

A new Belfast had sprung up in the years that Phoenix had been in TCG(S). The old Victorian slums of red-brick row houses and narrow streets crouching under the mills had all but vanished by 1990. The nineteenth-century working-class areas like the lower Falls, with their two-up, two-down houses, had been cleared away and replaced by developments of bright new homes with small gardens, indoor toilets, and three or four bedrooms each. The names of the streets were often all that was left to remind people of where they were. Those, and the political and sectarian passions which still erupted with deadly regularity into bloody violence.

However, the city's Catholic population had also undergone many changes during the 1980s. New anti-discrimination legislation gave them greater protection than ever before in the workplace. More Catholics were moving up into the middle class. Wealthy areas such as the Malone Road in South Belfast, once a mainly Protestant domain, were gradually transformed as the new Catholic middle-class families bought homes there in increasing numbers. Sinn Fein retained its grip only in areas of the city where unemployment remained high. However, it was aware of the social and economic changes that were affecting Catholics. Its vote had remained static since the mid-1980s. Some of its leaders had begun to question the wisdom of their committment to violence, particularly in relation to its political prospects in the Republic of Ireland.

Still, it seemed that no amount of slum clearance and geographical mobility could get rid of the Provisional IRA, or its loyalist rivals. The PIRA's Belfast ASUs that stalked the city in the early 1990s contained many new names, and a few old ones with which Phoenix would have been all too familiar from his previous experience. While Belfast looked brighter, more modern than ever before, with its rash of new homes and glittering shopping malls such as Castle Court, the Provisionals still retained control over the pockets of the city needed to pursue their goals. Not only that, but the city's economic resurgence offered tempting new targets for PIRA's bombing teams. The Provisionals were determined to show that, in spite of appearances, in spite of all the talk about old wrongs being righted and old grievances addressed, the city would never be free from death and destruction until their aims were met. Or, as Phoenix would have said, until they were defeated.

However, the British government had already ruled out this as a possibility. It was set on a course of containment leading to eventual accommodation with Sinn Fein, PIRA's political wing. Already, the British had begun to lay the foundations of a strategy aimed at bringing the Provisionals in from the cold. In October 1990 a representative of the government met with Martin McGuinness, a leading member of Sinn Fein who was also on PIRA's ruling body, the Army Council. The police believed he was in overall charge of the Northern Command, which ran PIRA's armed campaign in Ulster. McGuinness was told that the government wanted to reopen old lines of communication with PIRA. Though this did not influence the Provisionals to show restraint in their campaign, it did mean that the British authorities were more reluctant to use SAS units in countering PIRA violence. A month after the meeting, Margaret Thatcher was ousted from the leadership of the Conservative Party, replaced by John Major. The leadership change gave the search for a political accommodation new impetus, both in public and in private.

While such machinations went on behind the

scenes, Phoenix and his fellow officers were as usual dealing with the day-to-day reality of paramilitary killings and attempted killings. Soon after he arrived back in Belfast, Phoenix – now stationed at Castlereagh, in the east of the city – became acquainted with H, a leading PIRA activist in the city. H's ASU specialised in booby-trap bombs. Fortunately for the police, one of its members, a man whom they knew as 'Carol', was an informer.

Thanks to 'Carol', the police learned of a plot to murder an off-duty UDR man in which H's team was involved. An under-car booby-trap bomb (UCBT) was to be used. The UDR man lived in a small town in North Down. On the night of the expected attack, H and another PIRA member were in a car stopped by a police patrol near the town. Nothing was found when the car was searched, but the incident probably deterred the ASU from making a second attempt.

Two months later 'Carol' informed the police of a new target for the PIRA bomb team – a part-time policeman who lived in a village south of the city. The attack was scheduled for 1 November 1990, and was to take place at the shopping centre where the policeman worked. According to Ian, the Provisionals were, however, 'spooked by a worker at recce stage' and so abandoned this attempt as well. Undeterred, H's team – including 'Carol' – tried again the next day. When they arrived at the shopping centre, police observed H and a confederate, P, drive into the loading-bay where the target parked his car. Noted Phoenix, '[P] got out of the car with a UCBT in his hand and was in the process of planting it when the anti-theft alarm was activated. After some panic, he stuck it under the car and ran to his getaway car then off at a fast rate of knots out on to the main road to Belfast.'

On 19 November, Phoenix met with officers in B Division to discuss the way forward in relation to 'Carol', and the kind of operations in which he might be involved. The police needed to consider how best to use the kind of information that in the long run would save lives.

The police discovered an arms hide used by H's ASU. An HMSU squad was sent racing to the scene with orders to arrest anyone found in the house. According to Phoenix, 'On entry, they found [H] and [P] in an upstairs bedroom with gloves lying beside them. In an opposite bedroom they located a UCBT which apparently had been thrown there by the intrepid two when police entered the house. In the loft was another UCBT and a 9-mm handgun.' H and P were arrested and charged with possession of explosives and weapons.

Five days after this Phoenix's unit uncovered another arms hide, at the Whiterock Leisure Centre. It was part of a resupply that had come into Belfast. A Provisional IRA car had been driven from a hotel in West Belfast to the leisure centre, where it was under observation by 14th Intelligence. It was believed to be transporting weapons to a new dump. Det. were ordered to withdraw, and a HMSU squad burst in through the front and rear entrances. They found two AK-47 rifles, a 9-mm pistol and 600 rounds of ammunition. Two PIRA activists were arrested.

On 13 November Ian had to bury a friend and colleague – Davy Murphy, an RUC man. Like Phoenix, Murphy had loved hunting, and the two had gone on several duck-shoots together. On 10 November Murphy and another RUC man, Thomas Taylor, along with two civilian friends, Norman Kendall and Keith Dowey, were wildfowling in Castor Bay, near Morrows Point, Lough Neagh. They were ambushed by a group of Provisional gunmen. Their bodies were found at 2.10 p.m. All of them had been murdered.

After funerals like this Ian would go home to Susan, saddened by the waste of life but in a mood of counting his own blessings. The couple would discuss what they would do if such a disaster were to hit them. Ian would say, 'Well, if anything ever happened to you I would just turn into a hermit with my dogs.' Susan's reply was often 'I don't know what I would do. I just know that I would be lost – there would be no point to life without you.' In his usual matter-of-fact manner Ian had it all planned for Susan, and he often repeated the plan, which gave him comfort: 'You'd be OK. You would just travel and keep those Sagittarian feet from itching.'

As 1990 came to an end the Provisional IRA called its first cease-fire in fifteen years. It lasted three days, over the Christmas period. In part the Provisionals were responding to signals from their secret contact with the British government. Interviewed in the *Belfast Telegraph* as the last hours of the brief truce ticked away, the Northern Ireland Secretary of State, Peter Brooke, said it was time for 'new thinking about difficult issues, re-analyses of positions and goals, and re-evaluation of the validity of traditional aims in the context of the 1990s'. As 1991 began, rumours started to circulate about the possibility of the Provisionals bringing their armed campaign to an end. Paradoxically, this made them more dangerous than ever, as they now needed to demonstrate their continued commitment to political violence – and the more spectacular that demonstration the better.

Because of the political restraints that were being imposed upon the use of SAS units, Phoenix was finding it more difficult than ever to deploy them, even when he was convinced they were necessary. Before the PIRA truce, the police learned that an ambush was planned on an RUC patrol. Ian requested the use of the SAS. Phoenix's senior officer, told him 'he agreed in principle with the deployment'. However, after consultations with another chief superintendent, the officer reversed his decision and said that the SAS could not be used. In the event, they were not needed, as the PIRA ASU did not materialise and the attack was called off. But it would be an increasingly common pattern in the 1990s – decisions would be taken, then reversed because the police were under growing political pressure to avoid 'shoot-to-kill' incidents which might jeopardise the back-door diplomacy between the Provisionals and the government. In fact after 1990 the chief constable of the RUC had to give his personal approval before the SAS were deployed anywhere in the province.

Before long Phoenix would have another, much more serious, dispute with his senior officers, over an issue which struck at the very heart of Special Branch operations – the protection of sources. 'The first priority', said a colleague of Phoenix's, 'is to protect your source. The first question you ask about any operation is, Can it be carried out without compromising your source?' He cites a poem that Phoenix liked to quote by the Chinese general Sun Tzu:

> What enables a wise
> Sovereign or good general
> To strike and to conquer
> And to achieve things beyond
> The reach of normal men
> Is foreknowledge.
> Foreknowledge comes only through spies.
> Nothing is of more importance
> To the state than the quality of its spies.
> It is ten thousand times

Ian arranged a parachute display for a charity garden party with the proviso that the jumpers arrived with a bottle of Black Bush in their flying suits. He promised the glasses if they safeguarded the whiskey.

At peace in the wilds with gun and dogs – resting to look over the Irish Sea to Scotland.

The wine labels which Ian treasured on the crate of personally labelled wine presented to him by his friends in the SAS. Although he couldn't help commenting 'Nice labels, rotten wine'. He often said 'Life's too short to drink bad wine'.

DET. SUPER   IAN PHŒNIX

WHO DARES WINS

W.O.s' and   Sgts' Mess

22 SPECIAL AIR SERVICE REGIMENT

Vin de Table de France

GEORGES MONET

MIS EN BOUTEILLE PAR S.B.V A 78270 FRANCE

75cl℮   *Product of France : Produit de France*   12% VOL.

R

The devastated Loughgall police barracks after the IRA bomb had been detonated. It injured the volunteer policemen whom Ian had admired for their courage.

Dead IRA men after Loughgall.

'The Cap'n' with his colleague Bob Foster who died with him on 2 June. The hat was a farewell present from his team in TCG (South).

The last photograph taken of Ian by Susan. He is in the garden that he loved to tend and feeding his favourite hunting dogs, Finn and Bumbles.

The final picture of Ian and Susan with her parents. Five years after this photograph, Susan had lost all three of her loved ones.

Ian and Susan back in his favourite Malaysia. Photograph taken by their daughter on her twenty-first birthday in Singapore.

Ian opening his last good wine for those who made the trek to the beach after the final barbecue.

NEWS LETTER

SATURDAY, JUNE 4, 1994   **ULSTER EDITION**   EST. 1737 PRICE 30p (IR 40p in Eire)

EUROPEAN ELECTION

1 PAISLEY *Vote*

Smash The IRA/Sin Fein Conspiracy

Published by R.J Baggs, Election Agent, Hill Street, Ballymena

Their vital work will go on says RUC chief Annesley

TRIBUTES TO THE HEROES

D/Chief Insp D Bunting

THE names of all the victims of the Chinook helicopter tragedy were released by the authorities last night — as anti-terror chiefs assessed how to recover from the "catastrophic" blow caused by the disaster.

By PAUL CONNOLLY

Strict new travel guidelines for security chiefs are now expected in a bid to make sure entire tiers of the security services can never again by wiped out in a single incident.

As the RUC's top brass paid tribute to the Special Branch "heroes" who perished on the Mull of Kintyre, the Armed Forces and Northern Ireland Office released the names

D/Insp K Magee

D/Supt P Davidson

D/Chief Supt D Conroy

D/Supt I Phoenix

A/CC B Fitzsimons

D/Supt R Foster

D/Chief Supt M Neilly

D/Insp S Davidson

Chinook disaster

Boeing Chinook Helicopter
- Fuselage length: 51 feet
- Length inc rotors: 99 feet
- Fuselage width: 12.5 feet
- Max speed: 159 knots
- Max passengers: 44
- Entered service: 1961
- Radar: None

Chinook slams into 1,405ft Beinn na Lice peak

Road

Fatal route

Fort George

Inverness

Intended route

Glasgow

Kintyre

RAF Aldergrove

Mull of Kintyre lighthouse

RAF Chinook carrying Ulster security chiefs

NEWS: Jim Peel

Chinook victim 'committed to freedom and fairness'

Poignant scene: The remains of the security force personnel come home.

Ian's champagne funeral

EXCLUSIVE
By Rosie Cowan

■ Helicopter victim's widow tells of her '28 year love affair'

THE WIDOW of one of the Chinook helicopter crash victims has told of her 28-year-old love affair with her husband.

Susan Phoenix saw she who deeply touched by the fact that more than 1,500 people came to her husband Ian's funeral and by the 500 cards and letters she received.

Detective Superintendent Ian Phoenix was one of 10 high ranking Special Branch RUC officers who died on their way to a key anti-terrorism conference in Scotland on June 2.

All 29 people on board the Chinook, including nine senior Army officers, six Northern Ireland Office staff and four RAF crew, were killed when the helicopter ploughed into the Mull of Kintyre mountains.

Mrs Phoenix (45), remembers with pride the warm, generous man who lived to serve the community irrespective of religion.

She told of the champagne...

The 51-year-old former paratrooper, who loved life to the full and intended to take the family on expedition to Vietnam and Borneo this Christmas.

And she revealed how she wept uncontrollably when she heard a radio report of the crash while driving home alone, not long after leaving her husband at RAF Aldergrove to board the Chinook.

Love

Mrs Phoenix also visited the crash site with the couple's two children, and praised the kindness of the local people.

"I knew him for 28 years and was married for 26. It was a 28-year-old love affair," said the Englishwoman who met her Donegal-born husband when she was an Army nurse at Aldershot.

"We were as much in love now as we were then. I always... always got excited when he was coming home.

"The night he died I left him to Aldergrove and then had dinner with my daughter. We were giggling about using his credit card when he was away.

"I heard the radio report as I was driving home alone and I was just hysterical. I can see his credit station and demanded a phone.

Fairness

Mrs Phoenix recalls her husband's generosity of thought as well as deed.

"Serving his country was very important to him. Politics and religion didn't matter, freedom and fairness did," she said.

"He was always prepared to give anyone a chance. I remember us picking up an Australian hitchhiker who was an IRA sympathiser and Ian brought him home for dinner to talk to him.

"He loved the good life, good food and wine but he always wanted to share everything. Ian mixed people not possessions.

"When we got the Sunday joint on he'd be thinking who we could ask round to share it...

...dried to drink had wine which is why we decided to drink champagne at his funeral.

"He was full of fun and always on the go. He was very fit and wanted to take us all out to the Far East at Christmas to some of the places he'd served as a Para.

"He ran the first Belfast marathon and had a gym in the garage. I don't think he could have stood getting old and sick."

Mrs Phoenix says she was comforted by the letters which arrived from friends all over the world in the aftermath of the disaster.

"I never realised how comforting letters could be," she said. "I want to thank everyone who wrote. Every letter has a special meaning for me.

"She says she does not think about the cause of the crash but prefers to think of it as an Act of God.

"I knew he would have wanted me to go to the site and I also found the home-coming service very moving.

"As a young nurse, I'd seen Ian jump out of a Hercules so many times, and I was somehow right by body when it came back to the..."

Ian Phoenix: 'Committed to freedom'

The *Belfast Telegraph*, 1 July 1994.

The *Campbeltown News*, July 1994.

RUC widow's praise for people of Kintyre

THE WIDOW of one of the victims of the Mull of Kintyre Chinook disaster has paid a moving tribute to people of the area.

Mrs Susan Phoenix lost her husband, 51-year-old Detective Superintendent Ian Phoenix - an experienced RUC officer and former paratrooper - in the crash back in June.

In an open letter, Susan Phoenix, from Larne, said she has been 'overwhelmed' with the 'love, comradeship and human concern' shown to her family since the death of her husband.

She continued: 'The people of the Mull have been a tower of strength. I have felt so guilty arriving at the lighthouse with groups of friends, but we have always been welcomed with love and open arms by everyone which. very special people indeed.

'The love and support offered to us by Roddie and Jennifer...

Detective Superintendent Ian Phoenix

Tributes for the man who lived life to the full

Colleagues of detective superintendent Ian Phoenix carry his coffin. 24327

WIND and rain lashed Roselawn Crematorium on Thursday for the final farewell to a man of "courage and conviction".

Detective Superintendent Ian Phoenix was one of the security elite who perished in

in a nearby field to ease congestion on the roads and local people stopped to watch the

A lone piper leads the coffin bearers to Roselawn. 24326

The *Larne Times*, 16 June 1994.

Susan being comforted after the first memorial service on the site of the Mull of Kintyre crash. With (from left to right): Rev. Roddie McNidder, Stella Rimmington (MI5 Chief), Sir Hugh Annesley (RUC Chief Constable), Group Captain Roger Wedge (Senior Royal Air Force Officer N.I.) and their wives.

The cairn erected to the memory of all those who lost their lives on the Mull of Kintyre, 2 June 1994.

Obituary, *Belfast Telegraph*, 4 June 1994. **PHOENIX. IAN** – As a result of an accident on the Mull of Kintyre Thursday June 2nd loving husband and father, friend to the world. Too big a man to fit on one small page. Airborne to the end. Funeral arrangements later. Family flowers only. Donations in lieu to the Northern Ireland Deaf video unit.

Cheaper to pay the best
Spies lavishly than even
A king's army poorly.

'Carol' was certainly one of the Special Branch's best
spies in 1991. On 24 April he forewarned the police
of a possible attack on an off-duty policeman in East
Belfast. This allowed the police to establish an OP
on the threatened man's home, and an HMSU unit
was placed in the house. However, the target began
to suffer such stress that he went to his doctor and
compromised the whole operation by explaining to
the doctor why he was under stress. Fortunately the
Provisionals abandoned the plan.

Three months later a more serious situation arose
when 'Carol' came to the police with information
about a planned attack on a pub frequented by
off-duty members of the British army. At 3.20 p.m.
on Monday 22 July two weapons were moved from
their hide to the Whiterock Road. Said Phoenix, 'I
assessed that there was an operation on for later in the
evening and accordingly briefed TCG staff, HMSU
and HQ to recce [. . .] bar and plan for a last-ditch
option should plans go astray and the ASU reach the
target.'

Ian made it clear what he thought the best option
was: 'intercept the team once sufficient ASU members
were present, either mobile or static'. At 5 p.m. he
received information from 'Carol' which implied that

the pub operation was on. This was confirmed by 'Carol'.

At this point Phoenix informed a senior officer about the police options. 'As usual,' commented Ian, 'he took the wrong conclusion and thought we were going to have the ASU shot.' Two senior officers then arrived at Phoenix's office, he said, 'to ensure I complied with their directions'. Meanwhile, he and Detective Superintendent Bill Gwilliam tried to explain to a senior officer 'our reservations as to the stopping of the vehicle too soon'. The vehicle driven by the suspects was to be stopped against their advice. As a result the vehicle and weapons were recovered but only gun couriers were arrested. In Phoenix's own words, 'In total, we may have compromised a source and failed to get the real gunmen, thereby allowing them to continue killing. This was passed to [the chief superintendent] that the HQ decision was in fact sanctioning further deaths.' The next day Phoenix noted 'the sombre mood' in the office, due to 'lack of positive direction and confidence in their TCG staff'. He and his colleagues were also concerned about the fate of 'Carol'. They had every cause to be.

A surveillance team was tasked to watch 'Carol's movements. On 8 August he was told by the Provisionals to go to Connolly House – a Sinn Fein office on the Andersonstown Road in West Belfast. It was assumed that he was to be 'debriefed' by the Civil Administration Team – the Provisionals' much feared internal security unit. The surveillance team was on the spot and observed him leaving a short time later. He went across the road to the Busy Bee shopping complex. The surveillance team reported back to TCG Belfast that 'Carol' was in the supermarket. They were mistaken. The informer had been snatched from the Busy Bee car park, and whisked to a flat in nearby Twinbrook. There he was guarded by two Provisionals who were awaiting the arrival of the CAT interrogators.

Fortunately, and quite fortuitously, a helicopter was passing over the roof of the block of flats where 'Carol' was being held. Meanwhile an army foot patrol was observed outside. According to Phoenix, 'This caused the captors to panic' and they untied their prisoner, expecting the security forces to arrive at any moment. 'Carol' did not wait to see if he would be saved. He flung himself head first through the bathroom window of the flat and plunged two storeys to the ground, landing on his head. A concerned resident rang for an ambulance, which arrived on the scene rapidly, conveying the semi-conscious man to the Royal Victoria Hospital.

When he came round he gave the nurse the number of his police contact. But when she rang the police did not respond, suspecting a set-up. Local police arrived and listened to his story, and before long he was in protective custody. Sheer good luck had saved him from the fate of dozens of other alleged informers who have suffered torture and brutal death at the hands of PIRA's security team. But the whole episode served to justify Phoenix's misgivings about the hasty interception of the pub ASU a few weeks earlier. 'Carol' had been saved, but a valuable source of information on the inner workings of PIRA in West Belfast had been lost due to unnecessary conflicts and the lack of foresight of some senior RUC Special Branch officers.

Not only that, but an operation on a Provisional IRA hide had been compromised. The hide was located in the ceiling of a toilet for the disabled in Andersonstown Leisure Centre. (Leisure centres seem to have been a favourite PIRA location for storing arms and explosives.) PIRA then took explosives that were in the hide, put them in a plastic bag, and hid them in the ceiling of an adjoining toilet. By now, however, it was too late. The RUC raided the premises and recovered the contents of the hide.

As for 'Carol', he was moved to a safe location in Britain. However, he is known occasionally to revisit his old haunts in the city, in a dangerous act of defiance of the Provisional IRA, which has yet to settle old scores with him.

A couple of especially dangerous gunmen had become active in the Provisionals in the previous year, and had carried out several murders of policemen in broad daylight in and around the heart of downtown Belfast. Two RUC men had been shot in the back of the head and killed while passing through security gates at the foot of the Falls. Another had been killed in the city centre when fired on at point-blank range as his car pulled up at security gates. The RUC had identified one of PIRA's top killers in Belfast as Peter Lynch, and suspected him of involvement in these shootings, as was Michael Bennet, nicknamed 'Skin'.

After the arrest of Lynch in a shoot-out in Belfast, the officers involved told Ian that they were taken aback at Lynch's ferocious hatred of them. Even as they staunched the flow of blood from the wound in his leg – in effect saving his life until the ambulance could reach him – they said he kept up a non-stop stream of curses, calling them 'fuckin' black bastards' and other obscenities. Ian told Susan he felt it was yet another illustration of just how naïve the British government were in thinking that they could negotiate any kind of agreement with people who thrived on a continual diet of propaganda and hatred.

During the summers in recent years Ian had managed to relax with another example of what he described as 'a good idea at the time' – he and Susan had had the bright idea of buying an old ferry boat in partnership with their friend McStash. Like so many of their previous 'good ideas', it turned out to involve a lot of hard work, painting and labouring on a thirty-eight-foot wooden hull. In between the work they all enjoyed some fishing trips and picnics along the choppy coastline of East Antrim.

The friends met several problems with their anchorage in the shelter of Larne Lough. One young police constable, who was a keen diver, recalls his first meeting with Ian. Chief Inspector Phoenix walked into the ops room and said in his usual gruff voice, 'Do you dive?'

'Yes, sir.'

'Well in that case come with me after work!'

So another friend was made, with one very nervous constable quickly discovering not only that Ian's bark was worse than his bite but that a lot of fun was to be had doing some unusual after-hours 'work'. The resulting dives to rescue the mooring and anchor chain from a murky, current-filled Larne Lough were hilarious scenarios. There were two divers – one professionally trained like the constable; the other self-taught but with lots of high-tech gear which never actually got used – and the constable recalls how the chap with the space-age diving equipment spent most of his time inflating his drysuit and floating like a massive balloon around the surface, while Ian almost drowned himself hauling the other, less well-equipped, diver in and out of the water. Susan simply remembers sitting on deck pouring drinks and making sandwiches amid a lot of laughter.

On 9 September 1991 Phoenix received his yearly appraisal from his senior officers. In that year he was giving it more thought than usual, as he had his eye on possible promotion. However, he was to be disappointed. He noted getting a 'reasonable' write-up from one senior officer and a 'good write-up and gradings' from another, Chief Superintendent Brian Fitzsimons. But, in spite of his record, there was no mention of any promotion. His willingness to challenge authority and to criticise its decisions in an outspoken manner was still proving to be a liability. He lamented to Susan, 'I should learn to play golf, for that's where most of the promotions are being made these days – on the golf course.'

His worst fears were confirmed three months later, when he was officially notified that he was not being promoted. Not only that, but he was also questioned about allegations that he was doing other work in police time. The allegations concerned a shop which sold specialist equipment for the deaf in the seaside town of Bangor.

Since 1988 Phoenix had become more deeply involved in his wife's work with the deaf community in Ireland. His own hearing had begun to deteriorate significantly, due to years of being exposed to gunfire and explosions, so he had learned to appreciate the problems deaf people faced in their everyday lives. Susan had also begun working on a PhD at Ulster University, and he had helped her draft proposals for a European-funded training programme for deaf youths. They had been working on the proposals late into the night with his wife's friend Gloria, and submitted the project to several committees, only to have it turned down – mainly because of a lack of cooperation from a number of groups in the deaf community. Phoenix would often compare his wife's having to combat petty rivalries in different bureaucracies with his own problems in the police force. His favourite joke became, 'If you want to do something, do it yourself. If not, form a committee.' He was instrumental in helping her to complete the first survey of deafness in Northern Ireland. Initiated by the Dungannon Development Agency, it had led to a conference on deafness held in the Europa Hotel – which donated free facilities – with specialists in the field coming from England to take part. Ian had attended the conference, during which he stood up and attacked what he saw as the lack of vision among some of the educationalists present.*

In 1990 he and Susan became even more involved in the deaf community when she borrowed £10,000 to invest in the Bangor shop. It was owned by a member of the deaf community whose sister was a

---

* However, Susan had been amused to see her husband at one point acting as the *restrainer* when one of their friends, Louise, the mother of a deaf daughter, became too vociferous during meetings with other parents from all over the country. Ian kept tugging her by the lapel, and saying, 'Keep quiet! Behave yourself!' He took a keen interest in the development of their young deaf friend's education, and Susan and Louise were amazed to watch Ian and the little deaf girl communicate with each other using pidgin sign language and lots of teasing.

friend of Susan, with whom she had worked over the years. The shop distributed text telephones for the deaf in Northern Ireland, but the business was ailing and Susan went into it hoping her injection of cash would help make it profitable, as she felt strongly that there was an outstanding need in the deaf community for such facilities. Her partner in the enterprise was too deeply in debt to supply any of the collateral himself, however. They had agreed that he would make his contribution by working in the shop while she provided the funds. Unfortunately Susan was eventually left holding the business debts and a shop which she did not need and a lease from which she could not escape.

They were left to pay off the bank mainly from Ian's income. In order to cut costs, their daughter put her career in journalism on hold for eighteen months and went to manage the business full-time. The misadventure put an incredible strain on the family finances and happiness. At one time it was so bad that they thought they were going to have to sell their home in order to meet the bank's demands.

In spite of these difficulties, the little business did manage to do some good, as Phoenix canvassed among his connections for the installation of telephones for the deaf in many government agencies. This allowed the deaf the kind of access to officialdom that they had not enjoyed before. Other, larger, organisations went on to complete the aims of improving communication access for the deaf population of Northern Ireland.

It was galling for Ian to find not only that was he being passed over for promotion but that a senior officer was suggesting that he was abusing police time. He rebutted the allegations angrily. He explained to his senior officer that, when he could, he would drop by the shop at lunchtime to have a sandwich with his daughter. The explanation was accepted. Had it been a different time he would have seen the funny side to such gossip, given his complete lack of any shopkeeping skills. But Ian looked on it as bitterly ironic that the accusations had come from an RUC officer whom he knew liked to cut his gardening costs by using confiscated fertiliser from Provisional IRA bombs to nourish his flowerbeds. He even had the material delivered to his home in RUC vehicles. This complete abuse of a position of power by a chief superintendent in the RUC disgusted Phoenix. However, he kept his mouth shut about the matter – saving it up for a book he had begun to plan to write on his retirement.

Failure to get promoted, financial crisis and malicious slanders by a petty senior officer were far from the only problems and tragedies Phoenix and his family confronted in 1990 and 1991. In October 1990 his close friend John lost his daughter, who was Ian's son's age, in a car crash in Donegal. Defying orders, Ian crossed the border to attend the young woman's funeral. The death seemed to signal a period of stress that was to last for almost three years.

As far as the Phoenix family was concerned, the potentially most serious development took place in September 1991, and, like his friend's terrible loss, helped them put their financial problems in perspective. A young RUC officer had left his car parked in the Queen's University area of the city. Inside, foolishly, he had left his special-services revolver, and a Filofax. The Filofax contained the names and addresses of the policeman's contacts. When he returned to the car, he discovered it had been broken into and the Filofax and the revolver were missing. It was feared that they had fallen into the hands of the Provisional IRA, who would instantly connect the Hereford addresses with the SAS, knowing well that the regiment's headquarters is there.

Police fears were soon justified. The police were warned that PIRA now had the names and addresses of many police and army officers involved in Northern Ireland undercover work, including those of Ian and Susan Phoenix.*

On 14 September Ian and Susan were informed that the Provisionals might have their address. Phoenix and his family had two options: either move house

---

* The police officer involved was put under such pressure because of his mishap that he later resigned from the force and went to Bible college. The loss of this young policeman from the force was much to Ian's regret, as he had always been fond of him.

or install extensive security. Having only recently finished renovating their home after fifteen years of hard work, they chose the latter course. Susan recalls a visit from two officials who came out to survey the house for the purposes of installing security: 'One of the most distressing things of all was to have two men from the ministry sitting on our couch discussing the angle from which Ian would be most likely to be shot. But it brought it home to all of us just how serious this was.' An elaborate system of security was gradually put in, debated as usual with lots of humour and a grim acceptance of 'the way it has to be'.

In the midst of these woes and anxieties, Phoenix continued to run Belfast operations against the rising tide of paramilitary violence that in the early 1990s was sweeping the North. PIRA was conducting a bombing campaign against Belfast and the North's provincial towns – the worst since the early 1970s, causing millions of pounds worth of damage. In the space of two months, six PIRA bombs went off in the centre of the city, including one on 4 December 1991 containing 1,200 lb of explosives which ripped apart the Grand Opera House, a landmark building where the Phoenix family had enjoyed many plays and operas, causing the cancellation of the Christmas pantomime. It also damaged the Crown Bar, another of the city's historic landmarks, blowing out all but one of its original nineteenth-century stained-glass windows. PIRA payed about as much respect to the culture of Ulster as it did to its inhabitants as long as own objectives remained paramount. Nine days later a 2,000 lb car bomb blasted the heart out of Craigavon, wrecking the RUC station and a nearby primary school and injuring sixty-six people. It left a crater forty foot wide and twelve foot deep.

Meanwhile the UDA and UVF had stepped up their assassination attacks, and by the end of 1991 they were threatening to overtake the Provisional IRA in the killing stakes. (They did, the following year.) But it was against a loyalist hit squad that Ian's unit scored a notable success as 1991 came to a close.

The police became aware of a UVF plot to launch a major attack against a Catholic target on the Falls Road. Surveillance had located a UVF arms dump in North Belfast from which the weapons were to come. A car was stolen for the planned attack and was subsequently covered by surveillance. It was not until over five weeks later, however, that a hit squad set out in the car towards West Belfast. Just before 8 p.m. on 2 December as the car headed up the Falls Road it stalled at the junction of Waterford Street. An HMSU unit quickly apprehended the four occupants, who were caught with two AK-47 rifles, a sub-machine-gun and a handgun, as well as a radio receiver. It seems their intention was to massacre a large group of Catholics standing not far from where the car was stopped.

Four months later another loyalist hit squad was

intercepted as it made its way to its target in South Belfast. This time, when confronted by a Vehicle checkpoint, the gunmen did a U-turn and attempted to escape. When they saw a second police vehicle approaching, they turned into another street and threw a sub-machine-gun and a balaclava helmet from the car. Two loyalists were arrested and their weapon was recovered. Their intended target was unknown. Like many whose lives were saved by the actions of Phoenix and his colleagues, he probably remains ignorant to this day of just how close he came to losing his life.

These arrests took place in March 1992. In July Operation Hastings was launched against a third loyalist squad, which was stalking a target in the area which borders on West Belfast. On 18 July the operation was brought to a successful conclusion when the police intercepted a heavily armed hit squad, comprising of five men armed with Browning pistols, sub-machine guns and a sledgehammer, as they cruised through the empty streets in the early hours of that Saturday morning. One of the gunmen was shot and wounded trying to flee. Apparently their intention had been to sledgehammer their way into their target's home and murder him as he slept. Again the identity of the intended victim remains a mystery, but police suspect that it may have been a member of Sinn Fein. The sledgehammer indicated that the loyalist hit squad was expecting to encounter heavily protected doorways or security barriers, which Sinn Fein members normally install in their homes. The loyalists were later charged with conspiracy to murder.

At around the same time Ian came home with yet another story which disgusted him. A group of local children in West Belfast had found a small Semtex bomb, obviously designed as a UCBT. They had begun to kick it around as if it were a football. 'They were lucky little kids that the detonator didn't explode. So much for the "defenders of the people" who are willing to risk lives in their own area in this way.' The police had eventually arrived and an army bomb-disposal team had rendered the 'football' harmless.

Somewhat more comical was the conclusion of an operation against the IPLO, the day after the 'football' bomb incident. A surveillance operator was covering an IPLO suspect in the north of Belfast when a hostile crowd gathered around him, mistaking him for a child molester. An HMSU squad had to be sent in to snatch the unfortunate policeman to safety.

The Provisional's assaults on the commercial life of the province remained relentless. As the Northern Ireland Secretary of State Peter Brooke's attempts to start inter-party talks floundered in July, it was revealed that compensation claims for damage resulting from the violence were running at twice the rate budgeted for 1992–3. By the end of that month the government had already paid out £24 million pounds in claims – two-thirds of the budget for the entire financial year.

A political impasse seemed to have been reached, and no let-up in the violence was in sight. An atmosphere of grim resignation had settled on Northern Ireland as it endured its twenty-third year of murder and mayhem.

However, a breakthrough which came about in the same month that the grim statistics of the financial cost of the Troubles was released considerably boosted the morale of Phoenix and his officers. E4A had accurate intelligence on the structure and membership of PIRA's upper echelons in the city – indeed, as will be shown in Chapter 9, the entire leadership structure of the Provisionals' organisation, North and South, had been charted. The difficulty now was to catch those who controlled the ASUs in compromising situations. One of the key figures in the Belfast Brigade of the Provisionals was its explosives officer. He had already been identified as being one of the masterminds of the renewed bombing campaign, but proving it was another, more difficult, matter.

Phoenix's surveillance units had knowledge of one PIRA ASU which led them to take interest in the activities around a particular area of West Belfast. On 22 July 1992 two men were followed from the the Lenadoon area of West Belfast. The police watched as, with two other unknowns, they entered a house halfway down a street. The four men then made their way at intervals, in pairs, through the rear door of the house into a house in the next street – St Katherine's

Road. Shortly afterwards, at 8.35 p.m., the police observed a man enter the St Katherine's Road house through the front door, carrying a bag. At this point a decision was taken to raid the premises. The police burst in to find four men, one of whom they identified as the Belfast Brigade's chief bomb-maker. They also recovered bomb-making equipment, diagrams and gloves. All were arrested. The bomb-making classes were suspended – indefinitely.

This was to be one of Phoenix's last operations before he made his next – and final – career move. A month before, in mid-June, he had been informed that he was to take charge of a new intelligence unit which had recently been set up, specialising in certain types of surveillance.

At the beginning of August he attended a series of briefings on the workings of the new unit, and then went to London for meetings with BOX. He was in London until the beginning of September. On the 4th of that month he and Susan left for a small lakeside village in Italy, Trevignano Romano, just outside Rome, where they had rented a house for a few weeks to enjoy a much needed escape from the pressures under which the last year had put them. They were still in debt thanks to the Bangor shop, and still aware that the Provisional IRA was likely to have their name and address. However, the family was resilient, and there was Phoenix's new posting to think about. It was not a promotion but another sideways move.

However, it brought him closer than ever to those who exercised political power in Northern Ireland.

Phoenix's transfer to the new unit came at a crucial moment in the history of Northern Ireland. A concerted effort was under way to convince PIRA to abandon terror as a weapon. It was an effort that involved leading Northern Ireland politicians, both the Irish and the British governments, and eventually the US administration in Washington.

Much to everyone's surprise, the general election of April 1992 had brought the Conservatives under John Major back into power for another term. Major appointed a new Northern Ireland Secretary of State, replacing Peter Brooke with Sir Patrick Mayhew. Mayhew was in many ways the opposite to Brooke. A military man turned lawyer, he was bluff, hearty and very much old-school-tie in his manner. However, the change at the top of the Northern Ireland Office did not lead to a change in the policy that had begun under Brooke of seeking accommodation with the Provisional IRA. If anything, that policy was accelerated. On 16 December 1992 Mayhew made a speech in Coleraine, Co. Derry, in which he praised the nationalist tradition and said that if there was a cessation of violence then Sinn Fein could be admitted to talks. There would be 'significant changes' if violence ended. He also reiterated the Brooke speech of two years earlier, restating that Britain had no selfish or strategic interest in staying in Northern Ireland, but remained there simply because that was the will of the Unionist majority of the population. 'Mayhew has taken leave of his senses' was the comment from the Revd Ian Paisley.

Mayhew's speech was seen as a direct appeal to the Provisional IRA's leadership. On 11 January it was followed up with another speech, in which Mayhew spoke about PIRA's campaign of violence. 'There is no way out,' he said. 'I believe the Provisional IRA leaders increasingly realise this, and many of them wisely want to stop. They face further fruitless years, dragging their children into equal miseries. But they feel driven by their dead and by those "behind the wire". I must tell them that unless they abandon violence there will be more blighted dead, more lives spent behind the wire, and another blighted generation. And they will achieve nothing else.'

Mayhew was not aware that other politicians had already decided to do more than appeal to the Provisionals in public. At around this time the leader of the moderate nationalists in Northern Ireland, John Hume, had made private overtures to Sinn Fein in Derry, his native city. Hume, a former teacher turned civil-rights activist, was one of the most prominent political figures in Ireland, with a reputation that went far beyond the borders of his own country. He wielded influence in Dublin, in Washington, in Boston and in Brussels, as well as in London, where he represented his Derry constituency at Westminister. He had been known since the beginning of his career as a fierce critic of the Provisionals. There was talk that he would be awarded the Nobel Peace Prize.

Phoenix's new work was to involve him in much that would cause him disquiet, as he discovered the compromises that politicians were prepared to make to achieve their agenda. At the same time, as his work brought him closer to BOX, he was alarmed to find out that it too was engaged in pursuing its own agenda, as it tried to position itself so that, whatever the outcome of the peace efforts, it would be the dominant intelligence-gathering force in Northern Ireland.

Chapter 9

Hidden Agendas

(1992–2 June 1994)

The new specialist surveillance unit of which Phoenix was now in control, was based in Special Branch headquarters in Belfast. It worked in close liaison with the government's internal intelligence service, MI5 – or BOX, as it was known. In theory, BOX provided the equipment while the surveillance unit supplied the targets to be attacked. However, as time passed, rivalries would begin to emerge, as well as some distrust, as the two agencies struggled over the control of information.

The new unit was interested in building up a thorough picture of the different branches of PIRA, especially its large financial network, which by 1992 was providing the organization with funds amounting to over £7 million per year, according to police estimates. From 1992 until mid-1994 the information gathered would allow the police to build up an accurate picture of the structure of the organisation's entire leadership, including its financial godfathers. One of the unit's chief tasks was to provide the police with the information necessary to help them undermine that financial network. During that period, the intelligence gathered would also thwart at least one major assassination attempt, and disrupt PIRA's English bombing campaign.

PIRA's chief of staff had been given *carte blanche* when it came to spreading the 'armed campaign' to England. According to a republican source, he had been told to create 'mayhem'. From the late 1980s PIRA activity there increased to levels not seen since the 1970s. This was part of an overall strategy which hinged on the belief that the more damage PIRA could inflict in England the sooner the British government would come to the negotiating table. In April 1992 two massive bombs in London caused almost £1 billion worth of damage – more than any bombing in the history of the Troubles. (*Belfast Telegraph* figures show that the London explosions forced insurance companies to pay out £800 million in damages, while £615 million had been paid in total between 1969 and 1992 because of damage caused by the violence in Northern Ireland.) Three people died in one of the attacks, which devastated the Baltic Exchange in the financial district, while the other was directed against a flyover at Staples corner in the north of the City. Anxious to repeat their performance, the Provisionals planned another bombing in the summer of 1992, but the explosives were intercepted *en route*. Subsequent attempts to set off large bombs in London failed that year, including one involving a tonne of explosives that was aimed at Canary Wharf in the east of the City, but smaller devices made of Semtex continued to disrupt life in the capital and in provincial cities. These too could be deadly, as the people of Warrington, Cheshire, found out on 20 March 1993. Two small Semtex bombs killed two boys, aged twelve and three, and seriously injured five people, one of them a woman who had to have her leg amputated, when they exploded in litter bins in a busy shopping street. A month later, a massive bomb detonated near the NatWest Tower in the City of London, causing an estimated £1 billion worth of damage.

Many of the big bombing attacks were organised from south of the Irish border or from South Armagh. Both presented surveillance problems: the first because it was outside the RUC's jurisdiction, and the second because it had proved particularly resistant to penetration of any kind. But by February 1993, Phoenix's surveillance unit had identified one key PIRA member who was linked to an ASU that was operating in Britain. He was Phelim Hamill. Unusually for the Provisionals, he was an academic – a lecturer in law who in the 1980s had been suspected of passing information to PIRA to assist them in targeting prominent members of the Northern Ireland judiciary.

Within weeks, careful monitoring of the lecturer revealed to police that he was in regular contact with Britain. His contact there was a man with previous form as a PIRA activist – Rab Fryers. In 1985 Fryers had been linked to a mortar-building factory which E4A had uncovered.

Interest in the activities of Hamill and Fryers was heightened when on 24 April a massive lorry bomb exploded in Bishopsgate, London, killing a photographer and causing over £1 billion worth of damage. The RUC were under immense pressure to counter the Provisional's attacks in Britain.

For weeks Ian's unit and BOX had been trying to gain information about Phelim Hamill. A surveillance team had been keeping watch on his home, to no avail, but within weeks of the Bishopsgate bomb they were able to monitor Hamill closely enough to establish that he was in contact with Fryers. Fryers's base was the Bridge of Allen area of Scotland.

On 7 May Hamill contacted Rab Fryers in the Bridge of Allen, via a public telephone in the small village. During the following nights Ian ran the operation against Hamill without pause. However, he was angered to learn that a member of the Scottish police Special Branch, who had been informed of the surveillance operation, had told MI5 about some of the Northern Ireland unit's surveillance. Phoenix was concerned. Experience had taught him that the police on the mainland were easily panicked and tended to move against a suspect too soon, before he could lead them to other members of the ASU. (This had almost happened during the tracking of the Brighton bomber – see Chapter 4.) He gave the Scottish Special Branchman what he termed a 'slight rebuking'.

The operation against Hamill soon ran into other difficulties. In their zeal to get evidence to bring Fryers to justice, the Scottish police took it upon themselves to take the handset of the public telephone, from which they hoped to obtain his fingerprints. They did so by cutting it off from the wires, leaving them dangling. When he found out, Phoenix was beside himself. There was concern that when Fryers found the handset gone he would suspect something was wrong. However, he did not – assuming it was just another, if odd, form of vandalism. As Ian and his men discussed what to do to salvage the operation, British Telecom showed up and quietly repaired the telephone, innocent of the situation around the phonebox. Soon, communications between Fryers in Scotland and Hamill in Belfast were resumed using the new handset.

Throughout June there were almost daily briefings on the counter-PIRA operation in Britain. At one point Ian noted in frustration that there was 'no joy' from their work. During the first week in July, however, the police learned that a courier was due to meet Fryers. Fryers was followed over a period of several days. During this time he took the overnight train from Stirling to London to connect with the courier. Police searched the sleeping compartment after he had vacated it, and detected traces of Semtex on one of the towels he had used. Meanwhile, Fryers had taken the tube to north London, and picked up cash and a car from the courier at Scratchwood Service station on the M1. He drove back to the Bridge of Allen, where he was observed unloading two suitcases.

On 13 July, Fryers made a return trip to London by car and arrived at Scratchwood the following morning. According to Phoenix, the surveillance team observed he had 'something concealed under his coat'. He was quickly arrested, and a Semtex bomb was found in his possession. (His arrest on 14 July was captured on a security camera.) The result was something of an anticlimax. Ian had hoped that Fryers would have been tracked longer, and perhaps have led to bigger fish or other ASU members. But the police in London were not prepared to run the risk of losing him, for fear of allowing another bombing to take place.

It took longer to trap Phelim Hamill. After Fryers's arrest, Hamill left his job teaching in Ireland. The security agencies (and no doubt his PIRA pals) were pleased when he landed a job in an English university. They wanted him in England in the hope that he would lead them to other ASU members.

In January 1994 Hamill arrived in England to take up his new post as a lecturer at the University of Central Lancashire. His new career was fortunately brief, thanks to his other, less public, position as a PIRA bomber. A month after arriving, he was stopped by police at a service station near Wakefield in West Yorkshire. In his car were found seventeen kilograms of Semtex, two booby-trap bombs and a pistol, as well as detonators and timers – enough to make seventeen explosive devices. He was carrying in his wallet a list, written on cigarette papers, of 274 names of possible targets. These included MPs and military installations. At his trial he claimed he had intended to merely bury the material in advance of the Provisional's cease-fire. However, the court did not believe him and he was sentenced to twenty-five years' imprisonment for conspiracy to cause explosions – a sentence which was upheld on appeal eighteen months later.

The break-up of the Hamill–Fryers English ASU had initially involved only two arrests. But, in the follow-up, other ASU members were arrested countrywide. It was a set-back for PIRA operations in Britain. Though the ASUs still carried out some operations – including one at the beginning of October 1993, when three small bombs went off in the Finchley Road area of London, injuring six people in what police described as a 'murderous attack' – PIRA's British operations declined. The organisation was able to mount only one significant operation in England after July 1993. That was when it set off a series of mortars near Heathrow Airport the following March. The mortars were not primed, however, and the action seems to have been intended more to put pressure on the British government than to do actual damage. But, coming just over a month after a successful visit to New York by Gerry Adams, it did more political damage to Sinn Fein than anything else. It provoked cries of outrage – especially from the Irish government, who were trying to nudge the republican movement into the peace process.

Undoubtedly, operations like that which led to the arrest of Fryers, and then of Hamill, made it increasingly difficult for PIRA to play what it saw as its ace – its capacity to bomb Britain – and thus they put pressure on the leadership to call a halt to the campaign of violence. This became clear in July 1994, a month after Ian Phoenix was killed (See Postscript.)

As the Provisionals were mounting bombing attacks on the mainland, the second part of their grand strategy was also in operation. While they were bombing in England, they were talking peace in Ireland. Part of this 'peace offensive' involved contacts between Northern Ireland officials (including the head of MI5 there) and PIRA chiefs like Martin McGuinness and Gerry Kelly. Sinn Fein and PIRA leaders were also in touch with some leading politicians in the North, as Ian's unit learned somewhat by accident.

In December 1992, the media disclosed that the Provisionals were bugging the telephone line of John Hume, the founding member and head of the SDLP, the moderate Catholic nationalist party, and one of Ireland's foremost political figures. Ian had also learned of the extensive nature of the contacts then being established between the Provisionals and leading political figures. He obtained permission to gather intelligence about a number of persons involved in these negotiations. Among the first intelligence that Phoenix's unit gathered was yet more information about the Provisionals involved in political talks.

It was not the first time Hume had spoken with Sinn Fein leaders. In January 1988 he had held a brief series of talks with the president of Sinn Fein, Gerry Adams, during which he had tried to convince Adams that there was no moral or political basis for the campaign of death and destruction being carried out by PIRA. Since Britain had signed the Anglo-Irish Agreement in 1985, it was 'neutral' on the question of Northern Ireland. But Adams's thinking appeared to many to be changing. He was supported by other prominent Army Council members, such as Martin McGuinness. Though generally spoken of in the press as a 'hawk', evidence suggests that from quite early on McGuinness was identified with the movement towards peace within the Provisionals. In 1989 a letter from a leading member of the Belfast Brigade which was smuggled out of the Crumlin Road jail concludes, 'Hoping that this talk of bringing the armed struggle to a conclusion that McGuinness and co. are talking about bears fruit as I've thrown the hands up on at least two occasions. But I've an awful feeling this war is set for at least another decade.' In the event, it would take

another five years – and hundreds more deaths – before
the Sinn Fein leader opened up further talks with con-
stitutional nationalists that would lead, eventually, to
a (unfortunately temporary) cessation of violence.

Both BOX and Ian's unit were aware that there was
emerging within the republican movement a school
of thought which believed that the armed campaign
had run its course; it was leaning towards some kind
of cease-fire, sooner rather than later. On 28 January
1993 that year Phoenix asked a senior civil servant
at the Northern Ireland Office for permission to
increase surveillance on a number of key figures.
It was granted. Phoenix told the official concerned
to 'severely restrict' those who saw the intelligence
gathered as a result.

A month later Phoenix filed a report based on what
intelligence the unit had gathered. He was sufficiently
concerned by what he had found to ask that the report
be passed on to the Northern Ireland Secretary of
State, Sir Patrick Mayhew. On 15 February an official
at the NIO replied, quoting Mayhew as saying, 'I am
very interested in this valuable report.'

The Phoenix report had indicated that Sinn Fein
and SDLP leaders had discussed among other things
the Provisional IRA's bombing strategy, which was
aimed at forcing the British government to open up
talks with Sinn Fein. Another topic of conversation
was the general population shift, characterised by the
movement of Protestants to the east of the province.

As the year progressed, Ian maintained a close interest in the talks.

In April it was made public that Hume and Adams had met and were engaging in talks, though neither the extent of the MP's contacts with Sinn Fein nor the full nature of the discussions was revealed.

On 23 May 1993 a 500 lb car bomb devastated the heart of Magherafelt, a mainly Catholic town in the South Derry area, destroying the Ulster Bus depot, one of the town's oldest buildings, and causing an estimated £5 million worth of damage. Three weeks later Phoenix reported that he felt that there was a 'complete coming [together] of minds' between the Provisional leadership and Hume. By July cooperation between the SDLP and Sinn Fein was evidently such that the SDLP withdrew an anti-drugs statement it was about to release when it was learned that a Derry Sinn Fein councillor, Hugh Brady, had been arrested carrying cannabis. Twenty-one grams were found in each of his socks. The SDLP did not want to embarrass Sinn Fein, which had launched an anti-drugs propaganda campaign with Brady playing a prominent role. Brady was later fined £250. He was suspended from Sinn Fein and forced to resign his seat. In 1995 he was assaulted and badly beaten by a PIRA 'punishment squad'. (However, his treatment was in stark contrast to that administered to others the Provisionals accused of being involved with drugs, seven of whom were shot dead that same year.)

The growing understanding between the two parties was risky both politically and physically. Earlier in the year the UDA had denounced the 'pan-nationalist front' and had begun targeting the homes of SDLP members. By 21 September there had been fifteen separate attacks against party members, including two against the home of the party's West Belfast MP, Joe Hendron.

Phoenix was aware of more meetings between Mitchel McLaughlin (one of Sinn Fein's councillors in Derry City), Martin McGuinness and John Hume during July. That summer John Major's government was manoeuvring to gain the support of Ulster Unionists for the House of Commons vote on the Maastricht Treaty. Phoenix was concerned and thought that Sinn Fein was 'more in control of the situation' and might be using Hume. In the event, Major did win the support of James Molyneaux's nine Unionist MPs, but denied doing a deal. Hume was seeking a meeting with the Irish Prime Minister, Albert Reynolds, who appeared to want to claim credit for the agreement. The SDLP leader cancelled a visit to President Clinton in order to have another meeting with Adams.

John Hume was to see Reynolds on the 19th and then was off to London to talk with Major, after which he was scheduled to meet with Adams. Eight days later Phoenix learned that his surveillance of Sinn Fein was being officially curtailed – it was said because of operational difficulties. However, Phoenix commented that it was being done 'most likely for political reasons', thanks to pressure from the Northern Ireland Office and London. Ian voiced his concern that there had been a complete lack of condemnation from Hume in relation to PIRA's recent bombings and attacks. He felt that the government was being particularly naïve in its negotiations with Sinn Fein. He told Susan that it made him cringe when he thought of the discussions which must be taking place. He felt that they should be talking to the moderate nationalist party more seriously, rather than to those who were only steps away from the gunmen. However, the British government continued to take a positive view of the contacts, and the continuing discussion between Hume and Adams did help produce a dramatic, if short-lived, change shortly afterwards.

At the beginning of September 1993 a US delegation led by former congressman Bruce Morrison arrived in Belfast, whereupon the Provisionals suspended their campaign of violence for a week. Morrison met with senior Sinn Fein officials, and held talks with Adams. Since the election of President Clinton – to whom Morrison was politically close – the USA had been playing an increasingly important role in Northern Ireland. Clinton had originally supported the appointment of a US 'peace envoy' to go to Northern Ireland to help get negotiations started, but for the first six months of his term of office he was content to watch and gather information as to what was happening before making any larger commitment. The Morrison visit was in effect a fact-finding mission on Clinton's behalf.

Adams was confident enough to proclaim on 13 September that his talks with the SDLP leader were 'the only real political initiative in the province'. Twelve days later, Hume announced that his talks with the Sinn Fein president were suspended and that he had prepared a paper outlining the progress that they had made, which would be submitted to the Irish government. He then left for the USA to brief the Clinton administration. Momentum was building up that it was hoped would eventually push the Provisionals towards a suspension of their campaign of violence.

Powerful Irish-American influences were coming to bear on President Clinton to persuade him to play a more active role in backing the Hume–Adams initiative – first by lifting the visa restrictions that prevented Adams from visiting the USA. The previous spring Adams's application for a US visa had been turned down. Edmund Lynch, an American lawyer from New Jersey, was spearheading a campaign in the USA to have the visa restrictions lifted. He was due to visit Belfast from 30 November to 4 December and was expected to meet 'with senior figures in PSF [Provisional Sinn Fein]'. After his return to the USA he was scheduled to meet with Jane Holl, the Director of European Affairs for the US National Security Council, in Washington DC, on 14 December. 'The purpose of the meeting', recorded Ian, 'is to discuss the reasons for the refusal to grant Adams a visa as contained in a letter to the former Mayor of New York, from the President of the United States.' He went on 'Lynch's group are likely to argue against this visa denial on two grounds: (1) There is no credible evidence that Adams is participating in IRA activities. (2) Any contact which Adams may have had with the IRA is consistent with his activities to persuade the IRA to give up its military campaign.' Phoenix believed that Lynch would argue that Adams' visa denial is the chief obstacle to the continuation of Irish American support for the Clinton Administration, which was eager not to damage that relationship. Holl told Lynch that Clinton had expressed interest in the Hume/Adams initiative and also advised him that should members of the US congress invite Hume and Adams to visit Washington, the US administration would reconsider its visa denial.

Eventually, an invitation was issued to Adams and Hume to appear before a private foreign-affairs group in New York. Adams was granted a visa and arrived in the USA for the first time at the end of January 1994. He received a tumultuous welcome, and was a major New York media story during the weekend of his visit. On his return Adams argued that the strength of Irish America and the Clinton administration would be added to that of the Irish government and the SDLP – uniting nationalist opinion like never before – if only the armed campaign was ended. The creation of such a pan-nationalist front had always been Adams's goal. He saw it as a means of levering the British out of Northern Ireland. Most observers believe that the strength of the welcome he received in the USA helped put pressure on the Provisional's Army Council to declare a cease-fire six months later.

However, in spite of the Sinn Fein leadership's attempts to distance itself from PIRA violence, police intelligence still linked leading members of the party to the campaign of violence. A constant flow of information updated the security forces on the meetings between Sinn Fein leaders and top members of the military wing. For example, Phoenix met with the head of Special Branch to inform him that there were indications that top Sinn Fein leaders were still assisting PIRA members in operations. The people in question were among those who were in regular political debate with British government officials.

On the 23 October 1993 a PIRA bomb went off prematurely in a fish shop on the Shankill Road, killing ten people, including the bomber, Thomas Begley. PIRA said its target had been the UDA, which had its old headquarters above the shop. This, and other intelligence, made the police extremely sceptical about Sinn Fein's attempts to build a new image as the party of peace and present itself as an entirely separate organisation from the Provisional IRA, for by 1993 surveillance had built up a detailed picture of the republican movement's structure – financial, political and military. It showed considerable overlap between the leadership of Sinn Fein and the Provisional IRA.

Four of the seven members of PIRA's Army Council also held high positions in the political party. Police intelligence identified them as Gerry Adams, Sinn Fein president; Pat Doherty, a Sinn Fein vice-president; the veteran Joe Cahill, who had been in the IRA for most of his life; and Martin McGuinness. The other three Army Council members were PIRA chief of staff (COS) Kevin McKenna, his adjutant, Micky McKevitt, and Thomas 'Slab' Murphy.* McKenna had been COS since about 1987.*

Belfast men were still prominent on the Council, with two of its members – Adams and Cahill – coming from the city. Murphy and McKenna were from Tyrone and Armagh. McGuinness represented Derry City, Doherty Donegal and McKevitt Co. Louth. The fact that Belfast is prominent is because the city is the key to IRA strategy. The movement's

---

* By late 1995 Adams and McGuinness were no longer sitting members of the Army Council. Both of them have denied ever being members of the Army Council. Adams has also rebutted allegations that he was in the Provisional IRA. An ailing McKenna had taken a back seat, with control being effectively being handed over to another Armagh man. Another Belfast man who was known as a hard-liner was elevated to the Council. This came shortly after an Army Council meeting held in Donegal in October 1995, at which it was decided to resume bomb attacks in England.

leaders know that maintaining a strong control of the city's nationalist areas is essential if their campaign is not to be reduced to another futile border war like that of the 1950s. That is not to say that the rural areas are insignificant – especially those along the border across which arms-supply routes run. In this respect Armagh and Louth are particularly crucial for the Provisionals, as shown by the fact that two of the seven Army Council members came from there.

The Army Council sets PIRA's policies and determines the overall direction which it takes. The actual day-to-day running of the Provisionals is in the hands of the General Headquarters Staff, under the control of the chief of staff. Including the COS and his adjutant, this staff consists of twelve members. The COS oversees ten departments, each with its own director. Based on police intelligence, these were identified as Operations, Intelligence, Adjutant-General, Quartermaster-General, Training, Finance, Overseas Operations, Overseas Liaison, Engineering, and GHQ Staff Officers. There is some overlap between the Army Council and the departments. In 1994, for instance, four members of the Council were functioning as heads of department on the GHQ. There were also two separate structures: the Northern and Southern Commands. In 1994 both were headed by Ulstermen – Martin McGuinness was identified by intelligence as head of Northern Command, and Belfast man Dermott Finucane was in charge of

Southern Command. (Finucane had been arrested and convicted of attempted murder in 1981, but had escaped from prison two years later.) Directly under them they each had a deputy. Northern Command had six men in charge of operations, Southern Command four.

Another prominent member of PIRA, Gerry Kelly, was in effect second-in-command to the chief of staff. Gerry Kelly had been an active member of the Provisionals since about 1971. In October of that year he was identified as part of a Provisional IRA honour guard which took part in the funeral of two women volunteers, Maura Meehan and Dorothy Maguire, who had been shot dead by the British army. In 1973 he was arrested and convicted as part of a bombing team which exploded two car bombs in London on 8 March. One person died as a result of the bombing, and 250 were injured. It was the first PIRA bombing attack in Britain. Kelly was regarded as so important that his transfer to a Northern Ireland jail was one of PIRA's conditions for the establishing of the cease-fire negotiated in late 1974. He escaped from the Maze Prison in September 1983 and was rearrested in Holland six years later. He was eventually extradited back to Northern Ireland. By 1994 Kelly was free and part of the Sinn Fein negotiating team which met with NIO ministers after the PIRA ceasefire of 31 August. He was not a high-ranking member of the party, and his role during the talks was described as that of a 'secretary'. He was believed to have been present as a representative of the chief of staff, Kevin McKenna, who maintained a certain distance from the peace process, both during the run-up to the 31 August cessation of violence and after it was declared. Kelly was also known to be very close to Sinn Fein president Gerry Adams.

During this period Phoenix's unit had several notable successes in gathering intelligence about members of the Army Council and the GHQ. These successes did not come easily, and dedication and quick wits on the part of the operatives involved were always prerequisites for achieving the unit's aims. This was true regardless of how sophisticated the technology of surveillance had become. The resulting intelligence was crucial. It provided the police with detailed information on the thinking of the PIRA leadership and, more importantly, it led to the disruption of major PIRA operations and the saving of lives.

Throughout 1993 the complex PIRA organisation was moving slowly, ponderously, towards some accommodation, with the pressure building up to call a halt to its armed campaign. In November there was an initiative to persuade the loyalist groups to call a cease-fire. The police hoped the onus would then be thrown on to the Provisionals and Sinn Fein. The media coverage indicated that Joe English, the head of the UDA, the largest loyalist group, had met with the Revd Roy Magee in November to consider the loyalists calling the first cease-fire.

The Provisional Army Council (PAC) were due to meet the following weekend to discuss the political situation. They planned to meet, and any decisions made would be relayed to the Revd Magee. However, it seems that the loyalists were kept waiting for a reply from PIRA to their suggestions forwarded by Roy Magee. Phoenix commented – prophetically as it turned out – 'Interesting times ahead.'

In spite of the mounting pressure on the PIRA leadership, it soon became clear that the Army Council had decided not to call a cease-fire. Instead, it elected to have a seventy-two-hour truce over the Christmas period. It would be another ten months before it called a halt to the campaign of violence.

In the meantime, the killing continued. If anything, it threatened to get worse. After the Shankill Road fish-shop bombing had left ten people dead, the UDA responded by massacring seven people in a pub in the small village of Greysteel in north Co. Derry. At this time it was believed that loyalists were still attempting to procure weaponry, in view of a recent seizure of UVF arms in Teesport in England. The UVF arms haul was the largest ever seized in England. It's believed comparable had that something fallen into the hands of the UDA, giving it a frightening potential to wreak havoc.

Earlier in 1993 the police had discovered that the

UDA had come into a large sum of money – some £56,000 to be exact. In view of this, the police discussed the possibility of a 'sting-type op against the UDA . . . Explosives would be a carrot to induce them to part with their money.' Apparently this did not go ahead, and the money may have been used to pay for an arms shipment later in 1993.

An earlier UDA money-raising venture turned out less successfully for the organisation. It stole a large amount of cigarettes and drink from a bonded warehouse, and one of its top gunmen, Joe Bratty, planned to sell the stolen goods and use the money to take a vacation in Rio de Janeiro. But, according to Phoenix, 'because of internal UDA thieving of the drink and cigs he has cancelled Rio and bought a caravan in Millisle'. Millisle is a small seaside resort on the north coast of Co. Down – a favourite holiday spot and caravan site for local people.

Bratty was a notorious figure in the Ormeau Road area of south-east Belfast, where he lived. Local Catholics blamed him for many sectarian killings which took place there in the early 1990s, including a massacre at a betting-shop which left five Catholics dead. He survived several attempts on his life in 1992 and in 1993. On 17 October 1993 PIRA took over his mother's house near the Ormeau Road, waiting for him to make his regular Sunday visit to her. When his brother-in-law showed up instead, the gunmen took him into the backyard and shot him. He was lucky to survive the attack.

Bratty once told an *Irish Times* reporter that if Ireland was ever united it would be among the biggest countries in the world! Perhaps his trip to Rio would have improved his sense of world geography. But he never did get to take it – nor, for that matter, to spend much time in his caravan in Millisle. On 31 July 1994 a PIRA ASU shot him dead, along with Ray Elder, another reputed UDA gunman, as they walked across the Ormeau Road. Elder had been arrested in connection with the betting-shop murders two years before, but had subsequently been released without charge.

The rising tide of loyalist violence meant that in 1993 and 1994 Protestant hit squads were killing more people than the Provisional IRA. But for the RUC the Provisionals still remained the number one threat, because of their potential to drastically heighten the level of violence and widen its scope.

Alongside the campaign to disrupt PIRA's English bombing operations, the new surveillance unit was involved in a complex series of moves to undermine the Provisionals' financial network. On 6 May 1992, under the direction of the CID anti-racketeering unit, C-13, based at Stormont, a massive sweep took place throughout businesses, clubs and bars suspected of putting money into PIRA's coffers in the South Armagh and South Down areas. It was one of the biggest security operations ever organised, involving a thousand police officers and soldiers. Thousands of documents were seized for closer examination, and the police also impounded £150,000 worth of pirated videos – some of them pornographic – which were involved in a smuggling ring linked to the Provisionals.

Behind the scenes, throughout 1993 and 1994 Phoenix and his men quietly and unobtrusively conducted their work, though not without some internal conflicts. C-13 had a Special Branch unit attached to it. Phoenix argued that this should be transferred to the specialist surveillance unit, which now had the chief responsibility for the anti-Provisional racketeering operation. This was blocked. He noted, 'I'm sure that petty jealousies were involved. Everybody will lose because of their short-sightedness.'

In 1993 Phoenix discussed 'planned investigations of top PIRA finance people'. Not only did this lead to the identification of the financial structure of the Provisionals and those who controlled it, the Continental banks which were used to process the organisation's money were also identified. Two men Dm and D – one PIRA's financial adviser and accountant, the other chief finance officer – were given special attention. Meetings were known to have been held with contacts in Europe, to discuss PIRA's financial needs.

By end of that year, PIRA's chief finance officer, D, was reported by Phoenix as being 'self-exiled in the south because of our initiatives against Northern Command finance people'. A few days later the police were discussing approaches to some of PIRA's finance officers with the aim of coming to a mutually acceptable arrangement. Within a month Dm had joined D on the other side of the border. '[Dm] is now suicidal,' Phoenix observed, with more than a touch of his sardonic sense of humour – adding, 'He has lost his work as a result of our investigations. We will be sending him a letter shortly offering him a job and money.'

At the beginning of 1994 the Special Branch held meetings with European federal police about the state in which the PIRA bank accounts were held. The meetings were described as being 'very positive and fruitful'. Gradually, PIRA's money flows were being staunched. The amount of damage being inflicted on the Provisionals can be gauged by their response. As Sinn Fein spokesmen talked peace throughout late 1993 and early 1994, their PIRA colleagues were concocting a major assassination plot.

It became apparent that PIRA was targeting a high-ranking CID officer who had headed C-13, the RUC's anti-racketeering squad. He had frequently been interviewed on television during the May 1992 sweep against businesses linked to PIRA's money-raising operations. The Provisionals wanted revenge for the successes the police had achieved against their racketeering operations by killing the man most publicly identified as being responsible for them. If they succeeded, it would be regarded as a propaganda boost for the republicans – proof that no one was safe from them – and a major blow to the morale of the police.

PIRA had identified a vulnerable point on the officer's daily route to work each day. He was a man of very regular habits, who always stuck to the same routine. In Northern Ireland, that could have cost him his life. Immediately, moves were made to counter the murder conspiracy. The option of using the SAS was debated. The head of Special Branch rejected it. It was undoubtedly the political climate that was influencing his decision: he was anxious not to do anything that might upset the hopes of coaxing PIRA into joining the legitimate political process.

A surveillance operation was set up to protect the officer. PIRA's plans kept being delayed, however. But in early February 1994 police assessed there was an increase in activity in the area through which the target drove to work.

Early on 10 February the officer's car left his home with a member of an HMSU hidden in the back, carrying a Heckler & Koch G3 rifle. Not far behind was a brown Transit van that looked like it belonged to building workers – it had a roof rack and was carrying ladders, scaffolding and pipes. In fact it contained a police squad. At 6.55 a.m. the officer approached Belmont Avenue – on time as ever. It was a cold, dark wintry dawn. As the car reached the avenue, a yellow van pulled out in front of it. It was carrying three PIRA members who planned to carry out the killing. They were armed with a coffee-jar bomb, two rifles and a pistol. Immediately, the officer's car turned off and the brown Transit van behind it accelerated forward, cutting off the vehicle carrying the murder squad. The would-be assassins scrambled from their van at the same time as the police jumped out of theirs. One tried to escape by crawling under it. Another – later identified as Davy Adams, the nephew of the Sinn Fein president – made a dash for it along the street but was wrestled to the ground after a chase. There was short, sharp fight, during which Adams received injuries to his leg. It was all over very quickly. Only one escaped – the scout, who had been separate from the actual hit team. He was arrested two years later, during an attempted robbery.

When a senior officer arrived at the scene, he commented to the policemen who made the arrests, 'There's blood on the road.' He pointed to where Adams had been brought down by a vigorous tackle. One of them replied, tongue in cheek, 'It's frosty. We think he slipped.' In view of what the ASU had planned for the senior officer, any would-be murderer would seem to have been lucky to escape with such a minor injury.

Arrested along with Adams were Robert 'Cheeser' Crawford and Paul Stitt. Two others, Gerard Bradley and Patrick Donaghy, were arrested afterwards at the home of the owner of the yellow van, which had been hijacked. Both Adams and Crawford had already served prison sentences. In fact, Crawford had been released in 1990 after serving fifteen years for a double murder. He had been convicted of a brutal sectarian killing in 1975. This had occured during a period in the mid-70s when the Provisional IRA carried out retaliatory murders of Protestants in revenge for the killings of Catholics by the UVF and UDA. The wave of murders continued into 1975; North Belfast being the scene of much of the sectarian bloodletting. On 20 June, an eighteen-year-old Catholic, Anthony Molloy, was shot dead at his home in Ballymena Street, off the Oldpark Road by gunmen claiming to be from the Protestant Action Force – a cover name for the UVF. Two days later, two young Protestant men, Thomas Irvine aged twenty-three and Alan Raymond also aged twenty-three, were standing on Westland Road, which runs between a loyalist estate and a Catholic area. A crew drew up and PIRA gunmen opened fire, killing both in cold blood. One of those convicted of this casual sectarian killing was Robert 'Cheeser' Crawford.

Another prominent PIRA member was linked to the murder bid. In the yellow van the police had found a mobile telephone. One of the officers pressed the redial button, curious to see who it was that had last been in contact with the hit squad. The phone rang at a number that was traced to a flat of someone who was a close friend of many prominent members of Sinn Fein. He met regularly with Gerry Kelly, a prominent member of the Army Council. He was arrested and brought to Castlereagh for questioning. Detectives who were involved in interviewing him commented to Phoenix that he seemed high on drugs, which made him behave very confidently when he was first brought into Castlereagh. However, no charges were brought against him and he was released. He was 'promoted' within Sinn Fein, of which he was a member. Kelly, his confidant, went on to play an important role in the peace talks between the Provisionals and the British government later in 1994.

Adams, Crawford and Stitt were not so fortunate. At their trial, which ended on 18 May 1995, Adams and Crawford received twenty-five years each, and Stitt twenty-two years. The judge described Adams as 'a very dangerous man' and called the plot a 'sophisticated, carefully planned and serious murder plan'. Bradley and Donaghy received shorter terms of imprisonment.

'The tout hunt begins,' noted Phoenix about PIRA's response to the arrests, 'and all involved [in the attempted murder] will be stood down.' He adds, 'Tried to impress upon the authorities the need to highlight the S. Fein role in the operations.' He thought this could be profitably exploited by the police, if handled right – as could the deepening anxiety within PIRA. The organisation was very worried about how its plans had been undone. It was an opportunity to create friction between the Belfast Brigade and the GHQ staff and to 'widen and increase the animosity' they evidently felt towards each other as they sought to shift the blame for the recent débâcle. However, Phoenix curtly notes that his plans received a 'negative reaction' from some senior officers. On another occasion he got the support of senior officers to disseminate intelligence through the RUC press office, but at the last minute key figures backtracked and nothing was done. Phoenix lamented, 'God knows why they promote such indecisive people into positions of power.'

Phoenix had come to expect this. He had long fought for some of the intelligence his unit had gathered in relation to Gerry Adams and company to be exploited to the full in the propaganda war that was being waged against Sinn Fein. He wrote, 'We are in such an important position to influence the destiny of our country but the RUC bosses especially in the Special Branch are incapable of using our strategic position for the good of all.'

By early 1994 the specialist unit had garnered an extraordinary amount of information on the Provisional leadership – including, incidentally, their private lives. But what concerned Phoenix most was the relationship between Sinn Fein and the military wing – a matter he returned to time and time again, in an effort to get the information about their connection into circulation. This relationship went from the top to the bottom of both organisations. That the inner council of Sinn Fein contained four members of the PIRA Army Council – Adams, Doherty, McGuinness and Cahill – indicated that some high-ranking party members were frequently in touch with leading PIRA operators active in the planning of attacks. Then there were the examples at local-leadership level, where gunmen such as 'Cheeser' Crawford and operation planners moved from the party to the PIRA and back again, according to convenience. In most cases the intelligence that this portrait was derived from was concrete, and not based on the word of paid informers.

Ian set up an investigation under the control of his detective chief inspector, who was the liaison officer with the anti-racketeering C-13 unit. He drew up a report showing the paramilitary background of many of those involved in some legitimate community associations and this helped block funds going to the associations with direct paramilitary links. However, most of the information gathered on the paramilitaries and their links lay idle in police files and was never exploited. This was mainly due to political pressure from above, but lack of decisiveness within the police hierarchy about this and other matters was also a factor, according to Phoenix. After failing in September 1993 to get a decision on the use of a particular device, he noted in despair, 'The art of decision-making seems to be a dying trade as far as the Special Branch and the police are concerned.'

In Phoenix's eighteen months running his special surveillance unit there was much to celebrate in the successes which the unit enjoyed. Unfortunately, these successes were marred by several serious disputes, both within the Special Branch and between that organisation and its ally, BOX.

There had been the continuing disagreements between Phoenix and his senior officers about the use of the intelligence on the political situation within Sinn Fein, and the relationship between that party and PIRA, all of which he thought should be exploited. At one point in April 1993 Phoenix learned that there were meetings between Sinn Fein and the SDLP to develop an 'electioneering' strategy – because of the Hume–Adams talks, the former rivals for the nationalist vote were considering a joint approach to dividing it up: something unthinkable a few months before. As a result, there was 'turmoil' inside Sinn Fein, He 'went to see [C] at Stormont to see if it could be circulated to the press'. In the end the police were not allowed to leak any of this to the press, which he thought was yet another missed opportunity. Phoenix concluded that the reason was that it did not suit the political Establishment in London or at the NIO. He strongly suspected that political interference had already forced one major operation directed against a leading member of Sinn Fein to be curtailed, though 'technical problems' were used as an excuse. Phoenix was convinced that surveillance operations in general were being restricted because of political pressure coming from above, so it came as no surprise to him when he was informed at the beginning of September that plans to increase the strength of his unit had been 'put on the back burner'.

He was worried also about the control of information his unit had gathered. Without informing him, one senior officer was allowing others who did not belong to Phoenix's unit to have access to very sensitive intelligence. One of those involved was passing information to a Belfast journalist without having been granted clearance to do so. When Phoenix discovered this he was furious and had a row about certain senior officers' lack of judgement.

A serious dispute arose in April 1994, when there was a complaint from a detective superintendent about the amount of overtime E4A operatives worked on taskings for the specialist surveillance unit. Out of 1,286 hours of overtime worked by E4A officers, 749 of them where for the unit's taskings. This complaint was accompanied by others suggesting that the unit's aims and targets were 'unrealistic'. Two detective chief inspectors attached to Phoenix's unit responded under his guidance with a breakdown of the hours worked and defended the quality of intelligence which they had gathered over a period of fourteen months. During that period, four major operations had been undertaken – three against leading figures in the Provisional IRA, and the fourth directed at the UVF. Two of these operations had brought to the fore six major PIRA players, who had then themselves become subject to surveillance. This had saved the lives of several members of the security forces. The detective inspectors pointed out that if overtime was high it was only because the unit was being forced to try and work within nine-to-five office hours, which was unrealistic, since a large amount of paramilitary activity took place in the evenings and at weekends. RUC managers had to understand that terrorism was not an activity that was confined to office hours. The report suggested that working schedules should be revised to include late and evening periods.

Ian himself responded to the criticism that the taskings set by his unit were 'unrealistic'. He called it 'misleading and incorrect', and pointed out that when he had suggested two of the most important operations these too had been put down as 'unrealistic'. 'These became realistic', he wrote, 'when they were told how to do it.' He also spoke about the low morale within the E4A team that was tasked to carry out operations, and complained that this was made worse by such ill-informed criticisms. 'Their comments', he said of those who had questioned his unit's work, '. . . appear to absolve themselves from management decision by blaming others. Perhaps this is a strategy taught by Bramshill to promising young career officers.' He concluded, 'The targets are all highly motivated terrorists, with intelligence from more than one source indicating their involvement, and for detective superintendents and team leaders to state otherwise is a sad reflection of their commitment.'

The range of Ian's concerns as head of his unit was wide, and did not only include weighty matters of state, terrorism and organisational infighting. He also took it on himself to improve the conditions under which his men and women worked. For instance, he spent a considerable time in 1993 trying to get air conditioning installed in the office, where he felt conditions were overcrowded. He succeeded only after a long struggle with bureaucracy. Throughout 1993 and 1994 there was a problem of a more profound nature which overshadowed these internal disputes, however. It was a crisis that involved not only policing policy but the relationship between Northern Ireland and the rest of Britain. The issue was the role of MI5 in the struggle against terrorism.

On 8 May 1992 the Home Secretary, Kenneth Clarke, announced in the House of Commons that MI5 would take the lead in gathering intelligence to counter PIRA operations throughout Britain, replacing Scotland Yard's Special Branch. In the aftermath of the Cold War, the internal security agency was eager to find new areas in which to exercise its expertise. Phoenix's posting as the head of the new RUC specialist surveillance unit more or less coincided with this change in responsibilities, which was to have an immediate, and for Phoenix unwelcome, impact on RUC operations. For one thing, it ran counter to plans for the decentralisation of intelligence-gathering for which Phoenix was trying to win support. However, there were still more serious issues involved.

There had been a dispute between the RUC and BOX during the running of the mainland operations against an ASU which was planning bombing attacks in London during the early summer of 1993. BOX was concerned as to who was 'running the show', according to Phoenix. Shortly after this, on 4 June, Phoenix was told that BOX's unit T2 wished to have more direct access to his unit's information. This would mean that MI5 not the RUC could effectively take control of intelligence in Northern Ireland. Observed Phoenix, 'They were somewhat surprised at our insistence that it would not be welcomed.' BOX later appeared to have tried to pass it off as a misunderstanding about the issuing of warrants. Phoenix did not believe them, and expressed his alarm to his boss, the head of Special Branch, at the prospect of the police losing control over such a vital source of information. According to Phoenix, 'The boss was adamant that no direct access would be allowed.' However, BOX pushed ahead with its demands, and proved Phoenix's concerns to be well founded.

A few days later, Phoenix again brought up the subject with another senior Special Branch officer. Said Phoenix, 'I expressed my doubts and concerns re plans for direct access from the mainland. He asked a BOX agent to show me the telexes on the subject. During the course of our conversation I told him of my concern of a hidden agenda, in that the phones of MPs, senior civil servants, police officers could be tapped as a means of the future political talks. I realised that it was a fait accompli only if we allow it.' He appended two question marks after this remark. Thanks to the BOX agent's operational experience, he was one of the few members of MI5 for whom Ian had great respect and affection. Ian was always ready to welcome debate and open discussion, and quite happily agreed to disagree with people whom he recognised as having an honest commitment to the future peace of his country.

The 'hidden agenda' that concerned Phoenix related to the government's overall plans for Northern Ireland. The government had held secret talks with the Provisional IRA throughout 1993. Discussion had taken place about what it would require for PIRA to call off its campaign of violence. London would have to agree to declare for a United Ireland, to be introduced over a period of years. Dublin and London would have to commit themselves to containing any loyalist backlash directed against the nationalist community. Phoenix suspected that the British were concerned that any settlement with PIRA – whether on these terms or others – would meet resistance within the police force and among the North's Unionist Establishment. Without the support of the RUC, no settlement could be guaranteed to work. Hence MI5's desire to remove control of some aspects of intelligence from the police and place it in their own hands – so that they would have first access to sensitive information, deciding what and what not to disseminate. That is, they could withhold from the police whatever they chose, and intercept whomever they chose.

The matter became one of the subjects for discussion at the top-secret conference that was held that year at Machrihanish Air Force base near the Mull of Kintyre between 24 and 26 June. The intelligence chiefs took a Chinook helicopter from Aldergrove Airport, Belfast, to spend two days going over pressing problems in the war against the paramilitaries. BOX claimed that it was not happy with the Special Branch's 'passage of intelligence' and 'would willingly put some of their people into support us. Kind of them,' Phoenix noted drily. 'They treat us like thick Paddies,' he observed once to Susan. He was having none of it. BOX's offer was 'resisted by RUC', he wrote. This resistance reflected his determination to maintain police independence.

Phoenix continued to fight BOX interference in or control of police operations, and insisted that restrictions be placed on the dissemination of intelligence his unit gathered. Such moves upset MI5, who expressed concern that Phoenix's unit 'will be independent of them'. Phoenix's objections were not only based on an anxiety about the overall intentions of the British government and its internal security agency: He was always concerned about allowing individuals who were no more than civil servants to interfere in intelligence-gathering operations. He distrusted their judgement. He once wrote in a paper on terrorism, 'There is a continual source of annoyance for those operational agencies who are forced to liaise with civil servants with little or no operations experience or cognizance.' He regarded some of those working for BOX in this light – as pen-pushers who would be more concerned with forwarding political agendas, or their own careers, than with the fight against terrorism, which he saw as the primary role of intelligence-gathering. If such people had access to vital information without police input or control, he feared that they would not necessarily use it for the good of Northern Ireland.

His fears were intensified by a chance discovery in the spring of 1994. During a meeting with BOX, one of their agents let it slip that there were several operations in place about which the police knew nothing – neither the identity of the targets nor the type of intelligence being gathered. 'For all we know,' he once commented to Susan, 'they could be tapping the phone of the Secretary of State or the chief constable.'

When Phoenix was no longer there to oppose the BOX takeover, resistance to it crumbled. Since sometime in 1994 all intelligence information has been rerouted through BOX headquarters in London and is no longer under the control of the RUC. What Phoenix feared has come to pass.

In spite of problems between BOX and the Special Branch, and increasing restrictions on Phoenix's unit's surveillance operations, the intelligence compiled on PIRA had reached impressive proportions by 1994. That intelligence had been used in several outstanding operations which had frustrated PIRA plans, saved lives, and led to the arrests of many activists. Yet, when the time came for promotions to be handed out, once more Phoenix's name was passed over. He had not received a promotion since 1987. In that time, as well as his work with the new unit, he had completed a successful tour of duty in TCG(S), one of the hardest postings in the service, where he had made significant inroads into the East Tyrone PIRA active-service units. His frustrations were evident as he wrote in a private diary that 'I do not fit the SB criteria for promotion. One must be rather ineffective, quite indecisive, and terribly unimaginative.' He added that it was a 'bonus' if you 'play golf with your boss'. It was around this time that he began seriously contemplating retirement. He hoped to look more seriously at international terrorism and to devote some time to writing a book about his life and experience as a policeman.

In spite of Phoenix's fulminations and frustrations, he had a rather good-natured acceptance of life – enjoying his friends and his family, planning holidays abroad, gardening, pottering around their beautiful home during his free time, or taking walks along the pebbly beach with Susan. There, the timeless sounds of wind and sea allowed him to forget the world of terrorism and violent death for a while.

On 26 April 1994 Ian Phoenix was fifty-one years old. As usual, he resisted any fuss being made, preferring just to open a good bottle of wine with a few friends. That year, a close friend, Frances, was celebrating her fiftieth birthday at around the same time. A get-together was arranged at an Italian restaurant in Belfast. A lot of their mutual friends attended – John and his wife, Diane, among them. John and Ian had been close for some twenty years, but especially since the tragedy in 1990 which had taken the life of John's daughter (see Chapter 7). As the evening wore on, Frances lamented about passing the milestone of fifty years. Ian replied, 'Age? Don't worry about age. I can honestly say that if I died tomorrow I'd have no regrets. I've had a marvellous life, I lived it to the full, I have been so fortunate in my family and friends. What's another birthday?'

Earlier that month his brother Joey had died in Blackburn, following a long illness during which he had a heart and lung replacement. Perhaps this had provoked thoughts of his own mortality. In fact, after returning from his brother's funeral, Ian had commented to a close colleague. 'You know, death doesn't scare me.'

Phoenix decided to throw a party on May Day. It began as a plan for a modest Sunday lunch – which meant, by Phoenix standards, a guest list of at least twelve people. It soon expanded, and before long fifty people had been invited. The lunch became a barbecue. The guest list gives some idea of the range of Phoenix's acquaintances. Among the friends were five RUC men and women (ranking from chief superintendent to constable), two RAF wing commanders and their wives, one of whom was a nursing administrator, out-of-work friends, an artist and teacher, several psychologists, self-employed businessmen and businesswomen, university lecturers, shop assistants, an engineer, an FBI agent from America, and at least fifteen children of varying ages. John (the engineer) arrived with a van full of miniature motor bikes to keep the kids amused, but in fact the children had to fight off the adults to get their turns on them.

Phoenix did not normally socialise with police officers, except for a handful of friends and neighbours, but this was to be an exception. The chief superintendent had previously invited Susan and Ian to his home, and Susan told her husband that he should return the hospitable gesture. Phoenix had to overcome his feeling that socialising with the bosses was a form of crawling. Fortunately he liked the officer in question, and the two got on well together.

As the barbecue came to an end, since it was a warm, sunny day – what Ian called a 'white-wine day' – he decided to lead a contingent of friends down to the beach, while others stayed in the garden to sip port and some trekked across the fields to view a small menagerie a neighbour kept on his farm. One of those who accompanied Ian down the steep grassy slope to the shore was a fellow Special Branch officer, Phil Davidson. As they helped two ladies down the slope, Ian remarked to his colleague, 'When I go, this is where I'd like to have my ashes scattered.' Little did they know that just over a month later they would die together on the ill-fated flight to Fort George.

The group struggled down to the deserted shore, with its shifting, sliding drifts of coloured pebbles, and its crags jutting out into the waves. As they settled down on the rocks, suddenly Ian pulled a bottle of champagne and a carton of plastic cups out of his knapsack. 'That'll teach them to skive off from a healthy hike,' he chuckled, nodding back towards the others who had chosen to remain in the garden or take the more leisurely ramble over the fields to the farm. A second later the cork popped and the champagne frothed forth, seething like the surf at their feet. They drank, and looked across the sea towards the coastline of Scotland rising up on the clear horizon.

As they cleared up later that evening, he remarked that it had been a really good day. 'Why don't we organise a breakfast party next time?' he said. 'Everyone will have to arrive on an unusual mode of transport.' He enthused about the prospect of horsemen galloping up to the gate, boats beaching down at the shore, motor bikes roaring up the laneway, and even parachutists dropping down from the sky. Not surprisingly, that was the idea that caught his fancy the most. He went through the summer-house to gaze in the gathering twilight at the lawn and then up at the sky, wondering out loud if a parachutist could land there. He put his arm around Susan and said that it looked like it was going to be a long, hot summer. He was intent on enjoying it to the full.

A few days later he turned again his attention skyward, as a small aircraft flew overhead. It was flown by his son, who was on a training sortie with his university air squadron. 'Good to think that that's our lad,' he said quietly, sharing the moment with his wife. There were tears of pride shining in his eyes. That same weekend they were driving from a shopping mall listening to Radio Ulster when a familiar voice came over the air waves. It was his daughter, doing one of her radio reports. 'She's good, isn't she?' he said, beaming. 'Let's have a glass of wine on the patio and celebrate life in the sunshine. I love you all very much you know.'

She knew. Since February, Phoenix had known that

in June he would be attending a top-secret security conference in Fort George, near Inverness. It would be the second such conference he had attended. As at the conference held the year before, at Machrihanish, he expected there would be a clash between BOX and the Special Branch over control of information, among other things, as well as discussions on the rising threat of loyalist violence and the nascent peace process. He, like his colleagues, was aware, that it was a volatile period. The prospect of peace brought with it its own dangers. The flight to Scotland, in a Chinook, was scheduled for around 5.30 p.m. on 2 June.

The day before, at headquarters, he went over pressing matters. One was the setting up of a computer network at headquarters for the collation of information. Two tenders for the job had been put in – one for £862,000 the other for £1.8 million. Also on the agenda was the recruitment of a new PIRA source. Phoenix suggested he be offered £2,000 to entice him to a first meeting with a handler. After a discussion, this was approved.

On 2 June, at the morning briefing with the specialist surveillance team, intelligence relating to terrorist finance was discussed. A detective chief inspector who was also due to fly to Fort George later that day and was at the meeting asked for some matters to be put off until they came back from the conference. At around 1.30 p.m. a long-time and trusted colleague received a telephone call from Phoenix asking if he could borrow his Barbour jacket. 'I want your best one,' Phoenix said, 'to keep me warm while I go walking in the hills.' He'd planned to do a bit of hiking between conference meetings. The colleague said certainly, and the two arranged to meet for a coffee. The two men had worked together on and off for over sixteen years, and Phoenix was like a father to the younger man. As his colleague handed over the jacket, Phoenix smiled and thanked him. Then he stuck his hands in its pockets and said, 'There's no money in it – it's no bloody good to me!' But he took it anyway, chuckling as he threw it into the boot of his car.

They briefly discussed the PIRA peace moves and how they might be pushed forward. At 2 p.m, as Phoenix left to go home, have lunch and pack for the trip to Scotland, his colleague called, 'Have a good weekend. See you Monday.'

The passengers on the Chinook when it took off later that afternoon included the head of the RUC's Special Branch, Assistant Chief Constable Brian Fitzsimons, and eight other high-ranking Special Branch officers besides Ian Phoenix: Detective Chief Superintendent Maurice McLaughlin Neilly, Detective Inspector Dennis S. Bunting, Detective Inspector Stephen Davidson, Detective Superintendent Philip Davidson, Detective Superintendent Robert Foster, Detective Chief Superintendent Desmond Conroy, Detective Inspector Kevin Magee, and Detective

Superintendent William Gwilliam. There were six MI5 agents on board: J. R. Deverell, M. G. Dalton, J. S. Haynes, Ann James, N. B. Maltby and S. L. Rickard. They were accompanied by a group of nine British army intelligence officers: Major R. Allen, Colonel C. Biles, Major C. J. Dockery, Lieutenant Colonel R. Gregory-Smith, Major A. Hornby, Major R. Pugh, Major G. Sparks, Lieutenant Colonel J. Tobias and Lieutenant Colonel G. Williams.

At 5.55 p.m. – thirteen minutes after the Chinook had lifted off – in RAF Aldergrove they put its passenger list through the shredder. It was a security precaution. At that time the Chinook was just a few minutes away from the fog-wrapped Mull of Kintyre and Beinn na Lice, the hill which rises on its southern tip. The name is Scots Gaelic for Hill of Stone.

Chapter 10

On The Hill Of Stone

(2 June 1994 and After)

In spite of an RAF investigation and report, and an inquest which went on for three weeks, it remains a mystery why it was that at approximately 6 p.m. on 2 June 1994 the Chinook HC2 ZD576 flew at approximately 100 miles per hour into the Hill of Stone on the Mull of Kintyre, killing all twenty-nine people on board – among them Ian Phoenix.

Ian Phoenix's life was devoted to solving mysteries. It ended in mystery. Only what happened shortly before and immediately after the crash can be established with reasonable certainty through witnesses' statements.

At 5 p.m. the Chinook's crew were driven to the aircraft. Flight Lieutenant Jonathan Tapper and Flight Lieutenant Richard Cook were both experienced special-forces pilots. Tapper, who was the captain on the flight, had 2,081 flying hours with helicopters; Cook, who was acting as the handling pilot, had 2,096 hours. Tapper had served in the Oman. More importantly for this flight, which was to take them across the Irish Sea to the Mull of Kintyre then up the Great Glen towards Inverness, he had recently landed the Chinook near the Mull lighthouse, on the H-shaped landing-pad to its north, so he was well-acquainted with the terrain they had to cross. The equally experienced loadmaster crewmen were Malcolm Graham Forbes and Sergeant Kevin Hardie. Twenty minutes later, dressed in orange survival suits, the twenty-five passengers boarded the helicopter for the flight to Fort George. HC2 ZD576 lifted off at 5.42.

Dorothy McVeigh had only been in the garden of her home at Rathkyle, Co. Antrim, for a few minutes when she heard the noise of a Chinook helicopter approaching. 'I looked up and saw the helicopter coming over the top of a tree, very low. It seemed to be just 100 feet off the ground. The noise was almost unbearable as it travelled in the direction of Greystone Roundabout. I could see clearly the passengers in the aircraft, and looking through the windows I could see the sky beyond.'

A minute or so later, a few miles east of Mrs McVeigh's home, in the coastal village of Glenarm, Thomas Palmer heard a helicopter pass close by. 'It sounded to me as if it was hovering or was landing or in difficulty.

There is a hill at the back of our my house, and the sound came from the back of it . . . I stood for a short time expecting to see it, but it didn't appear. We see and hear planes and helicopters all the time. I have seen and heard Chinook helicopters before. This one sounded totally different. I cannot fully explain the difference in sound.'

A few miles further north, in her house in the pretty little seaside village of Carnlough, Ann Tyler saw the Chinook heading towards her. 'I looked out and saw a twin-bladed helicopter flying past my house. This helicopter was low. It was flying in the glen, and I could see the top of the glen over the top of it. The sound of it changed as it passed by my home and I thought it was going to land in a field . . . I moved to the landing and watched it. It flew down, slanting towards Carnlough harbour. It was flying low the whole time. We have had planes and helicopters flying round here quite a bit. I have not seen any as low as this recently unless they were actually going to land . . . The weather here was clear, but the Mull of Kintyre was obscured by mist. Normally I can see the Mull and the lighthouse unless there is a mist.'

At 5.47 p.m. a watch supervisor at Aldergrove Airport reported that the Chinook HC2 ZD576 had left the airport's control zone. 'Bye-bye,' she said. As far as is known, these were the last words spoken to HC2 ZD576. The last words ever heard from the aircraft came about eight minutes later. At 5.55, just as the passenger list was being shredded back at Aldergrove, Flight Lieutenant Tapper called Scottish Military Aircraft Traffic Control Centre at Prestwick Airport. 'Scottish Military, good afternoon. This is Foxtrot Four Zero,' he said. The call received no reply. It remains a mystery (one of the many surrounding the flight) why no one responded.

At around that time, Mark Holbrook and Ian MacLeod, two yachtsmen, were on board a thirty-foot ketch called *Serini* at approximately two nautical miles south-west of the Mull of Kintyre lighthouse. They had just encountered a small fleet of six fishing trawlers.

'We could clearly see the lighthouse and its white perimeter wall,' said Holbrook. 'Visibility at sea level at this time was one mile. There was low cloud obscuring the top of the Mull. This was quite dense and appeared to be following the contours of the land mass behind and above the lighthouse . . . As we approached the first boat my colleague altered course to manœuvre well clear of the first boat and I then took the helm. We then turned the engine on and following several manœuvres my colleague went below. After manœuvring around the fishing vessel, with my colleague below, I then saw what appeared to be a twin-rotor-blade helicopter. I am not aware of hearing it, but I was aware of being drawn to its presence by its thump. I believe the range of the helicopter to be 300 yards. It appeared to be at a height – bearing in mind that my last reference was the lighthouse, which is charted at a height of 91 metres – of between 200 and 400 feet. I did not have to tilt my head to see the helicopter, and I was aware of structures such as what I interpreted as individual panes in the windscreen and the under-carriage structures protruding below the body of the aircraft. The helicopter appeared to be in sunlight. I saw no clear markings and recall the basic colorations as a dull uniform grey or brown. The aircraft was moving in a straight line and in level flight and was proceeding towards what I could distinguish as the cloud localisation covering of the Mull land mass.'

Holbrook continued, 'I remember the aircraft being in level attitude and well below cloud level. At no time while I observed it did it move into cloud cover. I believe that I saw a single flashing light towards the rear of the aircraft which was either white or amber in colour . . . I remarked to my colleague that there was a "helicopter down here to have a look at us", and then returned to manœuvreing around the fishing boats. My colleague later confirmed the time to me as just on or just after 1800 hours . . . I would have held the helicopter in view for no more than five seconds, although this time interval was only set by my attention span. It appeared off my starboard side, although I am uncertain as to the exact heading of my boat at that time, and I saw the starboard side of the helicopter. I estimate my position at that time as being two nautical miles south-west of the lighthouse, north 55 degrees 16 minutes 20 seconds, west 5 degrees 50 minutes 20 seconds.'

During the RAF inquiry, Mr Holbrook was asked, 'At the time that you saw the aircraft, could you see the physical features of the cliffs of the Mull?' 'No,' he replied.

At the Mull of Kintyre lighthouse, the keeper, David Murchie, was getting ready to go off duty. He had five minutes before his replacement, Hector Lamont, arrived to relieve him. 'At approximately 1755 hours on 2 June 1994 I was sitting in my living-room with my wife, Margaret, when I heard the sound of what appeared to be a Chinook helicopter approaching,' Mr Murchie told the inquiry. 'I remarked that if it was going to attempt to land he would have problems, as the fog was so dense. At that point I got up [and] made my way round to the seaward side of the engine-room building where I could hear the helicopter approaching from the south-west. I would estimate the visibility at this stage to be fifteen to twenty metres at the most. The helicopter now sounded very close and did not seem to be terribly high. The noise appeared to pass to the east of the lighthouse. It became apparent that it was not going to land, because there were no noise changes similar to other helicopters that I have heard land before.'

Anthony Gresswell was on holiday with his girl-friend, Mary Green. They had parked their car at the end of the public road on a steep hill above the lighthouse, and then walked down to where the visibility was better. He was hoping to film with his video recorder. Mr Gresswell testified, 'I made a video of Mary with the lighthouse behind her. At the bottom, visibility was definitely clearer than at the top. However, it was still poor and was still misty. There was a foghorn sounding at the time.' Just before six, they decided to walk back up to their car. 'Virtually as we set off at the foot of the hill we heard the sound of a helicopter approaching from the left of the lighthouse. We were facing the lighthouse. We could not see the helicopter at all, but the sound was getting louder and louder. We thought it was coming in to land at the helicopter pad which was approximately fifty yards above us on the hill.'

Mary Green concurred. She said of the helicopter, 'It appeared to be flying very low – so much so that I thought it was going to land on the heli-pad at the lighthouse. I then made my way to the heli-pad and shouted to Tony to get the video ready to record the helicopter landing. The helicopter was very near, and I thought it was directly overhead. The engine sounded perfectly normal and I did not have any indication that the helicopter was in distress.'

Shirley Crabtree was the very last person to see Chinook HC2 ZD576 in flight. She was visiting the Mull with her husband, Alan, and, like Anthony Gresswell and Mary Green, they had parked their car at the top of the hill. Shortly before 6 p.m. they started to return to the car park.

'The weather was really bad,' recalled Mrs Crabtree. 'We couldn't see the hills on either side of us because of the thick mist. The mist was swirling around, because the wind was quite strong. As we were walking I heard a helicopter. It seemed to be flying from my right, from the sea, over the tops of our heads. It seemed very low and I thought it seemed strange . . . and I was very surprised that they were flying in that weather. I don't know how they saw anything at all. As it passed over I looked up, and I am sure I saw the rotor blade whirling in the mist and I thought I saw a white light which wasn't flashing. I only saw it for a split second, but I remember saying to Alan that it seemed only the height of a house above us. It flew off to our left.'

Said Mr Crabtree, 'It seemed to me that the helicopter was flying from my right to my left over a fairly steep rise on the left-hand side of the road. As it went over it sounded to me that the noise of the blades was slowing down.'

Russell Ellacott was on a touring holiday with his friend Tony Bracher, intending to walk, fish and bike around Scotland. On 2 June they were on the Mull, following a path that Mr Murchie, the lighthouse keeper, had told him led to a deserted village which lay on Beinn na Lice. They were forced to leave their bikes and walk. 'We walked over a ridge, and I found a piece of quartz rock on the hillside and started to dig it out with a key. I continued walking a short distance. I then felt something like a pressure all around me. On reflection it felt like the down-draught from a helicopter. I then heard a propeller turning around for about four or five seconds, and then I heard an explosion. I immediately saw an orange glow and became aware of dense, thick smoke.'

The lighthouse keeper's replacement, Hector Lamont, was driving over the hill, a few minutes away from the lighthouse. He recalled, 'As I carefully negotiated my way down the steep and windy last section of the road, past the big barrier, heading for the lighthouse, at about 1755 or 1800 hours I suddenly heard the sound of a helicopter directly behind me, so close I thought it was going to hit me, although I never saw it. Almost at the same time I heard a *whoosh*! kind of noise and saw an orange flash behind me. It wasn't a loud noise but I could just hear it above the sound of my diesel-engined Land Rover.'

Down below at the lighthouse, his colleague, David Murchie, having become concerned about the aircraft that had just passed over, reported, 'I then made my way to the north-west side of the building and heard a loud thud immediately followed by a whooshing and whistling sound that I thought to be the rotor blades striking the ground. At this point, my wife, who was standing out to the north of the building, began running towards me shouting, "The helicopter has crashed." I immediately asked her to telephone the emergency services, while I made my way to the area [where] I felt the crash had occurred.'

Margaret Murchie, his wife, testified that after hearing the helicopter pass over 'The next sound I heard was a dull thud then a "cracking" sound followed by a swish noise. The noise wasn't particularly loud. Within a few seconds of this I saw a fireball on the hillside to the left of where I'd heard the sound of the crash. Then everything went quiet. All this took place within about two minutes of when I first heard the helicopter while in the house.'

Anthony Gresswell, at his girlfriend Mary Green's request, had been about to video the helicopter landing. He recalled, 'I took my video out and prepared to film it landing on the pad, but could not see it so I did not press the record button . . . All of a sudden there was a crumpling sound followed by a splintering sound and then silence. I guessed immediately what had happened. I shouted to Mary that the helicopter had crashed. Mary started to run up the hill, and I shouted to her to come back. I turned round to run back down to the lighthouse and saw the lighthouse keeper and his wife, who had come out into the garden. I shouted to him that the helicopter had crashed. I turned around again and saw a ball of fire rolling down the hillside about 500 yards away to my left as I looked at the hillside.'

Anthony Gresswell and Mary Green joined David Murchie, and all three began making their way uphill through the dense fog towards the accident site. They met Hector Lamont in his Land Rover. Gresswell said, 'We all jumped in the back of the Land Rover. The driver turned it around and we set off back up the hill. We stopped when the driver spotted wreckage. Myself and the lighthouse keeper [Murchie] got out, and we climbed the hillside towards the wreckage . . . All we could see were fragments of the helicopter. Mary had driven off in the Land Rover and went further up the hill. The grass was alight and there was lots of smoke. We climbed the hill until we were above the wreckage and looked down to see if we could see anything. We talked to each other and agreed that nobody could have survived the impact. We then heard a shout from one of the two cyclists who we met on our way down . . . to the lighthouse approximately half an hour earlier.'

The cyclists, Russell Ellacott and Tony Bracher, on the mountain pathway searching for the deserted village, had been nearest the scene of the crash. Immediately after it had happened, according to Ellacott, 'I then saw things . . . shooting into the air. It was like a fireworks display. Visibility at this time was only about nine or ten feet maximum. Strangely, despite feeling this pressure and hearing an explosion, I did not see or hear the helicopter. With the density of the mist and smoke it was difficult to say how far I was from the point of the explosion, but I don't think I could have been more than 100 yards . . .

I said to Tony something like, "I think we've had a 'copter crash." Tony thought it was some sort of army exercise.

'We started making our way back along the path we had just walked, but could hardly breathe because of the smoke,' he continued. They came across their bikes, and found that their tyres had been scorched by the heat from the crash. According to Ellacott, 'The wind was very strong and blowing in a cross direction across the face of the hill. I said to Tony that "We will have to try and get above the smoke." We walked up the hill some distance until we were on a flat section above the smoke. I looked down and saw debris spread over a distance and a particularly big bit of metal that looked like the cone or nose of a helicopter.

'I more or less walked on a man lying on his back on the hillside. He had a gaping wound on the right side of his head, but it didn't appear to be bleeding. His legs were disjointed and were lying at a strange angle. His eyes were open and his mouth was wide. He had on a bright orange survival suit and was not burned. After this I saw another body about twenty feet away downhill . . . He was also wearing an orange survival suit – again not burned. In the vicinity of this body I counted another five or six in what appeared to be heaps, all wearing orange-colour survival clothing. I assumed that these were all bodies.

'Just then something went off, sort of exploded, and

shot up into the air from the big bit of wreckage. I was terrified. I realised we could not do anything for the people in the helicopter. I said to Tony, "We have to get out of here." I was frightened of other explosions . . . a vast amount of paper documents were flying about in the wind. Many of them were heading out towards the sea.'

They started down the hill, where they encountered Murchie and Gresswell and reported to them the scene of devastation that they'd found amid the burning heather. In the meantime, Mary Green had gone on with Hector Lamont in the Land Rover.

'We drove further up the hill,' Ms Green testified, 'and could not travel any further because of the thick smoke and nearby flames . . . I got out of the Land Rover and looked around the immediate area. The hillside was on fire either side of the road. The driver left me while he went back to the lighthouse to summon further help. I made several attempts to get through the smoke, but I could not breathe.

'The driver returned a few minutes later. I got in the Land Rover and we drove through the smoke, stopping where the road was blocked with debris. Together we removed a large piece of the nose-cone out of the road. I also saw bits of a golf bag and moved a golf club . . . There was a brown shoe and a "Brut" toiletries bag on the road. The whole road was littered with debris, and we cleared it to allow emergency vehicles to pass.

'At this point I found a dog-tag attached to a small piece of chain. It had a number written on it, and at this moment I realised that it was a military helicopter that had crashed.'

Shirley Crabtree, the last person to catch a glimpse of the doomed aircraft, seconds before it struck the Hill of Stone, testified that after her sighting, and the subsequent silence, she and her husband carried on up the road, only to find that 'the heather and bushes were burning. There was debris all over the road. It was in tiny pieces. There were long wires all over the place, and a heavy piece of metal. They all looked to have come from the helicopter. It seemed to have disintegrated.'

She suffered from asthma which made it hard for her to fight her way through the smoke, but she did.

'On the other side of the smoke we met the coastguard jeep, and he gave us a lift to the top of the hill by our car. There were two men there with bikes, and they were saying there were ten bodies lying up on the hill. We waited in the car until the emergency services were by, and then we drove back up the road to Campbeltown.'

The coastguard, fire service and police arrived at about 6.50 p.m. Shortly afterwards a doctor from Campbeltown drove to the scene. 'I was met by Calum Lawson, senior ambulanceman, Campbeltown, who advised me that he had not found any person alive at the crash site. Along with Calum Lawson and

Ronnie Hamilton, ambulanceman, Campbeltown, I was shown the bodies that had been located on the hillside [the Mull]. I was shown the bodies that were not burned, initially, examined them, and pronounced life extinct. I also saw several badly burned bodies at the crash site. I did not count the number of bodies that I examined.

'The most noticeable group of bodies – approximately six or seven – were located thirty to forty yards below the cockpit area of the helicopter wreckage. The distance was difficult to estimate due to the mist and smoke. These bodies I have mentioned were still smouldering, and from what I can remember were still generally intact. All these bodies were badly charred. I then pronounced life extinct after generally examining this group of bodies.'

The doctor's attention was drawn to one body lying face down near the cockpit. 'When Calum Lawson turned this body over I felt that the body was still warm, and when I listened to his chest I thought I could hear a faint heartbeat. Calum Lawson told me that he thought he could hear a . . . pulse. At this time, due to the search activity, helicopters and weather conditions, it was difficult to be sure of our findings.

'We then decided to attempt resuscitation. I put up and inserted an intravenous drip into his left arm while Calum Lawson attempted to intubate the lungs. Calum was unsuccessful, due to the severe facial/head injuries sustained by this casualty. Within a couple of minutes, Ronnie Hamilton provided a monitor for finding any heart activity. The pads were applied to the chest and the recording showed Astyole – no heart activity. I thereafter pronounced life extinct.

'I then examined all the other bodies that had been located and pronounced life extinct.

'I then spoke to Detective Sergeant Alaistair Barnett, who organised a count of the bodies at the site. A sweep of the area was carried out and I understood that twenty-nine bodies had been found . . . I telephoned Dr Jim Leisk, Campbeltown Hospital, and informed him that there was no requirement for any other doctors to attend the scene and for the hospital to stand down.'

The next day, a board of inquiry was established at RAF Benson. Its remit was 'To inquire into an accident involving Chinook HC2 ZD576 on 2 June 1994.' It had three members, with a further five 'in attendance'. These included two members of the AAIB (the Air Accident Investigation Branch). Members of the board of inquiry visited the crash site on 3 June, and again on two subsequent occasions during the following two days, to examine the remains of HC2 ZD576. The wreckage lay on the bare hillside, amid the scorched heather, until 7 June, when the president of the board of inquiry gave his permission for it to be removed. The board then deliberated for some eight months, interviewing witnesses and services personnel and studying a Chinook flight simulator in an attempt to establish various flight profiles that might help explain how the accident occurred.

The Chinook is a transport aircraft built by Boeing and used by the US military as a troop carrier. It can easily hold up to forty soldiers at a time. It is designed so that it can fly low at high speed to avoid detection by enemy radar. It can descend to as low as seventy feet above the ground in normal flight. During the Falklands War the Chinook had been used extensively.

Chinooks had crashed before. The most serious accident had occurred in November 1986, when over forty oil workers died after the Chinook carrying them plunged 500 feet into the North Sea. On that occasion faulty gearboxes were blamed. The investigation into the Mull of Kintyre accident, however, was hampered by the fact that HC2 ZD576 was not equipped with a cockpit voice recorder. It was regarded as a security risk for helicopters involved in special-services operations to carry flight data recorders, in case they should fall into enemy hands. But a recommendation had been made that they be installed after two accidents involving RAF Chinooks took place on 27 February 1987 and 6 May 1988. Though money had been set aside to refit the RAF's thirty Chinooks, the changes were never made. An RAF spokesman later told the press, 'It takes time, and voice recorders do not prevent accidents.' A further two accidents in 1989 – one at RAF Odiham and the other at Mount Pleasant in the Falkland Islands – apparently did not convince the Ministry of Defence that action was necessary.

The board of inquiry into the Mull of Kintyre accident would come to the same conclusion as its predecessors. It recommended that '*all* RAF Chinook aircraft are fitted with accident data recorders at the earliest opportunity.'

In the meantime, the board continued trying to piece together the last moments of the flight of HC2 ZD576. It completed its investigations in January 1995, and began to draft its findings. On 13 January these were delivered to HQ1 at RAF Benson. After discussions, the final report was finished seventeen days later and was handed over to the RAF on 3 February 1995. It was not made public for another four months.

The report consisted of four parts. Part I, some forty-three pages long, contained the main body of the board's findings and conclusions, to which had been appended the opinions of three senior RAF officers. Parts II to IV were compilations of evidence, including technical data, flight reports, forensic reports and witnesses' statements. The board concluded that the most probable cause of the accident was that in an attempt to fly over the Mull fog bank the two pilots, Flight Lieutenants Tapper and Cook, had chosen an 'inappropriate' rate of climb for their aircraft.

The events immediately before the crash were reconstructed. At approximately four minutes before impact HC2 ZD576 made a radio call to Scottish Military Air Traffic Control Centre. The purpose of this call has never been established; it was not prefixed by an emergency or urgency code, and it was not answered. At 1.75 km before impact, the pilots made a change of way-point (WP) – a computer-checked coordinate marking a stage on their journey. 'By changing the steering information to the WP at Corran the crew had removed immediate position information with regard to the Mull of Kintyre,' according to the report.

The board noted that as it approached land the helicopter had been in a shallow cruise climb at an airspeed of 150 knots, suggesting that the pilots' intentions were to overfly the Mull. The board speculated that 'The crew may have been deceived by a combination of factors into believing that a cruise climb would have provided them with adequate terrain clearance from the Mull of Kintyre. Whilst the Board discounted a major navigational error, in the circumstances even a minor navigational inaccuracy could have been significant.' The report noted that the data recovered from the aircraft's computers showed that there had been 'small lateral displacements to the right of their expected track' which 'may have led the crew to believe they were further to the west of the Mull of Kintyre than was actually the case'.

The board considered that:

this, coupled with the fact that their planned track to the lighthouse was almost tangential to the coastline, could have led the crew to underestimate the imminence of their landfall, and consequently the ROC [rate of climb] required to safely avoid the obstacle in their flightpath. Furthermore, if the NOH [non handling pilot – i.e. Tapper] had anticipated that a turn of 14 degrees to port would be under way immediately after the WP change was made, he may have believed that the resulting track change would have added to the safety margin by effecting a further lateral displacement from the landmass. These factors could have deceived the crew into believing that a cruise climb would have provided adequate separation between the aircraft and the Mull of Kintyre. The Board then considered the effect of the aircraft's speed on its climb performance, and the possibility that the crew did not recognise the implications of a cruise climb at 150 kts. The crew were unfamiliar with operating comfortably at high airspeeds, as the high vibration levels of the Chinook discouraged cruise flight above 135 kts. In the circumstances, an airspeed of 150 kts, coupled with a strong tailwind component, would have produced a high groundspeed and closure rate with the Mull of Kintyre. The Board established in the Chinook simulator, using the meteorological conditions prevailing at the time of the accident, that a level flight airspeed of 150 kt

required a high power setting, leaving only a small
power margin available for climbing ... The Board
therefore considered it possible that the crew may
have misappreciated the gradient of climb achievable
at their high airspeed.

When the Chinook crashed it was nose up at an angle
of thirty degrees. According to the board's findings,
this meant that four seconds before the moment of
impact the pilots had applied maximum power, giving
the aircraft an ROC of 1,000 feet per minute. The
duration of this thrust was four seconds, enabling
the helicopter to achieve a height gain of 145 feet
– not enough to clear the terrain into which it was
flying. It was also found that 'the impact parameters
indicate an element of left bank'. But the board
concluded that this did not suggest that the crew
had decided on a significant change of track but was
applied as a 'a response to either a late awareness of
their predicament or to make the small 14 degree
heading change to Corran', the next WP on the track
to their destination.

Within the framework of this explanation, other
factors may have played a part in creating the
circumstances that led to the crash, though the
board could not say positively that this was the
case. Among the factors considered was the fact that
in flying to Inverness that evening Flight Lieutenant
Tapper was extending his flight-duty time for that day
beyond the normal eight hours – if, that is, he had

intended to return to Aldergrove that same evening.
This is a matter of some debate. It is assumed that
Tapper had intended to return. Though he had
informed 230 Squadron DFC that he would remain
in Scotland if necessary, he made no attempt to reserve
accommodation there for the night of 2 June. The
board found that his tasking in Ulster that day had
not been such that it would have interfered with his
ability to undertake the flight to Inverness and back.
It did consider the possibility that he may have felt
under pressure to complete the Inverness tasking as
quickly as possible, but concluded that 'the known
facts regarding the intentions of Flt Lt Tapper, and
the possible effect of any associated pressure, do not
allow an objective assessment of any human failings
to be made in respect of Flt Lt Tapper's management
of crew duty considerations'.

The board also considered a series of other possibilities in trying to explain why Flight Lieutenant
Tapper had 'selected an inappropriate ROC to overfly
the Mull of Kintyre'. An accumulation of minor
navigational displacements, the fact that the Chinook
HC2 has low vibration levels, which could have led
to him into being deceived about the aircraft's high
speed, and some disorientation as to the location of
the Mull land mass were all hypothesized as having a
possible bearing on what happened. Possible technical
problems were also examined, and here the board did
have something concrete to consider.

During the tasking earlier on the day of the accident, the crew had reported problems with a no. 2 engine paser-turbine-inlet-temperature (PTIT) gauge and had gone to seek engineering advice at RAF Aldergrove. What exactly the problem was cannot be firmly established, since there was no maintenance work order-log entry for the fault. It is assumed that it cannot have been serious. Flight Lieutenant Tapper also asked that one of the navigation computers – a Racal RNS 252 Super TANS – be checked. He said it was giving 'unusual GPS [Global Positioning Systems] satellite tracking data. This check was completed, with no fault being found.'

Tapper's concerns about the SuperTANS' GPS should not be dismissed lightly: he was known as an expert on that particular navigational system. The system is installed in a console between the two pilots. It processes information from two independent navigational systems – the GPS satellite system, based on twenty-four satellites which circle the globe, and that of the Doppler Velocity Sensor, which, according to the report, 'provides velocities of the aircraft with respect to the earth's surface by transmitting signals from the aircraft, and measuring the returns reflected from the surface'. Earlier, in May, Tapper had gone to the Super TANS manufacturer, Racal Avionics, to seek advice on problems which he said he had been having with the system. He claimed it had been giving unusual data. As a result, the system was replaced three times on the Chinook HC2 ZD576 during that month. However, as with the gauge fault, no maintenance-work order was raised in regard to the 2 June complaint about the system's functioning – oversights for which the Board mildly censured those responsible. However, given the experience of the crew, it is understandable that they should respect the second opinion of their technical backup and avoid raising unnecessary paperwork if they had been suitably reassured.

The day before, during a tasking, a different crew flying HC2 ZD576 had complained about a 'lagging No. 1 Engine PTIT gauge problem. This problem was cleared during diagnosis when No. 1 and No. 2 gauges were interchanged by the groundcrew.' This was similar to the problem that Tapper's crew were to experience on the day of the crash, but the board decided that 'it was not a factor in the accident'. Likewise it concluded that the problem with the computer, which also went unrecorded, 'was not a fault in the system, and therefore not a factor in the accident'. The Board found that at power-down, 5.59 p.m., 'the SuperTANS and the navigation sensors appear to have been performing perfectly . . . The accuracy of the Doppler position also indicates that all had worked equally well throughout the flight. The pilot had performed the correct initialisation procedures, and was making use of the navigational facilities.'

However, the board acknowledged that the Chinook HC2 had a history of 'unforeseen malfunctions, mainly associated with the engine control system, including undemanded engine shutdown, engine run-up, spurious engine failure captions, and misleading and confusing cockpit indications'. It found no evidence of any such malfunctions during the fatal flight, but it concluded:

> Nevertheless, an unforeseen technical malfunction of the type being experienced on the Chinook HC2, which would not necessarily have left any physical evidence, remained a possibility, and could not be discounted . . . given the large number of unexplained technical occurrences on the Chinook HC2 since its introduction, the Board considered it possible that a technical malfunction or indication could have provided a distraction to the crew.

The possibility was raised of the crew having to deal with a false emergency at a critical time, as the aircraft closed with the Mull – a distraction which perhaps lasted long enough to prove fatal.

The Board had been careful not to point the finger of blame at Cook and Tapper. As regards Tapper, it had concluded that, while there might have been errors of judgement during the flight, 'it would be incorrect to criticise him for human failings based on the available evidence'. And it found that 'there were no human failings with respect to Flt Lt Cook'. In contrast two of the three senior RAF officers who appended remarks to the main body of the board's conclusions were harsh in their assessments of who was at fault. They rejected the board's conclusion that 'the crew, faced with the expected deteriorating weather, consciously elected to make a climb on track over high ground and in doing so used a speed and power combination that is unrecognisable as a Chinook technique'. The opinion of the station commander of RAF Odiham was that

> this was difficult to believe; such actions would go against all the crew's instincts and training. Moreover it is the very antithesis of the professionalism and careful planning that had gone before. Even taking into account the factors which the Board feel could have deceived the crew into believing a high speed cruise climb would have given them sufficient clearance over the Mull, I, and the few senior Chinook operators that I felt able to consult, find this suggestion incredible.

As an alternative theory, he postulated that at the time of the crash the crew were trying to follow the western coastline of the Mull rather than fly over it. But, he added, 'In arriving at this alternative scenario I am now faced with the same problem that faced the Board – how did the aircraft get to around 500 ft, at 150 kts IAS with an ROC of approx 1,000 ft per minute, which are the computed starting parameters for the final 18 seconds of the flight?' He concluded that Flight Lieutenant Tapper was to blame and must be held guilty of a failure of duty.

A second senior officer agreed. He wrote in his opinion appended to the report that:

> What does emerge from the Inquiry, however, is that there is no evidence whatever of any combination of possible minor problems, or of any major difficulty, which would have so taxed the skills of the crew that they had no option other than to keep flying towards high ground at speed at low level in deteriorating conditions of cloud and visibility. From this I am reluctantly drawn to the conclusion that the operating pilots could and would have avoided this accident had they followed a different course of action from the one they chose to pursue ... there is not even a hint of any circumstances which would have been beyond their professional skills to accommodate, or which would have justified them taking the risk that they did. Lamentably, all the evidence points towards them having ignored one of the most basic tenets of airmanship, which is never to attempt to fly visually below safety altitude unless the weather conditions are unambiguously suitable for operating under Visual Flight Rules ... the actions of the crew were the direct cause of this crash. I also conclude that this amounted to gross negligence.

When the board of inquiry's report was made public the relatives of the pilots were understandably distressed – not so much at the report's findings but at the conclusions of these two senior RAF officers.

To the families of Tapper and Cook this seemed unusually harsh and unfair, given the uncertainties surrounding the accident. In the weeks following the issuing of the report, the families asserted that the pilots had previously been perturbed by recurring problems with HC2 ZD576. The family of Flight Lieutenant Cook, who had been at the controls of the craft when it crashed, claimed that he had expressed grave worries as to its safety. He is said to have told his father on three occasions that if he was killed in a Chinook crash he should 'ask questions'. Mr Cook was also an experienced pilot, having flown for the RAF. Tapper's widow, Thamra, also said that her husband had expressed similar sentiments. Cook was so concerned, his wife said, that he took out extra life insurance, according to a report by David Walmsley in the *Belfast Telegraph* of 27 September 1995. The newspaper quoted an RAF colleague of Cook's who stated that before the doomed flight Cook had mentioned to him that he was worried about the engines. 'He then qualified that as not being concern for their engines but for their control units', said the colleague, according to the *Belfast Telegraph*. Mrs Cook said her husband was so uneasy about flying the Chinook HC2 that he would take his flight manual to bed with him at night to read.

There was another inquiry ahead – the inquest – during which people hoped some of the mysteries surrounding the crash would be cleared up. Originally it was due to begin in October 1995, but at the request of the pilots' families it was postponed until January the following year. The widows of Flight Lieutenants Tapper and Cook had suffered not only the loss of their loved ones but also the accusation that their husbands might have been responsible for the loss of so many lives. They wanted time to gather evidence which they hoped would vindicate the pilots' reputations.

The hearings began on 8 January 1996 at the Sheriff's Court in Paisley. The courtroom was packed not only with relatives and witnesses but with an assemblage of reporters from Britain and Northern Ireland. The sheriff, Sir Stephen Young, was in charge of the hearing.

For Susan Phoenix it was the beginning of the end of a period of grieving. It was not that the inquest would mean that she could cease to grieve the loss of Ian: rather she hoped that it would put to rest the doubts that harrowed her concerning the accident itself. She had to know what had happened to the man she had loved and lived with for the greater part of her life. She arrived in Paisley the day before the inquest was to start, along with Ann Magee, the widow of Detective Inspector Kevin Magee, with whom she had become close in the year following the disaster. The two women were the only ones among the RUC widows to remain at the hearings until they closed almost a month later.

It was not easy for any of the women. Susan had steeled herself to listen to the evidence, but when the senior inspector for air accidents testified she cried. She wept as she listened to his graphic description of the last seconds of HC2 ZD576. The fuselage began to disintegrate after the initial impact, during which the helicopter struck the mountain ridge slightly forward of the rear cargo ramp. This sent the Chinook into the air briefly again, as the floor of the cargo bay was ripped off and the craft continued to disintegrate. For between three and five seconds it was airborne before striking the mountainside a second and final time. As the helicopter broke into two main sections, it made what the senior inspector called a 'violent manœuvre', its massive rotor blades chopping through its fragmenting framework, causing terrible injuries. Finally, it came to rest some 300 metres from the first impact site.* The twenty-nine passengers and crew were dead on impact.

Susan imagined the scene vividly: the fireball blazing through the mist-shrouded Mull; the heather burning. 'They were all at peace before the fire consumed the heather,' she thought. The Chinook had split into several sections. The cockpit, the forward

* This is the figure used in the main body of the RAF's findings. However, the report of the RAF's School of Aviation Medicine, which examined the nature of the trauma suffered by the aircraft, its crew and passengers, says it came to rest 700 metres from the initial impact point.

rotary hub and the front end of the cargo bay were found on the ridge several hundred metres from the impact site. Near them lay the body of Flight Lieutenant Tapper, next to his seat and not far from Load Master Malcolm Forbes. Eleven bodies were found about thirty metres down the hillside towards the sea, near a section of troop seating which had been extensively damaged by fire. Three other sections were scattered in a radius of about fifty metres from the wreckage of the cockpit, with bodies close by. Ian's body was found not far the crest of the ridge.

When Flight Lieutenant Tapper's voice, taped by the Prestwick Air Traffic Control officer, was heard sending his last, unanswered message – 'Scottish Military, good afternoon. This is Foxtrot four Zero' – Susan leaned forward and stroked his father's hand as it clenched the back of the seat in front of her. This was the last sound of his son's voice. Why no one at Prestwick Airport responded to it remained unresolved. Unfortunately, as the hearings wore on, it became evident that the other chief mysteries of the flight would also remain unresolved. The phrases which were repeated most regularly were 'there is always a possibility that . . .', 'that may not necessarily be the case', 'it is not inconceivable' and 'yes, possibly'.

Other potential mysteries emerged that had not been mentioned in the RAF inquiry. Shortly after Flight Lieutenant Tapper's attempt to contact Prestwick a small blip was seen on a radar screen at the airport. Technicians call such things 'technical angels'. They are often found to be pockets of ionized air. The sheriff asked a witness – an air traffic control officer – if the blip could have been caused by a light aircraft, birds or possibly a small piece falling off of the Chinook. 'It's possible, My Lord,' he was told.

More details emerged concerning the problem with HC2 ZD576's SuperTANS system. The senior officer from 230 Squadron reported that on 3 May 1994 the GPS had failed to operate; on 5 May there had been another complication with the GPS, necessitating the replacement of the receiver and aerial; and 9 May the receiver had been replaced a second time. Within six days, four different receivers had been put into the Chinook. The officer commented that it seemed unusual, and had it been his squadron operating in Northern Ireland he would have had it thoroughly investigated. There had also been two replacement engines put in within three weeks of each other. Still, the Chinook was reported as being 'apparently serviceable' when it arrived in Northern Ireland on 31 May – three days before its last flight.

The next squadron leader who appeared as a witness had been part of the crew who had delivered the Chinook to Northern Ireland. He gave a graphic description of how the helicopter is flown, skilfully demonstrating with his hands the imaginary cockpit controls and explaining the meaning of 'yaw' and 'roll' in so much detail that the whole court felt airsick. He spoke highly of Tapper and Cook. When the sheriff asked if pilots could become distracted while changing controls, he replied, 'Possibly'.

The most controversial moment came when a squadron leader who was stationed in Aldergrove at the time of the crash said that the flight to Inverness was an opportunity for pilot training and would have been flown to maximise the potential to practise low-level flying. The court was stunned. 'It was a valuable training in low-level flying on an otherwise routine journey,' he said, as barristers and solicitors looked at their clients in disbelief. How could the RAF have given permission for a training exercise during a flight with so many key members of the security forces' intelligence personnel on board? He was asked if he had mentioned this to the RAF board of inquiry. He said he had. But it had not been thought to be significant enough to receive even a mention in the final report. However, a wing commander later testified that 'every time we fly we practise or hone our skills' and that, in any case, low-level flying was the safest option for the first leg of the journey across to the Mull.

It was his opinion that the crew had been attempting to fly around the Mull coast. Flight Lieutenant Tapper's unanswered call to the Scottish Military at Prestwick about five minutes before the crash could have been the first contact to prepare for the

WP change which would have necessitated the craft flying through a military air zone. Approach and tower frequencies at RAF Machrihanish had been noted on the maps the pilots had prepared, showing they intend to fly through military airspace. However, the wing commander believed that an accumulation of small navigational errors in the GPS and Doppler systems, coupled with miscalculations in the original plotting of the course, caused the pilots to misjudge the immediacy of the Mull. They then did not select the correct ROC to get over the obstacle. This would have been determined only during the last moments, as they had expected to fly around it. They had changed their WP on their navigational aid to prepare for turning left along the coast. So either they did not know where they were or something had prevented them from making the turn.

Jonathan Tapper's best friend and colleague was of no doubt which it was. He took the stand and defended Tapper's reputation with vigour and conviction, saying that he believed there had been a control jam which prevented the craft from making the necessary turn. He was cross-examined by the Ministry of Defence barrister, who insisted that the chance that his version of events was correct was 'millions to one against'. The witness agreed that it was easier to accept likely events than it is to accept unlikely events, but already the point had been made that the intense fireball had made the exact condition of many of the Chinook's instruments uncertain, possibly covering up any faults. Susan listened with admiration as he countered with humour and skill the barrister's points, standing by his conviction that Tapper was much too good a pilot to have made errors that would have led to the disaster.

When the wing commander was cross-examined by the Tapper family's barrister he agreed that only in a case where there is absolutely no doubt as to the cause of an accident can the deceased crew be judged negligent. There were so many doubts surrounding the Mull of Kintyre crash that it was not just to impugn the reputation of men who were not able to defend themselves. The wing commander also agreed that the possibility of a control jam could not be dismissed.

The three weeks of evidence and the parade of witnesses had come to this – yet another 'possibility' that could not be ruled out. On 26 January, the last day of the third week of the hearings, after every detail had been sifted through, the wing commander and the sheriff looked at each other silently. It was 4.45 p.m., only a few minutes before the hearings ceased. The wing commander leaned forward, resting the weight of his outstretched arms on the edge of the witness-box. The sheriff also leaned forward over his bench towards the witness – the last to be heard. A sad smile flickered across the wing commander's face. The sheriff looked as if he were beseeching him for an answer. He asked the RAF officer if he could offer any explanation, however far-fetched, as to why HC2 ZD576 was *where* it was, *when* it was. 'I cannot, My Lord. I wish that I could, but I cannot,' came the reply. They continued to look at each other as they shook their heads. 'It could be something beyond our imagination,' said the sheriff. 'Yes, it could,' the witness agreed.

Susan sat watching and listening as the final minutes ticked away. Vivid memories of the evidence surfaced again – the taped voice of Flight Lieutenant Tapper, and the last 'Bye-bye' from the Aldergrove air traffic controller; the shattered machine breaking apart, the heather blazing through the fog, and then the absolute and eerie silence. But for all this there was to be no explanation. No technical angel was going to appear and, with a wave of its wand, clear up the confusion once and for all and set her mind at rest. The tears welled up in her eyes. She would never know the truth about Ian's death. She was moved too by the inexplicable emotion she sensed between these two men who had a responsibility to explain what had happened but could not. They, like her, would never know the 'why' or the 'cause' of that disaster. Then the sheriff said, 'I've been in this job long enough to feel that truth is often stranger than fiction.' That enigmatic statement seemed a fitting conclusion. When the sheriff's report was issued, on 21 March 1996, it exonerated the pilots but did not offer any new evidence which might resolve the enigma of the crash.

At the end of the final week of the inquest Susan's son had crossed over to Scotland, and together they drove from Paisley north-west to the Mull of Kintyre. They had gone there with Susan's daughter the day after the accident to see the scene and to thank men like the RUC officers Paul and Trevor who had undertaken the gruesome task of identifying the bodies. They had also met Chief Inspector Jimmy Dorwood from Campbeltown, who had supervised the rescue efforts, the lighthouse keepers and their families, and the Revd Roddie McNidder, who had given them solace. Because of their kindnesses, these people would remain close to them for ever.

Now Susan and her son again took the road through Campbeltown, winding its way down the heather-clad promontory on which the sun was shining. It was a mild and windy day, and the Mull looked the very picture of peace and tranquility. Already there was a promise of the coming of spring. They parked, and trudged across the heather to the memorial cairn that had been erected the year before near the ridge that the Chinook had struck and near to the spot where Ian's life had ended. Beyond, just over that fatal ridge, the sea stretched blue, and further away Ireland was visible shimmering on the horizon.

Her son stretched out on the heather on the spot where his father had died. No words were spoken. None were needed.

The night of Ian's death, Susan woke while it was

still dark. Though he was gone, she did not feel alone. She had the strange but powerful sensation of a rush of energy that went through her. And he spoke to her, as usual, in his unsentimental and direct way. 'Well, Susan,' he said, 'get on with it.'

Chapter 11

As It Was

On 9 June 1994, the day of the funeral, the rain poured down from a low, grey sky. It was the kind of sky often seen over Belfast, with heavy rolling clouds so close that they seem to sit on your shoulders. It blotted out the light of early summer, turning June into November.

For miles around Roselawn Cemetery the police had established traffic-control points to help guide the steady stream of people that were coming to mourn the loss of Detective Superintendent Ian Phoenix. Over 1,500 arrived, braving the pouring rain. Policemen, former members of the Parachute Regiment, people from the deaf community, government figures, academics, reporters, friends from every imaginable walk of life, and relatives were gathering under clusters of dark umbrellas, on which the relentless downpour beat its own mournful tattoo.

I was there among them, with my wife, Mary, at my side, still reeling from the double shock of the discovery that our friend Ian whom we assumed was some kind of hearing-aid salesman was in fact a top-ranking secret policeman, and now dead. As we made our way towards the cemetery church and crematorium a black limousine approached. Susan's pale, tear-stained face was at one window. She turned and caught a glimpse of us. A smile of recognition, mixed with terrible sadness, flickered across her face as her children comforted her. We acknowledged her gaze as the car vanished around a bend.

At the church we stood outside as the coffin was carried in with Ian's RUC cap resting on the regimental colours of Northern Ireland's Airborne Forces Association. Six policemen bore it on their shoulders. One of them had been like a son to Ian. They moved with solemn and dignified precision, a piper walking slowly before them playing 'Dark Island'. We followed, shepherded along with hundreds of others past the watchful gaze of plain-clothes policemen who guarded the entrance.

The service was unusual not just for its stately restraint. Susan and her children were greeted by her old friend and colleague the Revd George Grindle from the Kinghan Church for the Deaf. He had been one of the first to offer her spiritual comfort after the crash. Her children had asked both George and the Revd (Group Captain) Richard Taylor to conduct the service. The choice seemed a perfect combination of Susan's and Ian's life together. Richard had been a source of inspiration to the family at several unrelated services in the past, his RAF background and service to the forces reflecting their own. George had known them all for almost sixteen years and knew that he would be needed to conduct a 'bilingual' service for the many deaf friends and colleagues who would certainly turn up to honour a man who had quietly supported them. His comforting praise for Ian's life was enhanced, for hearing people too, by his beautiful sign language. Bill, a colleague of Ian's in the Airborne Forces Association, spoke from the pulpit of his friend's humanity, generosity and devotion to justice. Ian's son read 'Requiem' by Robert Louis Stevenson; their friend Diarmuid had changed the penultimate line to suit the occasion:

Under the wide and starry sky
Dig the grave and let me lie.
Glad did I live and gladly die,
    And I laid me down with a will.
This be the verse you grave for me:
'Here he lies where he longed to be;
Home is the soldier, home from the field,
    And the hunter home from the hill.'

As the coffin sank into the bier which carried it to its final destination, a powerful sense of despair swept over Susan until she saw the look on the face of a SAS man who had served with Ian. He was a burly Glaswegian Catholic – a big, tough man of few words. His face had such a look of compassion that it somehow strengthened Susan's resolve not to give in to grief, to soldier on, in the comforting knowledge that so many other strong and special people loved and missed Ian Phoenix.

Afterwards, when the service had ended, Susan and her children stood to thank those who had gathered there to commemorate her husband. Mary and I were near enough the last of over a thousand people to shake their hands. When we reached them, the first thing Ian's son said was 'I'd like to apologise on behalf of my father and my family that he could not tell you and Mary the truth about what he did. It always troubled him.' We stood for a second, deeply touched that at a moment such as this, after the tragedy that had befallen his family, he had the consideration to want to reassure *us*. It was a measure of him that he did so, and a measure too of the man who was his father.

Some four hundred people then made the journey back to the Phoenix home, most bringing a bottle of Moët et Chandon champagne to celebrate life in the midst of death. It was rumoured later that all the off-licences for miles around were sold out of their supplies of Moët et Chandon for days to come. This was a send-off that Ian, whom some of his friends at the office had nicknamed 'Mr Moët', would have appreciated. Tables were loaded with an array of shellfish – including Ian's favourite: oyster – and the most exotic canapés, organised by Frances and a team of helpers. Two months earlier Susan and Ian had helped her celebrate her fiftieth birthday. Ian's colleagues took on the role of waiters and waitresses, squeezing between the crowds with large silver salvers. Others who were an important part of the Phoenix family's wide circle of friends gathered round to lend their support in every possible way. Susan's sister and her partner, Barry, drove through the night from Peterborough with their friends Geoff and Elaine. That loving support was to continue for the family during the terrible months to come. But at that moment nothing could help compensate for the loss Susan felt.

Yet somehow she roused herself and saw to her guests. It was a remarkable feast that Ian would have loved, she realised, moving among the people who were spilling out of all the doors of her home into the patio, the driveway and the surrounding gardens. She expected that at any second he would appear in the midst of his friends as usual – laughing, bantering, cajoling and teasing them; seeing to it that not a glass was empty, whether it be of champagne or orange juice. The conviction gripped her that she would walk into the dining-room and find him in his accustomed place at the table, champagne in his hand, a smile on his face. But he did not reappear to pass a joking comment on Alastair, the Prince Charles look-alike, or on Gary's Armani suit, or on Geordie's tan, or on Pete's ferret, or to talk with Bob about their lunch date, which had been planned for the following week. He was not joking. He would not keep that date. Her loss was real.

The day came for the scattering of the ashes. She lay on the sofa clutching the jar that contained them and cried for hours. She would soon have to part with them, and she did not want to let go. This was all she had of the physical being she had loved and lived with for over half her life. She was convinced then that it was possible to die of a broken heart. People wandered in and out of the room, unwilling to intervene in her grief. She was dimly aware of them coming and going. Through her blurred eyes she saw the little trophies of her life with Ian arranged around the room – the beautiful small wooden statues of the 'happiness people' from Singapore, where the family had celebrated their daughter's twenty-first birthday; the silver picture from Trevignano; the Indian batiks; the cushions they had bargained for in Egypt; and the Salvador Dali reproduction they had liked because it was of a chubby girl looking out of a window into what they had once imagined was a lovely future.

The thought that her children were waiting for her roused her from her grief. She rose from the mourning couch and put on her walking-boots. The piper was waiting for them once more, on the brow of the hill that overlooked the lonely pebble-strewn strand where she and Ian had passed many an hour together. A few friends were there, including young friends of her son and daughter. A little earlier Lady Mayhew, the wife of the Northern Ireland Secretary of State, had rung to ask if she might take part in the final ceremony. Susan told her she was very welcome to join them, but warned her that the scattering would take place over rough ground. When Lady Mayhew arrived she delighted everyone by throwing herself into the spirit of the occasion, donning Ian's old paint-stained shoes and walking-socks. The small group of around thirty people set out for the hillside overlooking the shore. They made their way across the ridge, the wind blowing off the sea, the waves crashing beneath them, until they came to a basalt rock that was partly buried in the grass. Susan and Ian had often walked past it, speculating how long it had stood there facing the blustering winds. Soon his name would be carved into the rock. It would be his only headstone.

On the spot, as Ian's dog frolicked around her feet, she read from Theodore Roosevelt's *Argus* words which her husband had cherished over the years:

It is not the critic who counts nor the man who points out how the strong man stumbles or where the doer of deeds could have done better. The credit belongs to the man who is actually in the arena, whose face is marred by dust and sweat and blood, who knows great enthusiasm, great devotion, and the triumph of achievement, and who, at worst, if he fails at least fails whilst daring greatly, so that his place shall never be with those odd and timid souls who know neither victory nor defeat. You've never lived until you've almost died. For those who have had to fight for it life has truly a flavour the protected shall never know.

The children supported Susan as they went down the hill up which Ian had so often hauled them after long country rambles. They scattered his ashes as they went. The piper stood on the brow of the hill, silhouetted against a cloudy summer's sky, playing the refrain of 'The Mull of Kintyre'. It was far from being a solemn occasion, however – Ian would not have wanted it to be. Some of the ashes fluttered to the ground to be trampled into the earth; other flakes clung to the grass. They neared the hill's foot. 'What was Ian really like?' Lady Mayhew asked Susan's friend Louise, slipping into a sitting position on a grassy bank as she did so. 'Well, let's say that right now you are sitting on him,' Louise replied. 'And he would have loved that!'

Susan had with her a lead plaque, on which her brother-in-law Barry had inscribed a simple message. It read, 'In memory of Detective Superintendent Ian

Phoenix who was killed in a helicopter accident during service to his country on the Mull of Kintyre June 2 1994.' When they reached the shoreline she pushed it deep into the grassy bank – to be found, perhaps, someday in the years to come, by future generations of hill-walkers.

The little ceremony was not yet over, however. The group, accompanied by Lady Mayhew, who showed no hesitation in clambering over any rocky obstacle in her path, went a little way around the coast, where cliffs drop sheer into the sea. They paused only when the round mass of the Mull loomed up on the horizon. Susan gazed at the Hill of Stone for a moment. Ian had died as he would have wanted, she reflected. He had lost his life with men with whom he had served, in a helicopter piloted by officers of the special forces whom he had always respected. And he had ended his life in the heather that he loved to roam. He would have been content with such a death. Her only wish was that she had been with him.

Bottles of champagne were produced, and once more the corks popped as they drank a toast to Ian's memory. Their friend Rory was there with a silver flute similar to that which Ian had played while a boy. On it he played 'The Fields of Athenry'. The Irish ballad that had been one of Ian Phoenix's favourite songs. The fact that it was a 'republican' ballad had made no difference to him – he had been an Irishman first and foremost, determined to enjoy what was best and finest in the Irish tradition. Its melody was borne on the wind along with the ashes of the man who had loved its haunting melody. Thus they consigned him to the peace of the 'long green grass'.

During breakfast on the last morning that Susan was to see Ian alive, he looked across the lawn to the flower-bed that flourished in one corner. 'What's that red flower?' he asked. It was a trumpet-shaped flower with bright red petals, sprouting from a perennial plant that they had tended together for several years. They did not know its name or its origin. Certainly it had never bloomed before the morning of 2 June 1994.

After he left for his morning meetings, Susan picked a few of the flowers and placed them on the kitchen window-sill for him to admire when he returned to pack his bags at lunchtime for the flight to Fort George. But in the haste of his departure, and then during the horrific night of tragedy that followed, the little flowers were forgotten about. The next day Susan was gazing tearfully out of her kitchen window at the far-off Scottish coastline when her friend Gloria slipped her arm around her shoulders. The flowers were sitting in front of them on the sill. Susan told how Ian had admired them on the previous morning. Gloria was able to answer Ian's question. The trumpet-shaped flowers were called Seven Drops of Blood. They did not bloom again, and the plant itself has since disappeared from the garden.

Not far from where the flower bloomed, in the centre of the garden, Susan planted some charred heather from the Hill of Stone. Her daughter had dug it out of the hillside on the first Sunday after the crash, when they had flown over to the Mull in a tiny Islander aircraft to see the wreckage. The heather has taken root, and thrives. In spring it brightens with gorse, and small mountain flowers flourish in the summer. Nature has prevailed, wiping out the last burned trace of the fireball that set the heather blazing that foggy evening.

For Susan, memories bloom over the traces of her love, covering up its loss though never replacing it. Their son was twenty-one in February 1994. To celebrate, she and Ian had taken the family and a family friend, Diarmuid, to Goa. They arrived on New Year's Eve, 1993. Their hotel was The Tamarind Lodge, set in a leafy oasis beside the paddy-fields. On the last day of the old year the Goans burn 'The Old Man' – a dummy stuffed with fireworks, which they light as the last seconds tick away. As the Phoenix family watched, they wished that 1994 would be a better year than that which was passing, with all its financial problems. They wished that with 'The Old Man' the problems would be consumed and become part of the past.

The fireworks being over, Ian, who had always been faithful to the Celtic custom of 'first-footing', produced his customary bottle of Blackbush whiskey and offered it to the other hotel guests, most of whom appeared to be somewhat bemused at his generosity. The Goans, however, were not so reserved, and their firecrackers and hourly cannon-fire went on for a full seven days, as did the ringing of the bells of the large Catholic church which stood nearby.

The nights were pitch-black, and the stars seemed close enough to reach out and touch. The only noise was from the dogs which barked as the family made their way past each isolated homestead on the return to the hotel at night. The Phoenixes were joined by Subir, an Indian friend of their son, who had shared a barbecue on their patio during an exchange trip some years earlier. He had undertaken a two-day bus journey from his village in northern India to be with them.

Ian had quickly befriended the local taxi driver, Dier, and proceeded to 'interview' him about local places worth visiting. On one journey they plunged into the surrounding jungle to find a high mountain waterfall. The taxi would take them only as far as an old, dilapidated railway station, where they had to leave it and finish the journey on an ancient passenger train. They returned on foot following the jungle railtrack. Before long, they were exhausted in the stifling heat. Fortunately, Dier was resourceful. He slowed down a passing freight train, enabling them to hitch a ride. They clambered on to the footplate as the train puffed and rattled its way through the dense forests. It was like a scene from a war-time jungle movie. They hung, laughing, from the ageing rolling stock, watching out for monkeys in the trees.

In the taxi, on the final leg of the trip back to the hotel, Ian and his son sang together 'The Fields of Athenry' and 'The Green Fields Of France', to Dier's delight. They sang heartily, against a background chorus of cicadas chirping in the trees as night fell. A few months later Ian's son would sing the same songs as he drove his mother back from the crash site on the Mull of Kintyre.

As the summer of 1994 drew to a close, Susan looked at the last rose of the season growing in her garden and realised that this year Ian would not walk in with it behind his back, as had been his custom, to present it to her, always shyly but still with a cheeky grin on his face. The long purple weeds and rogue daffodils would be left untouched at the bottom of the field and not be gathered into a makeshift bouquet as he returned from walking his dogs.

The doctoral thesis that Ian had cajoled her into finishing the previous summer was sitting on her office shelf. The PhD had now been awarded. She had dedicated it to his memory.

Three months after Ian's death, her father had died. Within another six months she had lost her mother, who passed away after a painful illness. This triple blow would have been enough to shatter most people, but her world did not end. That was not in her character. The love of her son and daughter helped her through those dark months, and Ian's words were always there as a simple admonition to live. 'Well, Susan,' he kept telling her, 'get on with it.'

In May 1995, almost a year after the Chinook disaster, her son was involved in a serious car crash, and she found herself with her daughter and a close friend sitting at his hospital bedside. Bandaged, bloodied and badly bruised, but alive, it took six months before he was fully recovered. (Afterwards, he put words to paper and expressed his experience in a poem. See Appendix 2.) He was, however, able to accompany his mother and sister to a memorial theatre trip which they had organised near the first anniversary of the Chinook crash. Ian had loved to take groups of friends to the opera in Belfast. Over seventy people joined the family. Each ticket contained a poem which Ian had cherished:

> If I should die and leave you here awhile,
> Be not like others sore undone, who keep
> Long vigils by the silent dust and weep.
> For my sake turn again to life and smile
> Nerving thy heart and trembling hand to do
> Something to comfort other hearts than thine.
> Complete these dear unfinished tasks of mine,
> And I perchance may therein comfort you.

At other times, memories take Susan back to Trevignano, near Rome, to the narrow streets and their huddle of medieval houses in the old village where they spent their last holiday as a couple. They would look down the street and see at the end of it a boat sail by on the blue waters of Lake Bracciano. 'A very a pretty little house,' she wrote in her diary, registering her first impressions of the place they had rented in September of 1992, 'with a lovely full library of books.' The house was actually a series of vaults in the wall of the fifteenth-century church, La Chiesa dell'Assunta. It overlooked the village and the lake beyond it, and had been part of a much earlier structure, dating back about a thousand years. Remains of a temple to the Roman god Apollo had been found on the site, so it stood on a place that had been sacred for many thousands of years.

They took the two bicycles out of the little cave under the house where the wine was kept, diligently repaired their punctures, and set off to explore the surrounding world of olive groves and vineyards and small plots of land where the *contadini* grew vegetables and fruits for the market. It was part of old Etruria, full of hidden Etruscan tombs and ruined Roman walls. They had arrived just at the beginning of the *vendemmia*, when the village reeks of fermenting fruit and on every cobbled street there are heaps of crushed grape-skins.

Their neighbour was Maria Assunta Montecolle, a

widow with a family of three boys. Maria Assunta was a strong-willed woman with a bright, cheeky smile, who had spent her life as the wife of a *contadino*. One day Ian saw the Montecolle family were stacking up their boxes of harvested grapes on the street outside. Seconds later he was in the street, ready to help them carry the crates into their cellar to be crushed and vinified. Before long he had outpaced Maria Assunta and her boys, though they were working hard. They yelled, '*Lentissimo*!' – Slow-coach! – with good-natured irony, in an attempt to get him to slow down a little.

Maria Assunta invited them to lunch afterwards, and somehow – she without a word of English; Susan and Ian with almost as little Italian – they managed to communicate their enjoyment of each other's company. As they parted, Ian handed his binoculars to Maria Assunta's youngest boy, Andrea, as a gift.

Three years later, in the summer of 1995, Susan and her son drove back to Trevignano. Maria Assunta was the first to greet her, with a big hug. Later they tasted the Montecolle wine, the harvest that Ian had not lived to appreciate.

It was shortly after that that I sat down on the terrace of my home – where a few years before Ian and Susan had watched the sun go down over the lake in the evening – and began to write this book.

Epilogue

Phoenix was dead, but his work lived on. He would have been delighted to see good police work on the mainland when on 12 July 1994 the cargo ferry from Warrenpoint in Co. Down docked in Southport, Lancashire. A lorry was among the vehicles which made their way down the vessel's ramp on to the dockside. It had come from South Armagh, and it possessed a secret compartment packed with nearly a ton of explosives destined for London. This was to be the Provisional IRA's pre-cease-fire blockbuster bomb. The explosives had been made by South Armagh Provisionals, who were generally responsible for most of the big bombing attacks in Britain. The Provisionals were moving towards declaring a suspension of violence, and wanted to go out with a bang to prove that they were not making the declaration from a position of weakness.

As the lorry left the port, the driver saw two policemen approach. He braked sharply and fled with his helper, abandoning the truck. Though both men got away, the explosives fell into the hands of the police. The British capital was spared another, devastating attack. Millions of pounds' worth of damage was prevented, and who knows how many lives were saved.

The interception was another demoralising blow to the PIRA leadership. They had been prevented from using their 'ace' card. The more difficult it proved to attack Britain, the more difficult it was for the PIRA leadership to resist the rising pressure from within and without their own ranks to call a halt to their campaign of death and destruction. Fifty days later, on 31 August 1994, the Army Council of the Provisional IRA announced a complete 'cessation of military operations'. The date had been chosen with care: it was the twenty-first anniversary of the death of a PIRA member, Paddy Mulvenna, a brother-in-law of Gerry Adams. On that date in 1973 British troops had shot him dead in Ballymurphy, West Belfast, fatally wounding his companion, a well-known PIRA gunman called Jim Bryson. It was Adams's way of commemorating his death.

Much has since been written and said about the Provisionals' decision to make this announcement.

Analysing the political reasons that lay behind it, the discussions tend to leave out a vital factor that influenced PIRA in arriving at that position – the success of the RUC in thwarting its operations. The cessation would not have been called had it not been for the operational difficulties that the organisation was facing, especially in Belfast. Those who worked with Ian Phoenix for many years affirm that by 1994 eight out of ten operations that the Belfast Brigade mounted were being thwarted. By 1994 the Special Branch was able to employ both technical and human resources, particularly in Belfast, to compromise many PIRA operations. Of course PIRA still had the capacity to kill and maim – sometimes on a frightening scale – and the police themselves would be the last in the world to underestimate its resilience: they know their adversary too well.

After the cessation of violence itself was ended, on 9 February 1996, PIRA demonstrated that it was still able to carry out bombing attacks in London. The police were caught off guard. But this was partly due to the fact that the officers who had replaced those killed in the Chinook crash had not been able thoroughly to acquaint themselves with their new responsibilities before the cease-fire was declared, which meant their skills had yet to be honed. Also, government cut-backs in overtime had led to the gradual curtailment of surveillance operations during the previous seventeen months.

It must not be forgotten, however, that before the 1994 cessation it was becoming increasingly hard for PIRA to pull off the big jobs, the spectaculars, not only in London but also in Belfast – the city that they always regarded as the key to maintaining their campaign. Big bombs in London were fine for shaking up the government now and again, but the Provisionals needed Belfast as a secure base from which to threaten the very heart of the governance of Northern Ireland. Support in the Catholic areas of the city for PIRA and other republican groups such as INLA made the contemporary campaign of violence different from that which took place between 1956 and 1962 in the so called border campaign, a short-lived disaster from which the IRA took years to recover.

Throughout 1993 and 1994 PIRA was being out-gunned in Belfast by the UDA and UVF, who were claiming more victims. It killed six people in the city in 1994, before the cease-fire compared to sixteen murdered by loyalists. 'We were being slaughtered,' commented one veteran Provisional from North Belfast, referring to the mounting fatalities among Catholics. In 1993 there were thirteen deaths at the hands of Belfast PIRA, but ten of those occurred because of the premature explosion in the fish shop on the Shankill Road. The organisation's ability to strike at 'prestigious' targets, such as on-duty members of the security forces, was declining rapidly. Of the six people it killed in the city in 1994, only one fitted that category – Constable Beacom, who died in a rocket attack on his patrol in the Markets area near the city centre. The year before, aside from those killed on the Shankill Road, the Belfast Brigade had managed to kill one off-duty member of the Royal Irish Regiment and two Protestant civilians. The last time a member of the British army had been killed on duty in Belfast was in August 1992. Before that it had been three years since the Provisionals had been able to kill a British soldier on patrol. The PIRA bombing campaign in Belfast, which had shown new vitality in 1991 and 1992, was in decline by 1993. The last major bomb blast to shake the Northern Ireland capital was in May of that year. During the sixteen months that elapsed before the cease-fire, there were no more successful PIRA 'commercial' bombings.

By the year of the cease-fire there was only sporadic PIRA activity in Derry, and in East Tyrone and North Armagh, once among the most active and dangerous PIRA areas, it had been almost wiped out. Between 1986 and 1992 the East Tyrone and North Armagh brigades had had twenty-two members killed, thanks to the work of TCG(S). South Armagh remained active, but even there PIRA's chief tactic was restricted one-shot long-range sniper attacks. In other words, the Provisionals were running the risk of being pushed into fighting something like the failed border campaign of 1956–62. Except, of course, that the organisation still retained the capacity to explode the occasional blockbuster in Britain – thanks mainly to the fact that of the two areas from where these attacks usually emanated, South Armagh and the Irish Republic, one was resistant to RUC penetration and the other was outside the force's jurisdiction.

The decision to call a halt to the campaign of terror in August 1994 was undoubtedly taken partly in response to these operational problems. That the Belfast Provisionals were especially supportive of Gerry Adams in this respect came as no surprise to those who were familiar with the problems the Belfast Brigade faced. Not only was the Belfast PIRA severely compromised, thanks to the police intelligence, but its attacks provoked violent retaliation from loyalists and from the city's Catholics who were bearing the brunt of this retaliation. So it was hardly a surprise that when the Provisionals did return to violence, in February 1996, the pressure to do so was coming mainly from the Southern Command in the Republic and from units in South Armagh – the areas least affected by the penetration of the RUC intelligence-gatherers and most immune from the loyalists' counter-terror.

Ian Phoenix went against orthodox opinion when he declared that he believed that the PIRA could in fact be defeated 'militarily'. Conventional wisdom holds that only a political solution can resolve the Northern Ireland conundrum. Political accommodation is necessary to undermine support for groups like the

Provisional IRA, who, it is argued, will feed off the discontent that the mainly working-class Catholics of Northern Ireland continue to feel. Northern Ireland has to be restructured to incorporate their nationalist aspirations. In the long term this is undoubtedly true – it is a politically worthwhile goal in itself, whether or not it is seen as a scheme to politically defeat violent republicanism.

There was no outright defeat of PIRA – no one would be smug enough to declare such a victory. Yet in one sense Phoenix was right: police and army counter-terror operations so constrained PIRA that it was forced seriously to consider abandoning violence as a way of achieving its political goals. It began its so-called 'unarmed strategy' in a blaze of self-righteousness on 31 August 1994, adopting an air of sanctimoniousness about peace that relatives of its victims found deeply revolting. But it could not mask the fact that its use of violence – what it euphemistically calls the 'armed strategy' – had been thwarted, thanks to the bravery and resourcefulness of officers like Ian Phoenix and his colleagues.

Postscript to the Paperback Edition

The bulk of this book was written during the period when the Provisional IRA and then the loyalist organisations had halted their murderous campaigns. It was completed under far different circumstances, as bombs went off in London and then violence resumed in Northern Ireland itself. Conscious of the nature of the material with which we were dealing, we agreed to rewrite or cut out material from Ian's diaries which either threatened the integrity of intelligence-gathering operations or posed a real risk to the security of individuals involved in those operations, informers, or indeed the paramilitaries themselves. Security became acute with the breakdown of the peace process when some of the operations we wrote about may have been reactivated to combat the rising threat of renewed terror.

However, there was no censorship as such. Nothing was removed because it portrayed the police or the security forces in an unflattering way. None of Ian's assessments of the inadequacies of the force he served or the political masters who determined security policies were cut out. A few critics have attacked the book because it lacked revelations about the 'shoot-to-kill' and 'collusion' allegations leveled at the police over the years. There is a simple reason why it does not contain those revelations. The diaries, never intended to be seen by anyone other than Ian, did not offer any evidence that the police in Northern Ireland pursued a 'shoot-to-kill' policy; nor did they reveal a hint that there exists high-level 'collusion' between the security forces and the loyalist paramilitaries. The diaries were copious and detailed, but they would have disappointed the critics of the RUC who allege that there is, behind the scenes, a tacit or even active acceptance of such policies. Had a shoot-to-kill policy been implemented at any time, it is quite evident from the amount of information Ian Phoenix and his colleagues had about the IRA and loyalist groups that there would be far more dead paramilitaries than there are.

The same applies to the collusion accusations. If the RUC Special Branch had made available to the UDA and UVF the kind of information on IRA membership that it possesses, the IRA would have suffered far more fatalities than it has. But it is quite clear from Superintendent Phoenix's diaries, which we read uncensored, that such a strategy would have been rejected by him if ever it had been proposed. Like the vast majority of his colleagues he despised and distrusted loyalist killers as much as he opposed the Provisional IRA. He would never have entrusted such people with the kind of information he possessed. Indeed, he was reluctant at times even to share it with BOX, concerned as he was with the vicissitudes of the British government's underlying political agenda.

For someone from a nationalist background to write a book in praise of an RUC man invited angry attacks from the usual quarters. They came as expected. Among the more amusing was an accusation from the President of Sinn Fein, Gerry Adams, challenging the assertion that I believed Ian to be a hearing aid salesman. Adams was quoted as saying he found it 'incredible' that 'Holland . . . a so-called expert on Irish Republicanism, can't even tell an undercover RUC operative from a hearing aid salesman.'

But the paramiliataries, however, seem to have the same problem, as evidenced by the fact that thanks to undercover policing, so many of them are currently in prison.

The implication behind this was not so amusing. It was that I was lying and that all along I had known Ian Phoenix was a Special Branch man. In Northern Ireland that can have the sinister connotations of 'collaboration'. The truth was simple, and far from sinister. But what seemed to anger and confuse certain people in Northern Ireland was that a book should be written presenting an RUC officer as a human being, and an interesting and sympathetic one at that. The problem with Northern Ireland is that one side denies the reality of the other side's experience and is able to do so usually through ignorance. It is a dehumanising process which in the end blocks the free flow of sympathy that should nourish our social and political relationships with each other, even when we are politically opposed to each other's goals. We need to acknowledge the other person's reality. Without such acknowledgement the Northern Ireland situation will remain intractable. *Phoenix* was a modest experiment along those lines.

For Susan, of course, it was much more. As 1996 began she decided to close some doors on her previous life. But there were painful, aggravating reminders of the most unsettled aspect of it – the continuing failure of the Ministry of Defence to meet the compensation claims of the relatives of the Chinook crash victims. The government's original position was that Ian and his colleagues were using the RAF Chinook as a civilian transport, like ordinary airline passengers and therefore their families were entitled to no more compensation than the victim of a civilian air disaster, which has an upper limit of £100,000. The families of the pilots themselves and of the military personnel on board were also deemed as unable to claim compensation since their loved ones were killed on duty. 'I was consumed with anger,' recalls Susan. 'No doubt this was dreamt up by some anonymous civil servant who thought he might get an OBE for saving the government some money.' Because Susan took a prominent role in speaking out against this decision, she received a flow of letters from former servicemen and women, veterans of past wars who had been badly treated by the MoD.

'I was disgusted to find out how inadequate war pensions had been for men and women who had fought for their country over the years,' she remarked. Along with Ann Magee, the widow of Detective Inspector Kevin Magee, who also died in the crash, she helped create a stir. The women were even more motivated when they heard that someone in Whitehall had remarked that 'the ladies in Northern Ireland are quiet and submissive and would probably not bother making a fuss about it all.'

In the end, the MoD rescinded its decision. The Minister, Malcolm Rifkind, stated that they were now prepared to consider compensation above the statutory level. However, families of the military personnel who died in the Chinook disaster were warned that if they applied for compensation then 'their pensions would be cut accordingly'. Such policies made her wonder what their men would have thought had they known that their years of service and of risking their lives would be rewarded by mean-spirited efforts to cut costs at the expense of their bereaved families.

Two years on, the matter remained unsettled. The women continue to wait, their solicitors continue to haggle, hopes are raised, then dashed, that it will be soon resolved. The greatest and most painful indignity of all is having to meet the MoD's demand made to each of the widows for an estimate of how much it costs to feed and clothe a man. In the grey, insensitive jargon of the civil service, this was expressed as having to 'specify the average amount per week which was expended upon domestic support and upkeep of the deceased'. Susan's initial response was that if the MoD did not know the cost of clothing and feeding a man over a given period of time then God help the armed forces! Everything from the cost of his socks to how many pounds of potatoes he ate every week had to be calculated. It was humiliating for women overcome with grief and shock to be expected to weigh the 'cost' of a loved one's life in the scales of petty bureaucracy.

In 1996 Susan took another step into a new life, away from the past life she had led with Ian. She spent some time in France, anxious to get away from Northern Ireland. Her experience convinced her the time had come to leave the lovely farmhouse that had been her and Ian's pride. In the winter she returned to prepare the 110-year-old house for leaving. She was trying hard to refocus her life. The last thirty months had tested her stamina to the limit. She needed to become part of another world, away from the one that she and her husband had built together.

She was not finding it easy. But it was not until she found herself alone in the roofspace of the farmhouse preparing to leave her home for the last time, that the overwhelming finality of what had happened hit her. Outside, the winds howled over the hill as always, a constant reminder of the wild northern landscape where she had made her life. And the sea beyond with the lonely strand on which she and Ian had often walked, still beckoned. In many ways, it had been such a complete, well-rounded, satisfying world, but now it was shattered. She had finally realised the need to rebuild, to start over again away from the farm and the seascape of which it was an integral part.

Although as we wrote the first chapters of this book Susan had forced herself to relate to me the story of her life with Ian, describing the world they shared together, it had been as if she were talking about someone else, as if the life she was remembering had not been her own. During those conversations, even when she spoke about her suffering she seemed to be reporting on someone else's. Now, two years later, the powerful need came upon her 'to feel a bit more like "me" rather than the inadequate half of "us".' And that meant moving away. The past was a place, and the future was a different place, a quiet corner of rural France where once they had fantasised they could retire together so that Ian could write his account of his experiences in the RUC.

When Susan was rummaging through the roofspace, she uncovered things that Ian had stored away that she had missed on her first hunt for material for this book. During that time she came across a telling anecdote about his days on TCG(S). Ian and his combined team of SAS operatives and RUC officers had just finalised plans for an operation against the Provisional IRA. They decided to drink a toast to its success. One of the RUC men gave the toast in Irish. An English officer was taken aback, surprised at the use of Gaelic in that particular situation.

'Look, we're not all against a United Ireland and the Irish language,' Ian told him.

'So what the hell are we doing here?' the SAS man asked, somewhat perplexed.

'You are here about terrorism and not politics!' Ian told him emphatically.

It is a story that illustrates the obvious truth that people are more complex than the simple categories into which they are often placed. On Ian's first passport against nationality he put 'British/Irish'. To some within the current Northern Ireland context, it might appear confusing that an RUC man could regard himself as both Irish and British, but it would not have appeared so to an earlier generation of Irishmen.

Political ideologues have a vested interest in categorising those they perceive as their enemies and they hate anything which seems to contradict their one-dimensional vision. It makes life simpler and people easier to dehumanise if one can fit them neatly into classifications. And of course, as Northern Ireland and other world trouble spots know to their cost, people are easier to kill once they are viewed only in terms of the category to which they belong.

Phoenix was a man who defied such easy classifications and loved diversity, especially when it upset the smug assumptions of the simple and bloody-minded purveyors of death and destruction. Otherwise, this book would never have been written.

Appendix I

Glossary

ASU – Active Service Unit.

BOX – MI5 and MI6, refered to as such because their address was a box number in Curzon Street, London.

CAT – Civil Administration Team, PIRA's internal security unit.

CTR – Close Target Recce (Reconnoitre).

Det – Military Specialist surveillance units detached from their own regiment.

DMSU – Divisional Mobile Support Unit.

DFC – Duty Flight Commander.

E – Special Branch department within police.

E3 – Special Branch's agent handling department.

E4 – Special Branch's surveillance department.

E4A – Covert surveillance unit within Special Branch.

HMSU – Headquarters Mobile Support Unit.

IO – Head of PIRA's intelligence gathering units.

INLA – Irish National Liberation Army.

IPLO – Irish People's Liberation Organisation.

LP – Listening Post.

OP – Observation Point.

OTR – On the run.

PAC – Provisional Army Council, PIRA's leading body. Has seven members.

PIRA – Provisional Irish Republican Army.

Recce – to reconnoitre a target.

RUC – Royal Ulster Constabulary.

Sinn Fein – Political wing of PIRA.

SDLP – Social and Democratic Labour Party, largest Nationalist party in Northern Ireland.

SAS – Special Air Service.

SSU – Special Support Units (uniformed Special Branch).

TCG – Tasking Coordination Group, comprising of SAS, MI5, Special Branch, and Military intelligence officers.

UCBT – Undercar booby-trap device.

UDA – Ulster Defence Association (loyalist).

UDR – Ulster Defence Regiment – amalgamated with Royal Irish Rangers to become the Royal Irish Regiment (R.I.R.) in 1992.

UVF – Ulster Volunteer Force (loyalist).

VCP – Vehicle Check Point.

Appendix II

This is the poem that was written by Ian Phoenix's son after a serious car crash almost one year after the death of his father in the helicopter crash on the Mull of Kintyre on 2 June 1994.

In the Smash Perhaps?

Lifted from the mauled car he rose up
Through the clouds which brushed against him leaving
their heavenly dew on his shattered face
Eventually he came down to a rugged shore to lie on the
clean, white and grey stones of the beach
The pebbles as always cool and soothing against his
bloodied cheeks, stained now by blood and not the tears
of before.
Shifting now he skimmed across the sea the waves
spraying on his face but salt not stinging
Soon he saw it stretched like a dark fist into the cold sea
A brooding Mull now bright and green, but bruised by

purple heather
He soared over rock and scrub looking for the prise
It was there blinking at him in the sun beneath the stone
cross
Suddenly he was floating in front of the shiny metal plate
His finger tip traced the beautiful name pushing out
against the world
And pushing him back across the sea
Laughing and smiling he tumbled across the waves and
hedgerows
The name spelt more than love and pride
A word was forming round his heart
And the word was life.
Another time ... perhaps. ...

Index